Franz Kafka

COMPANION STUDIES

Odette de Mourgues: *Racine: or, The Triumph of Relevance*
Ronald Gray: *Goethe, a Critical Introduction*
R. F. Christian: *Tolstoy, a Critical Introduction*
C. B. Morris: *A Generation of Spanish Poets, 1920–1936*
Richard Peace: *Dostoyevsky, an Examination of the Major Novels*
John Bayley: *Pushkin, a Comparative Commentary*
Dorothy Gabe Coleman: *Rabelais: a Critical Study in Prose Fiction*
W. E. Yates: *Grillparzer, a Critical Introduction*
John Northam: *Ibsen, a Critical Study*

Other volumes in preparation

Franz Kafka

RONALD GRAY

Fellow of Emmanuel College and Lecturer in German in the University of Cambridge

CAMBRIDGE
AT THE UNIVERSITY PRESS
1973

Published by the Syndics of the Cambridge University Press
Bentley House, 200 Euston Road, London NW1 2DB
American Branch: 32 East 57th Street, New York, N.Y.10022

Library of Congress Catalogue Card Number: 72–83576

ISBNS:
0 521 20007 5 hard covers
0 521 09747 9 paperback

Printed in Great Britain
by W & J Mackay Limited, Chatham

CONTENTS

PREFACE

No writer has entered into my own life so much as Kafka once did. That was nearly twenty years ago, and there have been changes since then. Yet the study that follows is not meant to be either a retraction or a withdrawal into a different subjectivity. I have not by any means completely maintained the view I had of *The Castle* when I wrote a small book about it, though I still see in it the same general pattern. What I hope to offer now is not, of course, any final statement, but a reasonable view which will at least be worth serious consideration, and at best be compelling. If general agreement is ever possible, I want to have contributed towards it.

The view is still a personal one; it could not be anything else. I have made suggestions for further reading wherever they seemed likely to be helpful, and accepted suggestions from a large number of writers, but I have introduced Kafka as I see him, not as though all views could be equally valid. I have also provided information about Kafka's own preferences among his works, and his criticism of them, partly to give backing to criticisms of my own. In addition I have included esoteric points and matters of biography which it is not necessary to know in order to enjoy the best of his writing, but which are useful when there is an obscurity. Apart from such usefulness, biography and esotericism are irrelevant, except to the specialist who assumes a responsibility towards the general reader. It is the general reader I have chiefly had in mind, though the argument is directed to specialists too.

My thanks go to friends who have read and criticised earlier drafts, especially to Michael Black, Eve and Harold Mason, John Harvey, and Arthur Sale.

R.D.G.

Cambridge
September 1972

KAFKA THE WRITER

Kafka's name has become a household word for the enormities of civilisation in this century, yet it was not in such terms that he was first presented. The original afterword to his posthumously published novel, *The Castle*, written by his friend Max Brod, concerned itself very little with questions of 'relevance', in the sense that word has recently come to have. It was as a religious genius that Brod presented Kafka, the two principal novels being portrayals of 'the two forms in which (in the sense of the Kabbala) the Godhead manifests itself; Justice and Grace'.[1] In just the same way, Kafka was presented to the English-speaking world by his translators, Edwin and Willa Muir, as a modern Bunyan. In an age when religious belief was either being lost or undergoing radical changes, the appeal of such a writer was great, even though there is no certainty that later generations will always be so fascinated.

In the 1930s, and increasingly in the forties, fifties and sixties, Kafka ranked high in the estimation of influential people, who placed him with the greatest writers of all time. 'Had one to name the author who comes nearest to bearing the same kind of relation to our age as Dante, Shakespeare and Goethe bore to theirs', W. H. Auden wrote, 'Kafka is the first one would think of.'[2] He must have meant, of course, 'our age, so far as intellectuals are concerned', for Kafka is one of the increasingly numerous writers in this century who explore a limited range of experience for the benefit of a small audience of similarly placed readers. But other writers have spoken without any such qualification. Paul Claudel, though seeing in Kafka a Jew who despaired because he refused the pardon of Christianity, wrote in terms of the highest praise: 'Besides Racine, who is for me the greatest writer, there is one other – Franz Kafka – before whom I doff my hat.'[3] Thomas Mann said much the same: 'If one considers that laughter, weeping laughter of a serious nature, is the best that we have, the best that we enduringly possess, one will be inclined, as I am, to account Kafka's loving fixations among the worthiest things to be read in world literature.'[4] André Gide, though he made no considered pronouncement, spoke in his *Diary* of 1940 of the profound impression made on him by Kafka's novel, *The Trial*,★ and later adapted it for the theatre.[5] Indeed, by 1955, it was possible to say 'Kafka is now one of the German-speaking authors most widely known and best assimilated in France, more even than Rilke, and on a par with Nietzsche. He is no longer a stranger; the French meditate on him as one of themselves.'[6] The same might have been said for Sweden and Japan, and if other countries were less profoundly impressed, it remains true that the bibliography of criticism published in 1961 is nearly 400 pages long, and includes items from every continent. Kafka has not only been read, he has been venerated.

The greater part of this secondary literature is not concerned with his writing at all, but rather with interpreting his message to humanity, or with disputes on his value as a religious guide, rather than with the quality of his novels and stories. This is partly for historical reasons. During his lifetime Kafka allowed only half a dozen very slim volumes to be published, amounting to less than would normally make a short novel. Although the works published after his death in 1924 were beginning to be known within the next ten years, the seizure of power by the Nazis in 1933 crippled their chances, and by 1939 both Austria and Czechoslovakia had also been stifled by Nazi censorship, so that his books could be openly read only in foreign countries. Not until after 1945 did German-speakers of the newer generations begin to hear of him. Friedrich Beissner has related how even then it was difficult for Germans to obtain copies, and how confusing it was to be confronted with a host of interpretations, largely by foreigners basing themselves on English or French translations, when the original versions being republished in New York were still unavailable in Germany.[7] 'Even interpreters for whom German was not, or did not need to be a foreign language', Beissner writes, 'showed themselves to be

★ German titles of Kafka's works are given in the Chronological Table.

unmoved by the literary quality, translating the words straight into the conceptual language of fashionable philosophy'.[8] Heinz Politzer made a similar point.[9] So far as Germany was concerned, the great reputation of Kafka began through accounts by foreigners who were more interested in ideas than in language.

Yet Max Brod had often insisted that language was at least as important as ideas. Ideas were important, and not only for the Jewish content Brod was able to find in them, though he did point to a distinctive feature in Kafka's mode of thought: 'Here, in Franz Kafka, and, let it be said, in him alone, amid all the literature of modern Germany, there is no fluctuation between opposite points of view, no looking at things from changing standpoints, no sleight of hand. Here is truth and nothing but truth.'[10] How right Brod was about that will be appreciated by anyone who recalls, by contrast, what fluctuations of standpoint there are in authors like Thomas Mann and Rilke. Kafka is relentlessly unwilling to take advantage of any foreknown scheme of 'salvation through damnation'.[11] But Brod was equally emphatic about the language: 'Cheap devices like turning out neologisms, compounds, swapping around of the parts of a sentence, he despises. "Despises" is not the word for it. They are simply not for him, as impurity is not for the pure, they are forbidden to him. His language is crystal-clear, and on the surface one sees no other endeavour but that of being right, clear, in conformity with the object. And yet dreams and visions of immeasurable depth flow beneath the serene surface of this pure stream of language. One gazes into it and is held fascinated by beauty and singularity. Yet one cannot say, at least not at first sight, wherein lies the peculiarity of these indisputably right, healthy, simple sentence-forms. If one reads a few sentences of Kafka, the tongue, the breath feel a sweetness never experienced before. The cadences, the periods seem to follow mysterious laws, the little pauses between the groups of words have their own architecture; a melody is expressed that does not consist of matter drawn from this earth. It is perfection, perfection once and for all, that perfection of pure form that caused

Flaubert to weep at the ruins of a wall on the Acropolis. But it is perfection in movement, on the march, I may even say on the attack.'[12]

There are passages in that tribute to a dead friend which have not stood the test of time. 'Sweetness' and 'health' would be disputed by many readers. But there is the claim, made by the man but for whose encouragement Kafka might not have written at all. If it had been taken up at once, and if Kafka's reputation had spread mainly on those grounds, there would be no need to establish the real quality of his writing. As things turned out, a great deal of his reputation was due to the efforts of Max Brod, both before and after his death, and while very little was written about him in Germany before 1933, his reception in other countries was mixed. Not that Brod was alone in his appreciation. Discerning publishers like Kurt Wolff and Ernst Rowohlt were interested in Kafka during his own lifetime, and so were writers such as Robert Musil and Carl Sternheim, to say nothing of the Prague circle of authors who knew him personally; Thomas Mann and Hermann Hesse both wrote appreciatively of him shortly after his death, and translations into French, English, Italian, Czech, Polish, Spanish and Swedish had appeared within twenty years of it.

Everywhere the suggestion in Brod's epilogue to *The Castle*, and in his other writings, that Kafka was using traditional religious terms, was accepted, not always readily. An English reviewer had read some way into *The Castle*, on its first appearance in translation in 1930, before it dawned on him that the novel had metaphysical implications.[13] Another found that it had a fine quality, 'elusive at times in its spiritual implications, but not more so than is proper in a sceptical or agnostic age'.[14] On the other hand these same reviewers, and others, spoke of 'exasperation' in confronting what appeared to be 'a Torquemada cross-word lacking a framework',[15] or described it as 'an elaborate and indeed a tortuous allegory' and (at first sight) 'an aimless rigmarole',[16] or complained of being 'lulled into unwondering acquiescence with a continual procession of involuted and endless sentences, of conversations where people speak for hours in vague surroundings, in unparagraphed pages'.[17] Such impressions – both of a fascinating if obscure allegory, and of irritatingly elaborate writing – remained the most usual ones in English literary journals for some fifteen to twenty years. Félix Bertaux, writing a survey of German literature for French readers in the early thirties, had given a very different account, speaking not only of Kafka's 'astonishing intensity' but also of his 'passion for clarity that is Slav or Jewish or perhaps even French'. 'There is no German writing', he added, 'in which pure reason is more obviously in control.'[18] This was a view which, for instance, the German satirist Kurt Tucholsky had shared. *The Trial*, he had observed, was 'not crazy, but perfectly rational . . . the fact is, it lacks that little dose of the irrational which gives rational men a grip on themselves.'[19] In England, by contrast (where, it has to be remembered, the most intense and the most clearly written stories, the 'terrible' ones, had not yet appeared) the impression was exactly contrary. Of *The Great Wall of China*, the next volume to appear in English, (a strange choice, since it contained so much of second quality) the *Times Literary Supplement* could only say that the total effect was 'strange and baffling', the metaphysical meanings 'elusive and uncertain', displaying the author's 'habit of looking at the universe as a problem in metaphysics rather than in its material aspects'; the style, which was 'careful and extraordinarily serpentine', was no more than 'well suited to his intricate turn of thought'.[20] *The Trial,* when it appeared in English in 1937, fared no better, so far as the writing was concerned: the 'remarkably elaborate and flowing style', and 'the serpentine flow' tended to 'weary the reader',[21] and with the publication of *America* comment was quite sharp, including phrases like 'exasperatingly undramatic incident and arbitrary small talk' and 'artlessly mechanical'.[22] Reason and clarity, the qualities Bertaux had found, were not being detected here.

Even after the War of 1939–45, when the *T.L.S.* devoted an editorial to Kafka, some hesitation could be sensed. In fact the excessive claim made at the beginning of the article, that 'in all

that he wrote' Kafka was concerned 'to the exclusion of everything else' 'with man's search for the absolute verities, for salvation and divine grace', seemed to betray in its exaggeration a
need to balance out what was said a bit further down the page,
that 'Kafka, let it be confessed, is frequently tedious',[23] unless
the tediousness resulted from that kind of exclusive preoccupation. And as late as 1948, when the *Diaries* appeared, Kafka
was contrasted unfavourably with the Swiss writer C. F. Ramuz,
and condemned 'not for his exploration of captivity but for his
failure to make a simultaneous exploration of freedom'.[24] So
far as the English literary press was concerned, Kafka had not
had an enthusiastic reception.[25]

By this time he had in fact become a *cause célèbre*, and a touch-
stone for readers trying to think their way out of the aftermath
of the Second World War. In 1946 French Communists
published an inquiry entitled 'Must Kafka be burned?', arguing
that he was a dangerous representative of 'black' literature,
likely to have a demoralising influence on society.[26] Attacks
were made from Christian quarters too, as by Erich Heller:
'It is the very spiritual uprootedness of the age which has
deprived us of all sureness of religious discrimination. To men,
suffering from spiritual starvation, even a rotten fruit of the
spirit may taste like bread from Heaven, and the liquid from a
poisoned well like the water of life.'[27] Equally early was the
criticism by Günther Anders, which concluded (in words taken
from the English adaptation) 'From great warnings we should
be able to learn, and they should help us to reach others. The
picture [Kafka] has drawn of the world as it should not be, and
of attitudes which should not be ours, will be of use to us if it
becomes imprinted on our minds as a warning. It is a picture
drawn by a good man, who finally came to doubt the value of
his work, and even pleaded for its destruction. His work could
never be of use to himself or to others as positive counsel; but
as a warning it may be truly helpful to us after all.'[28]

Edmund Wilson was more emphatic and allowed less for
Kafka's own insights into himself. Comparing him with Gogol
and Poe, Mr Wilson was able to find qualities in their writing to

compensate for their neuroticism, the one in his heroic conception of Russia, the other in his challenging, defiant temper, his alert and curious mind. 'In their ways, they are both tonic. But the denationalised, discouraged, disaffected, disabled Kafka, though for the moment he may frighten or amuse us, can in the end only let us down.'[29]

Meanwhile Max Brod and other friends of Kafka's had continued to write articles about him, especially in the American press, and his reputation grew also in France, where the harassed and oppressive climate of his novels and stories seemed to reflect the world in which Frenchmen lived during the German occupation. As Hannah Arendt wrote in 1944, 'Kafka's nightmare of a world . . . has actually come to pass.'[30] The stress was laid now not so much on the religious strain in Kafka as on his modernity: these were the terms in which W. H. Auden had written, in the passage already quoted.[31] But Miss Arendt no more neglected the quality of Kafka's writing than Max Brod had done. 'Without in any way changing the German language', she wrote, 'he stripped it of its involved constructions until it became clear and simple like everyday speech purified of slang and negligence.' His language had an 'easy naturalness'.[32] Within a few years, this note was echoed by a reviewer in the *T.L.S.*, who, without referring to the views of his predecessors or indicating how he came to a conclusion so contrary to theirs, encouraged readers to ignore the 'avalanche of comment' and read Kafka for himself. They might be surprised to find him 'after all the most accessible of writers; an admirable story-teller, master of a simple and rapid language, equally capable of wit and pathos'. Kafka's style was precise, swift and simple: 'his story-telling is as plain as that of the Bible', and it was pointless to inquire what he really meant: 'He means what he says; he must be swallowed whole.'[33]

The last remark makes its own comment on the reviewer's critical pretensions. One may doubt whether so frankly gullible a reader had anything of interest to say about either the ideas or the writing. But even Miss Arendt does not set out in detail the kind of thing that persuaded her to make her claim, and very few critics ever have gone into the question of what distinction Kafka's prose really has. One of the few to do so was R. O. C. Winkler in the only article on Kafka to appear in *Scrutiny*, where at least an attempt at an answer will be found. Winkler held that the basis of Kafka's method lay in the creation of a complex and continually changing dramatic situation subsisting mainly in the relation between the hero and the other characters:'Where the prose is not concerned with defining some element in an interhuman relationship, either external or introspective, but with describing the hero's situation purely objectively, it frequently becomes itself dramatic in movement.'[34] Here at all events is the central issue: does Kafka's prose embody the thought he expresses, giving it life and movement, or does it have more of the nature of ciphers, standing for the thing spoken of, rather than itself bodying it out?

The passage Winkler chose is typical enough of Kafka:

So ging er wieder vorwärts, aber es war ein langer Weg. Die Straße nämlich, diese Haupstraße des Dorfes, führte nicht zum Schloßberg, sie führte nur nahe heran, dann aber, wie absichtlich, bog sie ab, und wenn sie sich auch vom Schloß nicht entfernte, so kam sie ihm doch auch nicht näher.

So he resumed his walk, but the way proved long. For the street he was in, the main street of the village, did not lead up to the Castle hill, it only made towards it and then, as if deliberately, turned aside, and though it did not lead away from the Castle it got no nearer to it either.

But in his analysis Winkler, some may think, gave the kind of argument that is, though not false, applicable to a great deal of prose of no special distinction. He observed that the effect was to produce the sense of physical effort appropriate to the situation:

'The short phrases and the jerky movement of the sentence suggest the feeling of frustrated effort that K. experienced, striving to get nearer the Castle, but repeatedly being prevented. The end of the sentence gives us a closer view of the process: the movement forward – '*sie führte nur nahe heran*', the pause – '*dann aber*', the moment of suspense, – hanging from the tortuous syllables of *'wie absichtlich'*, then the sudden recoil, like a spring snapping back into place – *'bog sie ab'*, then the ensuing sense of disappointment and disillusion, embodied in the flat phrasing, *'so kam sie ihm doch auch nicht näher'*.

Admirable in intention, this still does not carry a ring of truth: the account in the analysis is much more vigorous than anything to be found in the German, and even misrepresents the novel a little, for K. does not, after this initial setback, repeatedly strive to get nearer the Castle: the one defeat is enough. Aware of this, Winkler invites comparison with Donne's third *Satyre*, which does have many of the effects noted in his account of Kafka. To quote Donne is to show what the difference is:

> . . . On a huge hill,
> Cragged, and steep, Truth stands, and hee that will
> Reach her, about must, and about must goe;
> And what the hills suddennes resists, winne so;
> Yet strive so, that before age, deaths twilight,
> Thy soule rest, for none can worke in that night.
> To will, implyes delay, therefore now doe:
> Hard deeds, the bodies paines; hard knowledge too
> The mindes indeavours reach, and mysteries
> Are like the Sunne, dazling, yet plaine to all eyes.

Effort, difficulty, stubborn resistance, determination, are there in Donne's lines clearly enough. The panting exhaustion of Kafka's prose is continued in the lines immediately following, which I give without the slightly greater articulation provided in the Muirs' version. Here everything piles on without any determining or determined mind to guide it:

At every turn K. expected the road to double back to the Castle, and only because of this expectation did he go on; he was reluctant [the English has, unjustifiably, the more vigorous phrase 'flatly unwilling'], evidently because of his tiredness, to leave the street, and he was also amazed at the length of the village, which seemed to have no end, again and again the same little houses, and frost-bound window-panes and snow, and the entire absence of human beings – at last he tore himself away from the obsession of the street, a small side-lane swallowed him up, still deeper snow, lifting one's sinking feet clear was fatiguing, he broke into a sweat, suddenly he came to a stop and could not go on.

The reader of the Muirs' translation will find a dozen places at which their version here differs from mine: by marking longer pauses, linking separate phrases, omitting a repeated personal pronoun, they supply a kind of coherence which the original does not have. It is true that Kafka was not writing verse, as Donne was, yet the dispirited quality of his German here would have come through, in no matter what form he wrote.

There is more to be done, if the distinction of Kafka's writing is to be seen – and without that his religious or other ideas count for very little, since it was as a novelist and short-story writer that he made his mark. The real nature of his language is best seen by comparison with his imitators, not so much with Albert Camus (in *La Peste* and *L'Etranger*) or Graham Greene (in *The Ministry of Fear*) or Rex Warner (in *The Aerodrome*) or Susan Sontag (in *The Death Kit*), or Hermann Kasack (in *Die Stadt hinter dem Strom*), or Elias Canetti (in *Die Blendung*), since these novelists took up only Kafka's themes, or his supposedly allegorical mode, or his general atmosphere.* More illuminating, because he not only takes up Kafka's subjects, but also imitates his style to the point of mimicry, is William Sansom. Sansom's early stories 'In the Maze' and 'The Inspector'[35] are not typical or among the best of his work. They are, rather, early pastiches, 'exercises in the manner of . . .', and like a professionally painted copy of a masterpiece they bring home the quality of the original by their divergences from it.

'In the Maze' is a story based on *The Castle*, in its subject-matter, and on 'In the Penal Colony' in its presentation. As in 'In the Penal Colony', a traveller is shown round a mysterious place – here the maze, in Kafka's story a place of execution – and as in *The Castle* there are overtones suggesting a general symbolism

---

* Others influenced include, in France, Adamov, Beckett, Blanchot, Ionesco, Michaux, Sartre; in Germany Walser and Peter Weiss; in Sweden Vesaas. Kafka in turn owes something to Dickens, Dostoevsky, Gogol, Kleist, Melville, Poe, de Sade, Strindberg.

about life and men's path through it. The first sight of the maze is closely modelled on the first sight of the Castle; like the castle, it is on a low hill, with houses beneath, and signifies more than itself:

Although the maze had seemed forbidding to the tourist from a distance, this quality of threat receded as they approached, until, when they had arrived almost beneath its shadow, the maze appeared to be an ordinary hedge of yew. Certainly it was high, higher than a man. Certainly it was dark; but then the yew leaf, in colour and in the immobile set of its leaves, is naturally brother to the cypress and the urn. Certainly the maze grew suddenly, a still sharp cliff of shadow against the young green of the attendant turf. 'I regret that you were frightened', said the topiarist, whose peak seemed now to have shrunk again to its original size. 'Normally, you should have lived in the halcyonry for some weeks. Realization would then have been gradual. But you are a tourist, and therefore imagine that you have no time. I made you a concession there'.

Together they mounted the wooden steps of a rakish gazebo that overlooked the maze. Finally they emerged onto an upper platform from which for the first time the tourist could survey the panorama from its clear beginnings to the confused distance of its far horizon.

The maze had no main entrance. In fact, there was no certain entrance at all. Each man who entered cut his own passage with his own pair of shears. Confronted by the penetrable mystery, he moulded his own way. Every man first cut himself a straight path, concise as a plumbline. Later, according to his degree of interest, he turned to the left or right, doubled back on himself, marched in squares, hurried forward, lingered back, clipping assiduously the convolutions of his chosen passage. One factor alone was constant. Each man clipped in straight lines. There were neither curves nor circles. As far as the eye reached, and forever further, men could be seen clipping their squared progress through the huge shrub. And always along the façade there were more men, each choosing a moment and a place of entry, each having climbed the hill from the halcyonry, each provided suddenly with shears, each confronted now with his individual task of penetration. 'Come', said the topiarist, taking the tourist's arm and guiding him gently back to the steps, 'Now you have some idea of the perspective, you will wish to examine our work in detail. Yes? Meanwhile I'll tell you about the night when the Arboretor listened.'

Kafka was incapable of writing like this. The absurdity of describing the actions of men who could be seen further than the eye reached can be put down to a slip in attentiveness, though it may also be due to a habit of asserting more than is known. Kafka is remarkable for the care with which he excludes anything that could not, from the experience of his characters, be said to be so. He rarely oversteps the mark in that way, despite the fact that his stories seem to have very wide implications. 'Forever further' would have been an impossible solecism. But it is not just a matter of logic and avoiding absurdity. At least as important is the difference in tone between the two passages. In 'but then the yew leaf . . . is naturally brother to the cypress and the urn', William Sansom brings in a neo-classical flourish, perhaps a touch of condescension towards the reader, a precious note, which is still heard in 'the young green of the attendant turf'. With this introduction the topiarist sounds embarrassingly like a *poseur*, though he is treated as a character who deserves respect.

One is often not sure Mr Sansom means the words he has used. Each man '. . . *moulded* his own way', though in fact he cut it. A straight path is no straighter for being '*concise* as a plumbline'. Marching in squares must have been impossible while clipping a hedge. But the mouthfuls of words still go on: 'clipping assiduously the convolutions of his chosen passage'; 'each confronted now with his individual task of penetration'. It is not the subject-matter that is at fault here. It is the inflation, the pompousness, and the inattention to words, a writer's only means of expression. Kafka's mode of writing has none of these faults, and though it has faults on occasions, this passage displays none of them:

On the whole the view of the castle which K. had from a distance matched his expectations. It was neither an ancient fortress, nor a modern stately home, but a rambling construction consisting of a large number of closely packed small buildings, only a few of them two-storeyed; if you had not known it was a castle you might have taken it for a small town. There was only one tower, so far as K. could see, whether it belonged to a dwelling-house or a church he could not make out. Hordes of crows were circling round it.

His eyes on the castle, K. went on, nothing else gave him any concern. But as he drew near the castle disappointed him, it was a really wretched little town, a huddle of village houses, only distinguished by the fact, if it was one, that they were all built of stone, but the paint had fallen off long ago and the stone seemed to be crumbling. Fleetingly K. recalled his home town; it was scarcely inferior to this so-called castle. If K. had only come sightseeing it would not have been worth the long journey, and it would have been more reasonable of him to have gone back to his old home, which he had not seen for such a long time. And in his thoughts he compared the church-tower in his native town with the tower here. The tower at home, definite, soaring upwards with its slight taper, then ending with red tiles on its broad roof, an earthly building – what else can we build? – but with a higher goal than the low cluster of houses and with a clearer expression than the confusions of everyday life. The tower above him here – the only one in sight – the tower of a dwelling-house, as now appeared, perhaps of the main castle building, was a uniformly circular construction, part of it peacefully covered with ivy, with small windows glinting in the sun – there was something demented about that – and a kind of balcony at the top, with battlements uncertain and irregular, brittle, as though drawn by an anxiously trembling or careless child, in a jagged line against the blue sky. It was as if some melancholy occupant, who by rights should have shut himself up in the remotest room in the house, had broken through the roof and risen up for all the world to see.

This is a precise and detailed picture – much more so than the picture of the maze. One notices too, half-consciously, that each paragraph runs to longer and longer sentences, as though the ideas came generously flowing, only to end with a briefer sentence, and a suggestion of menace. It is not untypical of Kafka's mind to move like this. There is also an irony here lacking in Mr Sansom's prose. That the castle matched K.'s expectations is said in such a way that the reader asks whether K. was too easily satisfied, especially when it appears that the building does not remotely resemble a castle, except for the battlements on the tower, which are almost an afterthought. At the same time, the reader is placed squarely inside K.'s own experience: 'If you had not known it was a castle . . .' – so that he is persuaded to share it, even as he realises the absurdity of knowing what can be seen to be false.

This involvement and detachment is a feature of Kafka's work that at once removes it from the pretentiousness of 'In the Maze'. And part of the attraction here is the avoidance of impressiveness. The castle of Kafka's novel has been taken by a large number of his readers to have some religious significance, whether as a symbol of God, or as the repository of something like the Holy Grail, and the comparison with the church tower clearly invites the imagination to run in that direction. At the same time, Kafka takes care that no such identifications are really possible. The church tower at home is 'definite' ('bestimmt'): it has the weight of tradition behind it, even though the recollection that it is still only an earthly building evokes the thought that the tradition is not conclusive, and it is not in doubt about itself as K. usually is about himself. The tower immediately before K.'s eyes, by contrast, is 'uncertain' ('unsicher'), reflecting the kind of man K. is, just as the castle reflects his expectations. It is not in the least attractive as one would suppose God or the Holy Grail to be. There is even something demented about it, and the whole appearance of the tower ultimately suggests (if one has read a certain amount of Kafka) an image not so much of a divinity as of a place from which just such a melancholy man as K. has broken loose. It is, in a sense, K. who has risen up in this novel 'for all the world to see': the castle reflects him before he has begun to be aware of his own likeness. But none of this is definite. There is no allegory as there is in the idea of men cutting their individual paths through a maze, and the reflections the reader is capable of catching are very many.

The most disturbing part of the passage is the hint at insanity. This, after all, is the castle which the whole novel is going to be concerned with. For much of the time it is going to seem a matter almost of life and death for K. to get into it, or at any rate to meet the senior official residing there, and here it is described at the outset with something verging on madness or evil in its appearance. It is rather like the end of Browning's poem 'Childe

Roland to the Dark Tower Came', when the knight reaches the goal he and hundreds of others have been trying to reach for generations, to encounter not the Grail but a loathsome enemy:

> What in the midst lay but the Tower itself?
> The round squat turret, blind as the fool's heart,
> Built of brown stone, without a counterpart
> In the whole world . . .

Yet it is clear that K. depends for his very existence on the castle's approval, and it is just as much of a fulfilment as a threat to him.

This does not sound as though Kafka had worked out beforehand an allegory of ideas that already existed before ever he came to write. The description, especially of the tower, is often independent of any conceivable allegorical sense. It is not a translation of some such thought as 'there's a divinity that shapes our ends / Rough hew them how we will', as the William Sansom story is. On the contrary it sounds as though Kafka himself was no more likely to be able to translate the words into other terms than the reader is. The image has come into his mind for the most part without antecedents (the tower or castle, of course, is an image of some antiquity), and he has written it down as it came to him, He sets K. to trace the path to the castle without fully knowing to what he is committing him, impelled by what some would call a daemon.

For all its ambitions, the passage from Kafka is not pretentious. And the integrity with which Kafka follows where his imagination leads is reflected in his treatment of people. Again a comparison with a William Sansom story is enlightening. 'The Inspector' is a tale based roughly on Kafka's novel, *The Trial*, though it is much shorter and attempts much less. Where, in *The Trial*, the plot is about a man, Joseph K., who is arrested one morning by a mysterious organisation that never brings any charge against him, but finally executes him, in Sansom's story a passenger on a bus is suddenly prevented from leaving it by a ticket inspector, and detained for weeks because he is unable to produce his ticket. The Sansom story is typical of what is now generally called a Kafkaesque situation: as in a dream, a mere triviality assumes unheard-of proportions. Being only a few pages long, it has no such possibility of development as Kafka's novel has, and there is no occasion to complain on that score. As before, the important contrast at the outset is in the tone, not only in relation to the characters, but to the spirit of the writing. Here are the opening sentences of *The Trial:*

Somebody must have been slandering Joseph K., for, without having done anything bad, one morning he was arrested. The cook employed by Frau Grubach, his landlady, who brought him his breakfast every day just before eight, did not come. That had never happened before. K. waited a while, observed from his pillow the old woman who lived opposite, and who was watching him with a curiosity quite unusual for her, but then, feeling both surprised and hungry, he rang the bell. At once came a knock, and a man entered whom he had never seen before in his flat. He was slim, yet solidly built, wore a close-fitting black suit, which, like tropical kit, was provided with various pleats, pockets, buckles, buttons, and a belt, and consequently, though one could not say quite what it was meant for, seemed extremely businesslike. 'Who are you?' asked K., sitting up half erect in the bed. But the man ignored the question, as though there was no choice but to accept his presence, and confined himself to saying: 'You rang?' 'Tell Anna to fetch my breakfast', said K., and silently turned his attention to discovering through careful attention and reflection who the man actually was. But the man did not expose himself so very long to his gaze; he turned to the door, opening it a little and telling somebody who was evidently standing just behind it, 'He says tell Anna to fetch his breakfast'. There was a short laugh in the next room; from the sound you could not tell for certain whether there might not be several people involved. Although the strange man could have learned nothing from it that he did not know already, he said to K., as though delivering a message, 'It is impossible'. 'I like that', said K., jumping out of bed and quickly putting on his trousers. 'We'll just see who these people in the next room are, and what Frau Grubach has got to say for herself, allowing this disturbance.' It occurred to him at once that by saying this he was, in a way, admitting the stranger had some right of surveillance, but this did not seem important now. At all events the stranger understood it in that way, for he said 'Wouldn't you rather stay here?' 'I neither wish to remain here, nor to be addressed by you, if you are not going to introduce yourself to me.' 'It was well-meant', said the stranger, and now he opened the door of his own accord.

As in *The Castle* there is a certain irony here: K. is impressed with the externals of the stranger even though he does not know what the trappings on the suit are for, and by the same token the Court which, as it turns out, has sent the man, is also distanced just a little. The outward aspect of the Court impresses K., yet the reader's attention is drawn to the irrationality of K. In the same way the bold front K. puts on is just a bit ridiculous. As he notices himself, later, he is giving in too quickly to the absurd situation: a saner reaction would have been to send the man packing, and K.'s would-be determined language is all wrong. His final words in this passage are impossibly circumspect and bound by the rules of etiquette. Yet throughout there is a sense of menace: the black suit, the unaccountable laugh, the possibility that there are men outside ganging up on K., and the sudden show of goodwill at the end are unsettling. The combination of courtesy and brutal disregard will continue to the moment when the executioners thrust a knife into K.'s heart.

The Sansom story is more trivial. The central character, having found his way blocked as he tries to get off the bus, at first resists, then gives in, as a hand grips his jacket. What Kafka conveys without actually naming it is here verbalised:

The fingers seemed to caress the cloth they touched as though they recognized and apologized for the assault that nevertheless they intended to pursue with vigour.

One sees what Mr Sansom wants to put over here, but one does not feel it as a whole situation. That is not the case with what follows:

At this point the clerk noticed that the tall man was wearing uniform of some kind. The canopy of the bus and the bright sunlight beyond shadowed his exact identity. As the clerk sensed the uniform, his arm, which he had begun to withdraw, slackened its tension and yielded. A sensation of old guilt, latent in even the most innocent passenger, disturbed the clerk's inner equilibrium. He felt his capacities shrink, and the words in his mind, although unspoken, were pitched several times higher than was normal.

'May I see your ticket, please?' The clerk was instantly impressed that this must be the Inspector. He now raised his eyes. The Inspector's face was closely shaven, round and greyish white, with a hard polish. His cold eyes seemed to search through the clerk, yet they fixed themselves on the knot of the clerk's tie rather than on his eyes, in order that their accusation, although authoritative, should not appear discourteous.

'I'm sorry', said the clerk. 'I left it upstairs. And now a sailor is sitting on it.' This was the truth. The clerk had placed his ticket on the seat beside him, and then a petty officer had taken the very seat. The clerk had not liked to disturb the petty officer, since the necessity of the ticket appeared less than the necessity of the petty officer's comfort.

Although the Inspector now frowned, his lips remained set in their solid smile. 'So a sailor is sitting on it? Well, I must say I haven't heard that one before!' He glanced back at the conductor bitterly. When his eyes returned to the clerk, they were cold and once more efficient. 'Now, sir, I must ask you for your ticket, please.'

'But a sailor is sitting on it,' repeated the clerk.

. . . The conductor coughed nervously. 'We ought to go now, sir,' he said. 'We're behind schedule.'

It was clear that the Inspector resented this intrusion. For he turned his face slightly away from the conductor, wrinkling his brow and affecting not to have heard the conductor's plea. But the conductor persisted. 'As a matter of fact', the conductor continued, in a lowered voice of apology, 'I can safely say that I remember selling this gentleman a ticket.'

Now the Inspector raised his shoulders, so that he seemed to grow a full inch taller, and compressed his lips with reserved indignation. 'That is not the point at all,' he said . . .

The English is unsatisfying here, at several places: 'shadowed' is needlessly ambiguous; 'he felt his capacities shrink' has little meaning; 'impressed that this must be the Inspector' is bad usage, and so is 'the necessity of the ticket'. At the same time, there is no menace here, though the Inspector is several times, later on, said to be tremendous; there is no humour, no particular tone at all. It is all as harmless as a mild dream of anxiety in which a misdemeanour is magnified. The people involved are taken from the comic papers, not from the cold, distant world that surrounds Joseph K.:

Two middle-aged women with straight corseted backs and untidy hats watched the scene. An old man chewed his gums and muttered his own solution inaudibly. A boy in greased dungarees gaped. . . . The two women stumbled to seize and sit in the seat immediately behind the petty officer. The boy began to gape at something out of the window that had attracted his bewildered eye. . . . The old man had discovered an advertisement that he now scanned with intense interest. He stood on the seat and ran his nose up and down the print, not more than an inch away.

There is a condescension towards these people, a vaudeville background to the not very seriously threatening situation of the clerk. Kafka, on the other hand treats his minor characters with as much seriousness as the major ones, though they behave extraordinarily. The old woman who watched K. while he lay in bed reappears a page or two later:

He walked up and down the empty space in the room a few times, and saw across the way the old woman, who had dragged a much older man to the window and held him in a firm embrace.

And later:

In the window opposite the two old people were once more lying down, but they had increased their numbers, for behind them, completely over-topping them, stood a man with an open-necked shirt, squeezing and twisting his reddish, pointed beard.

A little later still:

. . . Kullich suddenly pointed at the house opposite, where the large man with the blonde pointed beard had just appeared, and, momentarily a little embarrassed at showing himself now in his full size, retreated to the wall and leaned against it.

These mysterious witnesses are often in the background of

Kafka's novels, and it is never very clear why they are there. Occasionally they seem momentous, as at the end when Joseph K. is about to be executed:

His eye fell on the last storey of the house adjoining the quarry. Like a ray of light darting up, the two halves of a window flew open, a man, faint and thin at that height and that distance, jerked his body out and stretched out his arms even further. Who was it? A friend? A good man? Somebody who cared? Somebody who wanted to help? Was it a single individual? Was it everybody? Was help still possible? Were there objections he had forgotten?

These bystanders are not there to provide easy laughs, they are the sometimes hostile, sometimes benevolent, sometimes ambiguous society in which K. has to live, and their haunting presence keeps up the enigma of the novels. Even when they are like marionettes, as in the last passage quoted, which evokes a kind of jack-in-the-box, the melancholy is enhanced: a jack-in-the-box is all that K. has to count on at this last moment.

What emerges from these comparisons is that Kafka's writing is without condescension; it is pure in the sense that it adopts no superior attitude either to people or to things. If it sees people as puppets occasionally that is not a sneer at them but a matter-of-fact statement. The writing is clear, in the sense that it contains no absurdities, goes straight to the point, and is not obscured by false sentiment. It is simple, above all in comparison with a great deal of German prose, which has often tended to labyrinthine constructions. But it is not, so far, recalling Brod's praise of it, anything like sweet, and one is not at all sure it is healthy. The comparison with Mr Sansom's early tales certainly establishes Kafka's greater maturity, precision, detachment. Can more be done, reading such short passages?

The most terrible of all Kafka's stories is 'In the Penal Colony', written shortly after the beginning of the First World War. The story of an infamous machine of torture, it is at the same time a metaphor for the spiritual condition of those human beings who are obliged to suffer unspeakable anguish for the infringement of codes of behaviour beyond their comprehension. One of its sources is almost certainly a story by Edgar Allan Poe, 'The Pit and the Pendulum', though here the metaphor, if any is intended, concerns rather the inevitability of death. A comparison of Poe's prose with Kafka's will show further what issues are before the reader who is aiming at some personal decision about the claim made by Max Brod.

Poe's tale is related by a former prisoner of the Spanish Inquisition, condemned to a lingering death in the dungeons of Toledo. Swooning away as his judges pronounce sentence, he awakens to find himself in total darkness, fearing he is already in his tomb. He gropes his way to a slimy wall, and explores a large area of what seems to be a subterranean courtyard, only escaping by chance from a fall into the deep pit somewhere near its centre. For some time he is kept alive by bread and water which appears by his side after his fits of unconsciousness, until at length he finds that during his most recent sleep he has been made even more of a prisoner than before. He is now bound down, lying on his back on a low framework of wood. The pitcher of water has been removed, but a dish of meat, pungently seasoned, apparently in order to increase his thirst, has been left. Looking upward, he sees on the ceiling a painted figure of Time, from which, instead of a scythe, there is what seems to be the picture of a huge pendulum. But the pendulum, as he observes, is not painted, it is in motion, swinging from side to side, and appears to be one more of the designs of the monks against his life:

It might have been half-an-hour, perhaps even an hour, (for I could take but imperfect note of time) before I again cast my eyes upward. What I then saw confounded and amazed me. The sweeps of the pendulum had increased in extent by nearly a yard. As a natural consequence, its velocity was also much greater. But what mainly disturbed me was the idea that it had perceptibly *descended*. I now observed, with what horror it is needless to say, that its nether extremity was formed of a crescent of glittering steel, about a foot in length from horn to horn; the horns upward, and the under edge evidently as keen as that of a razor. Like a razor also it seemed massive and heavy, tapering from the edge into a solid and broad structure above. It was appended to a weighty rod of brass, and the whole *hissed* as it swung through the air.

. . . What boots it to tell of the long, long hours of horror more than mortal, during which I counted the rushing oscillations of the steel! Inch by inch – line by line – with a descent only appreciable at intervals that seemed ages – down and still down it came! Days passed – it might have been that many days passed – ere it swept so closely over me as to fan me with its acrid breath. The odour of the sharp steel forced itself into my nostrils. I prayed – I wearied heaven with my prayer for its more speedy descent. I grew frantically mad, and struggled to force myself upward against the sweep of the fearful scimitar. And then I fell suddenly calm and lay smiling at the glittering death as a child at some rare bauble.

. . . Down – steadily down it crept. I took a frenzied pleasure in contrasting its downward with its lateral velocity. To the right – to the left – far and wide – with the shriek of a damned spirit! to my heart with the stealthy pace of the tiger! I alternately laughed and howled, as the one or the other idea grew predominant.

There is a ringing tone, and an urgency about this prose. There is also some melodrama, an exaggeration which possibly shows that Poe was not completely sure of carrying the reader with him, though the situation is bad enough not to need the italicised sound, and the other suggestions of fantastic speed in the swing of the pendulum. The last sentence substitutes a merely apparent symmetry of contraries for an experience, and one may well ask whether it was the idea of a damned spirit or of a stealthy tiger that provoked the laughter: either would be an unlikely cause. This is in key with the rest of the story, for the prisoner escapes the pendulum by encouraging rats to gnaw at his fastenings, only to find that the metal walls of his dungeon are being made red-hot, and advancing towards him – the Inquisition spares no expense in devising its tortures – only to be rescued at the end by French troops who fortunately happen to have invaded the town at that precise moment and decide to see what is going on below stairs. Poe is aiming at making the reader's flesh creep – not wholly unsuccessfully – rather more than at creating an experience with a serious meaning.

Kafka, by contrast, is entirely serious. The machine in his

story can be set to inscribe on the body of a prisoner the commandment he has unwittingly transgressed, and thereafter it kills him and throws his body into a trench. There is no emotion in it at all. Near the beginning, the officer in charge of the machine describes it to a passing explorer (the scene is set in the tropics) in the plainest of terms:

'It consists, as you see, of three parts. In the course of time each of these parts has come to acquire a popular name, as you might say. The lower one is called the bed, the upper one the inscriber, and this mobile one in the middle is called the harrow.' 'The harrow?' asked the explorer . . . 'Yes, the harrow', said the officer, 'a suitable name. The needles are arranged as in a harrow, though remaining in one place, and with much more subtlety. You'll understand very quickly, I'm sure. On this bed here the condemned man is laid – I'll describe the machine first and then let you see it actually in motion. You'll follow it better like that. And then there's a cog on the inscriber that has been worn down; it squeaks quite a bit when it's moving, one can hardly understand a word anyone says; spares are difficult to obtain here, I'm afraid. – Well, then, here's the bed, as I said. It's covered completely with a layer of cotton-wool, you'll see why in a moment. On this cotton-wool the condemned man is placed, on his belly, naked of course, and here are straps for the hands, these here are for the feet and these for the neck, to hold him down. Here at the head of the bed, where the man, as I said, lies first of all with his face down, is this little wad of felt, which can easily be arranged so as actually to be jammed into the man's mouth. The idea is to stop him shouting or biting off his tongue. The man has to take the wad into his mouth of course, otherwise the strap breaks his neck. 'Is that cotton-wool?' asked the explorer, leaning over. 'Why yes', said the officer, smiling. 'Feel it for yourself.' He took the explorer's hand and guided it over the bed. 'It's a specially treated cotton-wool, that's why it looks so different; I'll tell you what it's for in a moment.' The explorer had already been rather taken by the machine; with his hand over his eyes as a protection against the sun he looked up at it. It was a large construction. The bed and the inscriber were the same size, and looked like two dark chests. The inscriber was about six feet above the bed; both were connected at the corners by four brass rods which almost cast rays around, in the light of the sun. Between the chests, attached to a steel band, was the harrow.

The striking quality here is the complete indifference to suffering with which the officer speaks. It is not even a question of irony: he describes the machine as though he were selling a motor-car, almost as though it were funny, and there is not the slightest suggestion that either the officer or the explorer cares what happens to the prisoner. In tension against this is the feeling which the reader is almost certain to experience as he takes in the violence that is being done to the prisoner's body, and the pain that the prisoner must undergo. This is increased by the gradual awareness – not in this passage – that what is being described is not a fictitious invention, but an image of human life which is possibly even being presented for approval. Approval, that is, not in the sense of finding it good. Approval is scarcely the word for so ambivalent a mood. Yet there is something in the whole story which suggests that suffering of this kind is not only a normal part of human experience, but actually to be greeted with the same indifference as the officer displays:

'Do you understand how it works? The harrow starts writing. When it has done the first layer of text on the man's back, the layer of cotton-wool rotates and slowly turns the body on its side, to give the harrow fresh space. Meanwhile the wounds of the part that has been written on are laid on the cotton-wool, which, thanks to the special treatment, immediately stops the flow of blood and makes the flesh ready for the deeper incision of the text. The claws here on the edge of the harrow then tear the cotton-wool from the wounds as the body is rotated again, fling them in the trench, and the harrow can start again. So it goes on writing more and more deeply for twelve hours. For the first six hours the condemned man lives almost as before, he merely feels pain. After two hours the felt wad is taken out, as the man no longer has the strength to shriek. Here, in this electrically heated bowl at the head of the bed, warm boiled rice is placed, of which the man can eat as much as his tongue can lick out. None of them ever miss the opportunity. I have never found one who did, and my experience is very wide. Only at the sixth hour does he lose the pleasure in eating. I usually kneel here, then, and observe the phenomenon. The man seldom swallows the last mouthful, he merely turns it over in his mouth and spits it into the trench. I have to duck down, or I get it in my face. But how silent he becomes at the sixth hour! The stupidest begin to realize what's what. It starts round the eyes, a sight to tempt you into lying under the harrow yourself. Nothing else happens, the man simply begins deciphering the text, and pouting his lips as though he were listening. As you see, it isn't easy to decipher the text with your eyes, but our chaps decipher it with their wounds. There's a lot of work in it, it's true; it takes six hours to do the whole thing. But then the harrow spikes him once and for all and throws him in the trench, where he splashes into the blood and water and cotton-wool. The judgement is finished, then, and we, the soldier and I, shove him in his grave.'

The practicality of some of this – the officer ducking to avoid the spit – is so closely thought out as to raise a defensive smile. Yet no passage in Kafka is more sickening, and for turning the reader's stomach nothing could match the precise details of circumstances. There is no sign here of the health Max Brod found, unless it is health to see that life is as tormenting as this, and to accept it so willingly that the willingness is no longer even apparent, having been turned into matter-of-factness. What is at stake here is a whole definition of health and sanity: of the way in which it is healthy and sane to accept the fact that people must suffer and die, nearly always for reasons that must seem incomprehensible. Kafka's officer – not necessarily to be identified with Kafka himself, but that is a point to take up later – so completely accepts the notion of torture that he can no longer be called human. He has achieved what theoreticians of literature sometimes call the conquest of tragedy, and repellent it looks. The confinement of his vision is so great that he expects the explorer to believe men capable of eating in the midst of such torments: that is how far he has moved from any aware-ness of human realities.

For all that, the experience of life as a torment is not in itself to be brushed aside as unhealthy. It may be the only way to health. There is a story by Tolstoy, *The Death of Ivan Ilyich* which is very similar in some ways to Kafka's *The Trial* and to 'In the Penal Colony'.* It is the account of a middle-aged

* See also the discussions of Tolstoy's story by Logan Speirs, *The Oxford*

magistrate who is suddenly struck down by a fatal illness, rather as Joseph K. is suddenly arrested on an unspecified charge: in each case the arbitrariness of the 'attack' is a matter of concern, leading in Ivan Ilyich's case to a sense that he is actually on trial, and that the justice of God is called into question by the injustice with which he finds himself treated. Tolstoy draws the reader in to the experience simply by bringing home how easily each man and woman lives without awareness that death must come, and may come at any instant, and how each one feels himself exempt, morally as well as factually, from the universal law of human insignificance. Ivan Ilyich is any man who lives an unreflective life, suddenly confronted with an intolerable affront to his self-esteem. Here he is, suddenly incapacitated with pain, for no reason at all, just as Joseph K. is suddenly threatened with what appears to be an unspecified moral charge that requires his extinction. Of course he is innocent, nothing can persuade him otherwise. Towards the end, the Russian is almost completely helpless; the screaming continues for three days, and cannot be heard without horror through closed doors two rooms away. The final moment recalls both Poe and Kafka, without the melodrama of the one or the flat tone of the other:

For three whole days, during which time did not exist for him, he struggled in that black sack into which he was being forced by an unseen, invincible power. He fought as a man condemned to death fights in the hands of the executioner, knowing that he cannot save himself. And every moment he felt that, notwithstanding all his struggles, he was drawing nearer and nearer to what terrified him. He felt that his agony was due both to his being thrust into that black hole and, still more, to his not being able to get right into it. What hindered him from getting into it was his claim that his life had been good. That very justification of his life held him fast and prevented him from advancing, and caused him more agony than everything else.

Suddenly some force smote him in the chest and side, making it

Review, no. 8, 1968, reprinted in *Tolstoy and Chekhov*, Cambridge University Press (1971), and D. Z. Phillips, 'Moral Presuppositions and Literary Criticism' in *The Human World*, Feb. 1972.

still harder to breathe; he sank through the hole and there at the bottom was a light. It had happened to him as it had sometimes happened to him in a railway-carriage, when he had thought he was going forwards whereas he was actually going backwards, and all of a sudden became aware of his real direction.

'No, it was all wrong', he said to himself, 'but no matter.' He could, he could do the right thing. 'But what *is* the right thing?' he asked himself, and abruptly grew quiet.

Tolstoy's character differs from Kafka's in this respect, that he is still unwilling, and remains unwilling to accept suffering: suffering is as obscene as it ever was in his eyes, right to the last, whereas Kafka writes as though suffering were desirable. There is the further difference, in the passage immediately following on this, that Ivan Ilyich begins to feel compassion, an emotion unknown to almost all characters in Kafka, who remain pre-occupied with their own intense suffering, or else aloof and apparently beyond it, in all but a very few instances. And the most significant difference of all is that Ivan Ilyich, in the moment before he dies, ceases to fear, ceases to be concerned with his pain, and is filled with a strange mixture of joy and agony, something which only a reading of the story itself can give in all its nuances and starkness. Kafka's Joseph K. neither feels compassion nor any release from the conviction of his own degradation.

It is possible, in Tolstoy's story, to do the right thing, even at the last instant of life. Is that the case with Kafka? If not, is he more truly tragic than Tolstoy or has he lost the sense of tragedy by seeming to transcend it (if these alternatives can be offered without suggesting they exhaust the possibilities)? Is his ruth-less rejection of sentimentality and condescension, the plain straightforwardness of his writing, ever a subtle yielding to an insidious temptation, the temptation never to allow a spurt of life to burst out? (There is more life in Poe's writing, though it may not be the most admirable kind of life.) Do readers of Kafka tend to yield to the same temptation? Can one answer any of these questions not by appeal to some dogmatic assertion that there ought to be some positive ending, some moral aim in a story? Is it possible to drop all the defences one would like to put up, and go along with Kafka's imagination wherever it chooses to go, without yielding at the same time to what must sometimes seem a deadening of the very quick of life?

Kafka is an extreme instance of a writer who abandoned himself to all the forces that could destroy a man, without trying to put in their way any of the conscious blocks that most of us use, as Ivan Ilyich did, to separate ourselves from unacceptable insights. We are likely to go wrong, though, if we try to rule Kafka out of court because of any objection we have to the defeats his characters suffer. If the comparisons with William Sansom and Poe show nothing else, they show that Kafka was too scrupulous an artist to be challenged on any grounds except that of the art of novel-writing and story-writing which was his deliberate choice of activity. His lasting quality will be found in a work that grows out of this basic integrity. But to see the work as a whole means taking into account more than individual passages. The patterns of whole stories and novels go towards making the full picture, and then too the pattern of Kafka's whole life as a writer has to be sought.

2

TOWARDS UNDERSTANDING

Kafka lived his life in extreme desolation, so extreme as to be beyond comprehension without a special effort of imagination and sympathy. He seldom writes in the expectation of sharing experiences that the reader already knows; the situations in his stories are often so incredible that only his complete confidence can overcome the doubts that other people are bound to have. A further difficulty for anyone enjoying a less melancholy life is that Kafka almost always seems not to be too discontent with his unhappiness; in a certain sense he actually wants it to continue, and yet to label this 'masochism' and leave it at that would be to escape with a word whose meaning was not really evident. There are religious and philosophical as well as purely personal issues involved here, and some of them reflect, if only in distorted images, issues of universal interest.

It is true, and helpful in a small way to know, that Kafka was influenced by the place and times in which he lived. This is difficult to determine, since others in very similar situations so far as place and time were concerned did not write as he did. It may be that a working life spent in the Austrian Civil Service contributed to Kafka's spare, unemotional style. Yet there were general forces at work. Born in Prague in 1883, he grew up at a time when Austria-Hungary, of which Bohemia formed a part, was on the point of dividing into its constituent nationalities, as it eventually did, after 1918. Czech nationalists were already pressing strongly for independence from Vienna, and there were divisive currents which could foster instability in individuals. In addition, Kafka did not even belong definitely to the dominant German-speaking middle-class of Prague. As a Jew – and Jews had only recently been allowed to live in the city – he was sent by his father, a well-to-do dealer in fancy goods (a 'Galanterie-händler'), to the German 'Gymnasium', or State grammar school, and to the German University of Prague, so that he might be the more readily acceptable socially. He remained a

German-speaker of Czech origin* in a city where German-speakers were in a small minority. Isolated or at least separated from the Czechs as a 'German', from the Germans as a Jew, from orthodox Jews as a man of independent mind, and from his own family by what he felt to be the implacable hostility of his father, he had a hard station in life to occupy. Yet there were other Jewish writers in Prague like Franz Werfel and Max Brod, both friends of his, who did not feel their situation with such dreadful intensity, and perhaps only Rilke, also born in Prague, though not a Jew, knew anything comparable.

Social and historical causes should not be ruled out, but it seems that Kafka's desperation had begun before any general external circumstances could have entered his consciousness. So one would think from his account of the writing of a novel in boyhood, and the reception it received. He knew even at that early age that a radical division existed between himself and the rest of the world. The novel itself could have become a fictional development of two sides of Kafka's personality, if he had ever written more than a few pages. It was to have been about two brothers, one of whom was to go abroad, while the other stayed 'in a European prison', which sounds as though it could have represented the condition in which Kafka found himself. The project never got beyond a few fragments, since he quickly grew tired, and it was finally crushed in the way he describes, in a passage written some fifteen to twenty years after the event:

so one Sunday afternoon when we were visiting my grandparents and had eaten the very soft bread and butter we usually had there, I was writing on the subject of my prison. Quite possibly I was doing it to a large extent out of vanity, and by pushing the paper about on the table-cloth, tapping my pencil, looking round under the rim of the lamp and so on I was trying to tempt somebody to take away from me what I had written, look at it, and admire me. The last few lines were mostly taken up with a description of the corridor in the prison, especially to the silence and coldness there; there was

* His family name is a form of the Czech word ('kavka') for a bird of ill-omen, the chough or daw (German 'Dohle'), a fact which he commented on. There are one or two references to this bird in his stories, including one in the Italian name (see p. 185 below).

also a sympathetic word for the brother who stayed behind, because he was the good brother.[1]

The description sounds as though it fitted closely enough to Kafka's own state of mind at that time, even if it does not fully match up to what he experienced later. Yet even here, the ostracism he often felt he suffered showed itself:

An uncle of mine who liked laughing at people finally took the paper, which I was holding very feebly, looked at it, handed it back to me without even laughing, and merely said to the others, who were following him with their eyes, 'The usual stuff'; to me he said nothing at all. I went on sitting there, bending as before over my evidently useless sheet of paper, but I had literally been pushed out of their society with a single thrust; my uncle's judgement repeated itself in me with an almost real meaning, and even though still feeling within the family I had a glimpse of the cold expanse of our world which I should be obliged to warm with a fire I had as yet not even begun to look for.[1]

Such dereliction seems to have been ingrained, indelibly printed through Kafka's whole being. His surroundings might increase it but they did not account for it.

Ingrained though it was, Kafka was able to resist the temptation to luxuriate in it. Baudelaire had defined that temptation when he spoke of 'l'aimable remords': there is a kind of satisfaction in feeling remorse and guilt and inadequacy which can flatter the ego as unsatisfyingly as self-conscious virtue does, and Kafka was more susceptible to that temptation than most people. Not only did he feel intensely, so that he could plead for mercy in the conviction that he was guilty in every corner of his being, he was accustomed to an atmosphere of thought in which despair was almost enjoined on any serious thinker. For some generations past, if not as far back as Luther, there had been a strong tradition in Christian theology whereby dereliction and unbelief came close to being identified with their opposites, and this was not merely a matter of recalling, within the framework of the whole of Christian belief, Christ's words of dereliction on the Cross. If Christ could believe himself forsaken of God, so might any Christian, but to endure in that forsakenness until it pleased God to release one: that was a traditional and possibly the best formulation, though active efforts to release oneself were also advised in some cases. With Romantic theologians like Schleiermacher, and with such a philosopher as Hegel, a certain degree of systematisation came into this. With Hegel in particular, the idea took shape that the more alienated ('entfremdet') from God a man became, the greater was the likelihood of a sudden reversal by which the same man would enter into the fullest possession of God. To define that process of thought in all its varied nuances in different authors throughout the nineteenth century would be impossible in a small compass. The general tenor is given by an exchange of dialogue in Thomas Mann's novel *Doktor Faustus*, in which Mann attempted to summarise and symbolise all the major trends in German civilisation in modern times. Here, at one of the climaxes, the central character Adrian Leverkühn, as a modern Dr Faustus, discusses with a figure who seems to be the Devil his own desperate situation, not unlike Kafka's in some ways. But Mann need not have had Kafka in mind: many other writers of the past hundred years or so would fill the part equally well and better. Leverkühn's point is that, though he is in a state so sinful that he might well despair, that very despair is his salvation. The Devil does not fail to point out the weaknesses in the argument:

[Leverkühn]: You rely on my pride preventing me from feeling the contrition essential to salvation, and yet you do not take account of the fact that there is such a thing as proud contrition. The contrition of Cain, firmly persuaded that his sin was too great ever to be forgiven. Contrition bereft of all hope, being firm unbelief in the possibility of grace and forgiveness, being the rock-like conviction of the sinner that he has gone too far, and that even infinite goodness is insufficient to forgive his sin – that alone is real contrition, and I draw your attention to the fact that it is closest of all to redemption, most irresistible of all for goodness. You will admit that the run-of-the-mill sinner can only be moderately interesting to divine Grace. In a case like that the act of Grace has little impetus, it can only be moderately active. Mediocrity leads no kind of theological life. A sinfulness so hopeless that it makes a man despair of all hope, there's your truly theological path to salvation.

[The Devil]: Clever. And where is the like of you to find the simplicity, the naive abandonment to despair that would be essential to such a hopeless way to hope? Isn't it clear to you that conscious speculation on the attraction exerted on goodness by extreme guilt, makes an act of grace impossible to the utter extreme?

[Leverkühn]: And yet it is only by such a 'Non plus ultra' that the highest pitch of a dramatic–theological life is reached, that is, the extreme of guilt and therewith the final and most irresistible challenge to the infinity of goodness.

[The Devil]: Not bad, Ingenious, I must say. And now let me tell you, it is precisely intellects of your kind that make up the population of Hell . . .[2]

There is a scene in Kafka's *Castle* which bears quite a resemblance to this, in a general way, when K., the hero, is confronted in a moment of utter helplessness and hopelessness with a chance of making full use of his inadequacy, a chance of bringing down the whole structure of authority that stands over against him, and achieving, as it were, complete power, Were he Leverkühn he would speculate on his chances; being K., and thus closer to Kafka, he ignores them. Kafka's own words on this subject were 'Don't despair, even at not despairing.'[3] Yet the situation he is in is similar, even though his individual reaction to it is distinctive, and Kafka is operating with the same ideas as Mann, despite his fundamental divergence. He comes very close indeed to Mann's novel when he writes that 'No-one sings so purely as those in the deepest Hell. What we take for the singing of angels is their singing.'[4]

Even so much categorising as that has its risks with Kafka, who was never precisely the same man in the same mood from day to day. There is a passage in one of the fragments intended for *The Trial* which anyone attempting to come to an understanding needs to take to heart. It is a passage from an unfinished chapter entitled 'The Struggle with the Deputy Director', and refers to the character whom Kafka designated in both this novel and in *The Castle* with the initial of his own surname:

The deputy director must not be allowed to rest in the belief that K. was done with; he must not sit comfortably in his office with this belief, he must be discomfited. He must realise as often as possible that K. was alive, and that, like everything that is alive, he might some day come up with surprising new talents, however harmless he might seem today.

Kafka is not to be packaged into any formula, even though he may have been tempted from time to time to speculate as Leverkühn did. What is so wrong about Adrian Leverkühn's expressed belief is its obvious perversity, so obvious that it is hard to see why Leverkühn persists in it, once the implications have been so fully explored. Mann's fictional character is fitted to a mould, much more than Kafka himself or K. could be. What distinguishes Kafka from the sheer calculating rationality of Leverkühn is, for instance, the desire to be reconciled to his condition simply because it was a necessary one and yet at the same time a condition which one could learn to love, as one might learn to love a leper. Only a complete reading of the diaries could give a picture of the variety of moods through which Kafka passed, though there are, as well as hopeful moods, constantly recurring thoughts that he is damned, that suicide is the only way out, if an impossible one, that all the gods of vengeance are coming down on him with outstretched fingers and claws, that he needs punishment and welcomes it, that no man has ever lived in so miserable an inward condition as he has. Very little of this is ever specific. Though the major part of Kafka's diaries, as of his writing career, fell in the period of the First World War and its aftermath, there are no references in it to the fighting (except for a frank confession that he passionately wishes every kind of evil to those engaged in it[5]), to the conditions on the home front, which must at times have been extremely difficult, or to the revolutions which flared up in Berlin, Munich, Budapest after the Armistice, or to the inflation which followed.

The misery is all within his mind, and is almost always concerned with the spiralling of his own self-criticism, or with violent self-reproach over trifles. These reproaches spring from a desire to love, an emotion which Kafka repeatedly accused himself of not knowing, yet they are in themselves, as he is aware, demonstrations of his own inability to love himself. It happens, for instance, that he is travelling in a train in the same compartment as a young nurse, whom he finds attractive, and who tells a story about one of her patients who snored, which prompted the other patients in the ward to throw slippers at him: you have to be strict with them, she said, or you never get anywhere. 'Here', says Kafka, 'I made a stupid, but in my case very characteristic, sneaking, cunning, offhand, impersonal, unsympathetic, untrue remark, far-fetched out of some remnant of my diseased disposition, and influenced into the bargain by the Strindberg performance last night, that it must do women good to be allowed to treat men in such a way.'[6] (He may well have been thinking of Strindberg's *The Father*, in which Woman is represented as exploiting men.) The nurse, he observes later, took no notice of his comment, which is interesting only for the flood of recrimination which it unleashed in Kafka. It does not sound as though it had been malicious, and if it was, another man might have quickly recovered his poise. Kafka's striving, rather on the prim side, is to make himself angelically without such promptings, and the result is a diabolical self-laceration. No wonder then, that he writes in terms like these, and no wonder that a certain pride – of which he will later be conscious and for which he will reprove himself – lurks in the background:

To come to terms in love, with a life like mine, is impossible, there has certainly never been any man who could have done so. When other men came to this frontier – and to have come here at all is pitiable – they swung aside, but I can't. And it seems to me I haven't actually come here at all, but was driven here as a small child and fastened here with chains . . .[7]

The attempt at self-purification drives him further and further into self-damnation; he finds himself no surer at the end of it. Yet he was aware how simple a thing might comfort him, and even be a release. There was very little that Kafka was not aware of, even though that little seemed to him the one unattainable salvation. At all events, he relates an occurrence, only a few days after the meeting with the nurse in the train, which shows what he felt to be real insight into both himself and others. No-one, he reflects, really shows understanding of him in everything. To have someone who did possess such understanding, a wife for instance, would be to have support on all sides, 'it would be to have God'. And then he reflects that his sister Ottla, to whom he was devoted, understands him quite well, his friends Max Brod and Felix Weltsch a certain amount, while his sister Elli understands only a few details, though 'with hideous intensity'. His fiancée, on the other hand, Felice Bauer, to whom he was twice engaged, but whom he could never bring himself to marry, does not understand him at all, despite the rapport which exists. At this point, however, he reflects that perhaps she does understand him without knowing it – and he recalls one occasion when he was longing for her unbearably, and travelled by the Berlin tube to a station where they had arranged to meet. Thinking she was at the street level, and wanting to reach her as quickly as possible, he was about to rush past her on the platform, when she quietly took him by the hand.[8] That is all the story, and to see why it meant so extraordinarily much to Kafka, something that he could call divine, presents some difficulties. It does seem apt, though, that a man so constantly preoccupied with looking for satisfaction at some higher level should find it unexpectedly at the place where he already is, just as Felice Bauer's gesture of restraint must have seemed completely right – no shout, no comforting word, no overt communication at all, it appears, and not even a sign that she knew what she was doing, which would have seemed an intolerable intrusion, and yet a tangible proof that he need look no further. His advice to himself not to despair even at not despairing springs from the same remote but firm certainty.

A similar indestructible certainty is at the root of another experience, this one from childhood, when he heard two women calling to each other across the gardens. It will come to mind frequently later on, and deserves attention now in some detail. Here it is, not as it appears in the diary – though the real experience was identical with the fictional one – but from a later piece of fiction in which he gives some reflections on it and gives it a wider significance. A man who has been praying in a church speaks to the narrator:

'There has never been a time when I have been convinced through myself of my own life. It's that I perceive things around me in such shaky images that I always think the things were alive once, but are vanishing now. I always have a desire, my dear sir, to see things as they may be before they show themselves to me. That's when they are beautiful and quiet, no doubt. It must be, because I often hear people speaking of them in this way.'

As I remained silent and only showed by involuntary facial twitchings how uncomfortable I felt, he asked 'Don't you believe that people talk like that?'

I felt I should nod, but could not. 'Really, you don't believe it? But listen – when I was a child, I opened my eyes after a short sleep in the middle of the day, and while still quite drowsy I heard my mother calling down from the balcony, in a quite natural tone, "What are you doing my dear. It's so hot." A woman answered from the garden, "I'm having tea outside" ['Ich jause im Grünen' – the Austrian 'jause' is untranslatable in its suggestion of ease and comfort]. They spoke without reflection, and not particularly clearly, as though it were only what anyone would expect.'[9]

Such calm enjoyment – with the suggestion that everything is equally peaceful until he himself destroys it with his own vision of it, haunts Kafka's imagination for most of his life. Yet for his own part, he could not rid himself of the perpetual affliction. Like the animal in his story 'The Burrow', which could sit outside its underground lair, its one place of safety, and observe minutely every danger to which it was exposed, he had nothing but this dual experience – fearing and knowing his fear – to contemplate:

I am as it were specially appointed to see the phantoms of the night not only in the helplessness and blissful confidence of sleep, but at the same time to encounter them in reality with the full power of my waking self, and with a quiet critical ability.[10]

At times it seems to him that there is nothing but to go on enduring, observing the dangers, though often with the belief that to do so without resistance, in a quietistic acceptance, will eventually lead to release.

A heavy downpour. Stand out in the rain, let the iron rays go right through you, glide along in the water that is trying to sweep you away, but stay erect and wait till the sun comes streaming suddenly, endlessly in.[11]

He reflects that Abraham's wife Sarah was to all appearance beyond hope of giving birth to a child, being well past the age of child-bearing, and yet was blessed; that even though one's prison-cell may be passed by day after day, that is still no proof that it will not some day be opened:

Be content, learn (learn, you're forty now) to rest in the moment (no, you used to be able to). Yes in the moment, terrible as it is. It isn't terrible, only fear of the future makes it so.[12]

The paradox remains all the time: the escape is always for-seeable, anyone could instruct him how to find it, yet it is never available. With time, tuberculosis takes its toll of him, and he reflects that bodily pain is the one undeniable truth. How strange, that the God of Pain was not the chief god of the primitive religions, but only of the later ones:

To each invalid his household god, to the lung-patient the God of Stifling.[13]

In such irony he confronts his situation. Incapable of breathing, he must accept that too as part of a divine imposition, and so he swings between hopeless acceptance of the given moment as inevitable, and belief that only by such acceptance could he escape from it to a better life. At times escape and persistence in the same condition seem indistinguishable. 'Who speaks of victory? to endure is all', Rilke wrote. Much of Kafka's personal experience, though without Rilke's rhetoric, is as negative.

The real release he looked for, if such a phrase is possible at

all, was in his writing. Kafka's sense of vocation was deep-going. Writing was to be his salvation, and for long stretches he could go on believing that without ambiguity, though the sense of futility always returned. This was not a purely thera-peutic device, either. As early as 1911 he makes up his mind that the desire he feels to write down his whole fearful condition, 'just as it comes up out of the depths', straight on to the paper before him, is 'not an artistic desire'.[14] There must, presumably, be some shaping, some control: he is not intending to write the kind of thing that might serve on a psychoanalyst's couch. Some impression of the teeming world of his creative mind can be had from the variety of fragments and stories which continually fill out his notebooks. The settings are world-wide: Prague, Italy, Paris, Russia, Turkey, the tropics, China, the United States, the Arabian desert; the chief figures are fantastically varied: a chimpanzee, a dog, a beetle, a mouse, a trapeze-artist, a bank-official, a lift-boy, a physician, a scholar. Themes grow and die away, hundreds are abandoned for the few that continue into fuller life: a rabbi begins to make a living creature out of clay, a man comes across a burnt-out hotel, a child is pulled down through the floor by unseen powers, an angel's arm bursts through the ceiling with a sword in its hand, a white horse gallops alone down a city street. To allow this to come through from the dark side of his mind, and yet not be irre-vocably engulfed, is his aim. The intention is to liberate him-self – 'The tremendous world I have in my head. But how to free myself, and free it, without being torn in half. And a thousand times sooner be torn in half, than keep it back in me, or bury it. That is why I am here, that's quite clear to me.'[15] He admires, at just about this same time, an author who shows details and has order and logical sequence. Writing is some-thing that gives him assurance, even if he writes only a little; he is amazed at it, and has a sense of confidently surveying everything about him.[16]

Later in life, in such a story as 'Josephine the Singer', he was to place in an ambiguous light the pretensions of the artist who sees himself as a superior being. But for a long time he continued to believe in the possibility of an apocalyptic outcome, destroying the present world only to achieve a new and greater one. A story like 'A Country Doctor', he observed, could give him a temporary satisfaction. Happiness he could only have if he could ever 'lift the world into the pure, the true, the unchangeable'.[17] What precisely he meant by those often-quoted words will never be certain, now. It may be that the only pure, true and unchangeable state he had in mind was death. Certainly this is the impression to be had from his conversation with Gustav Janouch, if it is to be trusted (Janouch himself is unwilling to vouch for it altogether), in which Kafka observed that whereas 'Literatur' was concerned with presenting things in a pleasant light, 'Dichtung' (that is, roughly, serious literature) was concerned with raising things into the realm of truth, purity, and permanence.[18] But it was only through writing that he expected such a relief, and in the end he still left instructions to Max Brod in his testament that his manuscripts were to be burned, and that nothing he had ever published was to be issued again after he had died. True, Brod ignored this on the grounds that Kafka was well aware that he would ignore it when he made the request, and it is in itself a mark of Kafka's abdication from a decision, that he should have entrusted the destruction of the manuscripts to someone else, when he could have destroyed them himself if he really intended to. But that is all part of the shifting ambiguity found everywhere in both his life and his work. Even writing both was and was not the way out.

It must have been in much the same mood that Kafka wrote the lengthy letter to his father in which he set out the whole relationship between his father and himself, exonerated and condemned them both and finally retained the letter, which was never delivered. Since so much in Kafka's writing is concerned with this relationship it is essential to read it, for all the continuing ambiguities. 'My writing was all about you', he wrote, 'I complained there only of what I could not complain of at your breast. It was an intentionally prolonged departure from you, yet although it was forced on me by you, it proceeded in the direction determined by me.'[19] How much of the account is true, how much due to a sensitive man's misinterpretation, need not concern us so long as it is not assumed that every word of accusation is necessarily objective. The father whom Kafka portrays is not so harsh as many fathers have been. He scarcely ever beat Franz, though the threat of pulling off his braces was worse than a beating, since the boy assumed, even when forgiven, that he had deserved to be beaten, and felt guilty for long afterwards. Nor do some of Herrmann Kafka's faults seem now more than peccadilloes: the inconsistency which allowed him to disregard table manners which he fiercely imposed on the children was less harmful in the lives of Kafka's sisters than it was in Kafka's own. In part, the sheer size of his father, a bull-necked man with close-cropped hair and pointed moustaches, very much as Kafka describes the superior official Klamm in *The Castle*, was intimidating, especially at swimming-lessons. And gradually the picture is built up of a man, as his son saw him, so full of self-confidence, so brash, so intolerant, and so terrifying as to assume the importance of a god – indeed Kafka says that his every word was a divine command. He was terrifying, whether or not he struck a blow, by his words alone: 'I'll tear you like a fish' was the least of his threats. His cynicism was just as offensive: not merely did he attend synagogue in the most perfunctory way, he spoke of marriage in such terms that Kafka, who desired nothing more earnestly than a wife and children, was for ever frustrated. At the age of 36, when he spoke of an intention to marry, his father suggested a prostitute instead to satisfy the lusts of the flesh, and offered himself to take the son to a brothel if he was afraid. In these circumstances, the chief hope of emulating his father vanished. To marry would be to achieve independence, to be on a level footing with his father. Yet marriage appeared to him in so objectionable a light, precisely because of his father's attitude to sexual matters, that to marry would be to become too like his father. Quite apart, then, from any feeling that marriage would prevent him from devoting his time to writing (or make him so happy that he would have nothing left to write about – the neurosis was self-defensive), Kafka was confronted by his father with ambiguity personified. Here was the issuer of divine commands who broke them with impunity, the representative of what the Talmud declared to be the proper married condition of every Jew, who at the same time denied to his son any decent intention in marrying. Kafka, like the hero of the Castle, became certain of nothing, 'needing at every moment a fresh confirmation of my existence',[20] much as K. needs the Castle's confirmation that he is what he claims to be. Yet with all this he did not with one part of himself see in his father the authority he saw with the other part. Kafka and his sister Ottla, he tells his father, are always talking of 'the dreadful trial going on between you and us . . . this trial in which you always claim you are the judge, whereas, at any rate to a large extent . . . you are just as weak and dazzled a participant as we are.'[21] By this means Kafka seeks once again both to accuse and to excuse. The letter is never free of this ambiguity, and it was in the long run never sent, perhaps never meant to be sent. What it does make clear is one major source of Kafka's extreme sense of guilt and inferiority: the practical impossibility, as he saw it, of ever making that self-assertion which for other men might have been satisfying, but in his case could only lead to an intolerable sense that, if he made it, he was likely to finish up resembling his father.

By the time Kafka had reached maturity, Freud's theories of the dependence of religious belief in a divine Father on earthly experience of a human father had become well known. Whether Kafka's writing is to be understood in purely Freudian terms, that is, as entirely about his human father and only by projection about any divinity, is a matter not to be decided by reference to the writing itself, which never mentions such terms, except for a derogatory remark about psychoanalysis in the diary and a not very enlightening reference to Freud's name in connection with the writing of 'The Judgement'. One may decide on other grounds that a Freudian analysis is profitable for understanding Kafka; his own words give no particular justification for doing that. On the other hand, since the point is sometimes disputed, it needs to be said that there are explicit observations of a purely religious nature in

Kafka's private remarks, though scarcely ever in his published works.

Unlike many of his contemporaries Kafka was seldom inclined to oriental religious speculations with their stress on self-annihilation or absorption in Brahma or evanescence in Nirvana: in so far as he reads or writes about religion, it is the Judaeo-Christian tradition that is in the forefront; he reads the Bible and the Talmud, Kierkegaard, Pascal, as well as Nietzsche (often a disappointed Christian) rather than the Upanishads or the Bhagavad-Gita. The Book of Job had a special attraction for him, and he writes of such events as the Fall of Adam and Eve, Hell, Paradise and the rejoicing of the Seraphim, rather than of concepts like 'the Naught'; indeed, according to Janouch, Kafka had an aversion from 'Oriental' religions. He was interested in the Yiddish theatre, his literary friends were often Jews like Max Brod and Franz Werfel, and he had sympathy with the cause of the Zionists. Yet he did not attend synagogue or church, writes in his diary of having been 'with the Jews' as though he felt himself distinct, and could express real contempt for Jews in general. His schooling at the State schools in Prague, especially at the German 'Staatsgymnasium', may have had something to do with this. Certainly none of his fictional works is explicitly about a Jew (though 'Josephine the Singer' is sometimes interpreted as though it were) and where any religious affiliation is mentioned at all, it is Christian not Jewish. The father in 'The Metamorphosis' and Joseph K. in *The Trial* both cross themselves; the cathedral scene in the latter novel is clearly a Christian building; K. in *The Castle* thinks of the castle in connection with a church in his home-country, not a synagogue. This may have been a means of tying the works to the general European tradition rather than to a less representative Jewish one, yet Kafka's works are coloured by the choice, whatever the explanation. The fairly frequent references in his diaries and conversations to Christ and the Messiah, on the other hand, show by their scepticism that he paid allegiance ultimately to neither Judaism nor Christianity. What is indisputable is his preoccupation with ideas in the monotheistic

43

tradition. Without the reinforcement of paternal by divine authority his problems might never have arisen.

What is distinctive in Kafka, in his religious thoughts as in his relation with his human father, is his ambiguity. A diary entry that begins 'Have mercy on me, I am sinful in every corner of my being', goes on to decry such a plea as 'ridiculous self-love', though it also defends it, half-heartedly, on the ground that every living being must have self-love, and to that extent is not ridiculous.[22] At the back of such a thought as this lies the recurrent idea, more akin after all to Buddhist thought, that all the created world is unworthy to exist, and only the total extinction of self is justifiable. Sometimes, in such circumstances, one is uncertain whether to read Kafka as speaking within the paradoxical tradition of Hegel and Kierkegaard and the German Romantic theologians, whereby the greater the lack of faith becomes, the greater dedication to God or the greater chance of salvation there is, or whether he means to speak without paradox, simply as an atheist. His reflections on Pascal are apt here:

'Pascal makes everything very orderly before God appears, but there must be a deeper, more dread-filled scepticism, than that of the [one word unreadable] man, who slices into himself with wonderful knives, it is true, but with all the calm of a pork-butcher. Whence the calm? the sureness of grasp on the knife? Is God a theatrical triumphal chariot, which, granted all the desperate toil of the labourers, is dragged on stage with ropes from a great way off?'[21]

Scepticism about God, this seems to say, should produce more fear and trembling than Pascal showed; Pascal's scepticism was too confident in its attendance on the revelation that was ultimately to come. Kafka's position, at this moment, seems to require a sense of damnation comparable to Michelangelo's, whose Christ in the 'Last Judgement' might have presided over the Court in Kafka's novel, if that organisation could have tolerated so resplendent and noble a judge. Yet even Kafka's scepticism does not seem, in the last analysis, to be meant solely sceptically; there is still, lurking in the background, some expectation that even the worst hell is a way to salvation.

This thought is akin to that of Kierkegaard, in whom Kafka recognised a kindred spirit as soon as he read him. The whole idea of 'dread' or 'Angst', as Kierkegaard defines it, is an in-increasing realisation of the deceptiveness of all earthly and finite aims, an opening up to infinite possibilities: a man must realise that literally anything may become of him. Kierkegaard requires not only an infinite scepticism but also recognition that terror, perdition and annihilation, far from being mere possi-bilities, are constantly at hand, ready at any moment to become fact. Life is a process in which men are continually confronted with a nameless fear, an increasing recognition of infinite guilt, such as Kafka's *alter ego* Joseph K. endures. The basis of *The Trial* is readily seen from such a passage in Kierkegaard as this, contrasting human notions of courts and justice with the more intense trials undergone inwardly:

. . . No Grand Inquisitor has in readiness such terrible tortures as has dread, and no spy knows how to attack more artfully the man he suspects, choosing the instant when he is weakest, nor knows how to lay traps where he will be caught and ensnared, as dread knows how, and no sharp-witted judge knows how to interrogate, to examine the accused, as dread does, which never lets him escape, neither by diversion nor by noise, neither at work nor at play, neither by day nor by night.[24]

In Kierkegaard's terms, every man who has awakened (as Joseph K. literally wakes one morning) to the realisation of the infinite demands made on him, and the infinite possibilities that lie before him, has begun to undergo a trial whose possible end may be total damnation. Yet the whole process is an educa-tion, in which the individual learns to throw away 'the shrewd-ness of finitude' – the calculating element which Kafka thought to find in Pascal, or which is displayed in Adrian Leverkühn's dialogue with the Devil – and to rely on faith alone. A man who thinks in finite terms will calculate; his good and evil will always be means to his own ends. When faith comes, so Kierkegaard asserts, dread will eradicate what it has itself pro-duced, and calculation will cease. Yet to do so, dread must always oppose the merely finite perceptions of ordinary life. Joseph K. in *The Trial* is never accused of anything specific, just as Kafka's self-torturing was seldom concerned with any particular evil, apart from self-love, for as Kierkegaard writes:

The man who merely by finiteness learns to recognize his guilt is lost in finiteness, and in the end the question whether one is guilty or not cannot be decided [finitely] except in an external, juridical, exceedingly imperfect way. He therefore who only learns to recognize his guilt by analogy with the decisions of the police justice or the supreme court never really comprehends that he is guilty; for if a man is guilty, he is infinitely guilty.[25]

Here is another indication of what a 'trial' meant, in the terms Kafka was used to seeing. Yet the extreme difficulty with all Kierkegaardian theology is the paradox of the acceptance of infinite possibility, including infinite guilt, along with faith that the worst leads to the best: 'He who sank in possibility . . . sank absolutely, but then in turn he floated up from the depth of the abyss, lighter now than all that is oppressive and dreadful in life.'[26] If the abyss is infinite, the rational sceptic in us wants to know, how does one ever rise from it? Kierkegaard himself admits the risk that a man who enters upon the trial of dread may end in suicide, if he mistakes any of the countless counterfeits of dread for the real thing. The path as he describes it often looks like one devised by some malicious spirit, against whom we need to be constantly on guard: it is not a path that seems likely to promote generosity, magnanimity, confidence, but rather wariness, expectation of torment, fearfulness, something like a spiritual hypochondria (and significantly, Kierkegaard defines his position so as to exclude hypochondria of this kind – it is close enough to his meaning to need that distinction).

Kierkegaard's theology is a form of Christianity which has been influential; whether it is genuine Christianity is not a matter to treat here. The point is that Kafka, in so far as his world is capable of being interpreted in religious terms at all, rather than in terms of his relations with his father (or in some other terms altogether), is to be seen against such a background as this. The defeat or destruction of so many of his heroes may not be the purely negative thing it seems to be, or it may be that it appears so only from the point of view of the reader who has not himself made Kierkegaard's movement of infinite resignation. Kafka himself, at least at one moment in his life, certainly felt that he had made that movement, judging by a passage in his diary where he says that the best things he has written have their foundation in his ability to die content. In the fiction, there would be a death which the reader would find unjust, and by which, Kafka imagined, the reader would be moved:

'But for me, believing as I do that I shall be able to be content on my death-bed, such descriptions are, privately, a game; I enjoy dying in the dying man, and calculatingly exploit the reader's concentration on the death; I am much clearer in my mind than he is, since I assume he will cry out on his death-bed, and my cry is therefore as perfect as it can possibly be, nor does it break off like a real cry, but continues, beautiful and pure.'[27]

For the time being, with a certain condescension, Kafka sees himself as having taken dread to the point where he can comfortably contemplate extinction, though very likely the rusé attitude towards the reader would have struck him as a yet further evil, later on. There is no end to infinite guilt. From such a point there is a possibility of rising again, if Kierkegaard's belief is held. And perhaps that is what Kafka intends, when he speaks of the purity and beauty of his cry. Yet the thought must occur, that if a pure and beautiful cry (of lament: the German here is 'Klage') is all that is to emerge, this is a long way removed from the words, placed by Kafka in quotation marks, in his diary for 16 December 1913: '"The thunderous cry of delight of the Seraphim"'. Is this cry of lament all that he has to offer, even to himself, let alone the reader? The answer to that question is to be sought partly in his life, partly, and more accessibly, in the works of fiction in which he explored the ramifications of infinite possibility.

3

EARLY STORIES AND 'THE JUDGEMENT'

Kafka's demands on himself as a writer were exacting. Of the total quantity of his works, which make some six volumes in the Collected Works, though these do not include the manuscripts confiscated after his death and presumably destroyed by the Gestapo, nor those burned by himself or by Dora Diamant on his instructions, he himself approved only some forty short stories and vignettes – less than two hundred pages – for publication, and then usually reluctantly. Some of his rejections were savage, not least the request to Max Brod to destroy all his work and never let any of it be republished, though he allowed validity to a small number of pieces, 'The Judgement', 'The Stoker', 'The Metamorphosis', 'In the Penal Colony' and the story 'A Hunger-Artist'.[1] This could sound like a roundabout way of seeking approbation, since no reasons for these rejections and acceptances are given, but there is less trace of that in his letter to Felice Bauer about his astonishment, on re-reading *America* (or *Lost Without Trace*, as he normally titled it), at finding that 'only the first chapter proceeds from an inward truth, whereas the rest, apart from a few shorter or longer passages of course, was written as it were in remembrance of a great emotion that is completely absent, and is therefore to be rejected.'[2] He was similarly critical of the final pages of 'In the Penal Colony' and 'The Metamorphosis', and although he approved of these for publication, he refused to allow more than the first chapter of *America* to be printed. Since his death, a large quantity of his other writings, some of it specifically rejected by him, has seen the light, and is commonly treated without argument as though it were on a par with the rest, as indeed it is, for most research purposes. Yet even the earliest of his published work is often to be preferred to some of the ruminative deliberating of more ambitious pieces which he did what he could to suppress.

These early pieces resulted from the meeting with Max Brod shortly after Kafka had begun study at the University of Prague. What has survived from these student years is very little indeed: a couple of dozen pages, most of it intended for a larger work, *Description of a Struggle*, which never came to anything; but with Brod's encouragement he published the separate pieces in literary magazines, collecting them with some slightly later pieces in a slim volume, *Meditation*, published in 1912. Already in 'Children on the Highroad', though it stands in its own right, there are premonitions of future themes, as this extract shows:

We thrust head first through the evening air. There was no day-time and no night-time. One minute our waistcoat-buttons would be rubbing against each other like teeth, the next we would be loping along, keeping our distance, fire in our mouths, like beasts in the tropics. Like cuirassiers in wars of long ago, stamping and riding high, we would chase each other down the short alley and get up speed for the slope up the main road, beyond. Some jumped into the ditch, and had no sooner vanished down the dark slope than they would be standing like total strangers up on the footpath, looking down at us.

'Come down from there!' – 'You come up, first!' – 'So you can push us down, not likely. Got too much sense, we have.' – 'Too much funk, you mean. Just come and try it, come on!' – 'What, you lot, think you'll throw us down? Like to see you do it.'

We made the attack, were pushed in the chest, and lay down in the grass in the ditch, falling of our own free will. Everything was warmed through, you didn't feel warmth in the grass nor cold, you simply got tired.

If you turned on your right side and put your hand under your ear, you felt like going to sleep. You did want to arise again, with lifted chin, but then to fall into another ditch, a deeper one. Then you wanted to launch yourself into the breeze with one arm aslant in front of your body, and both legs blown awry, and fall into a still deeper ditch. And you didn't ever want to give that up.

You scarcely thought yet of how you would stretch out in the last ditch for a real sleep to the very limits, especially your knees, and you would lie, close to tears, on your back, as though ill. You would blink when a boy with elbows pressed to his hips jumped over from the embankment to the road, with dark soles.

Several of the themes of the stories in *Meditation*, and of Kafka's later work, are presaged here: the children are conscious of themselves as heroic warriors, and the deflation of heroic afflatus is to be a frequent topic; already the narrator shows that wish to lie down and die that Joseph K. will show. As writing, however, this extract has features not found in the later work. Metaphors, Kafka observed, were one of the things that made him despair about writing: he did not say why, but here similes follow thickly on one another. They are vivid ones, in fact, but his later writing scarcely ever has any. If the rejection of these had anything to do with a distaste for connecting things together – in Kafka's world there are as a rule only isolated beings – then that is reflected in the aversion, later, from any shared experience. Here the talk is all of what the boys in general did: 'you' ('man') did this or that, and though it is clear enough that only the narrator was involved, the pronoun makes a suggestion that it was not too uncommon to feel as he did. Again, the vivid, naturalistic dialogue would obtrude in the later works, where speech comes closer and closer to narration until at times they are indistinguishable. 'Children on the High-road' has nothing that is distinctively Kafka's in the actual writing, as distinct from the themes, though as an evocative, atmospheric piece, it has an extremely attractive quality.

By contrast, the originally unpublished remainder of 'Description of a Struggle', written in 1903 or 1904, and 'Wedding Preparations in the Country', written in 1907–8, are obscure and baffling, the mode of narration clumsily old-fashioned. Kafka seems to write here without careful revision, as in this conversation between first-person narrator and a stranger, which begins mysteriously, with a hint of an uncanny posture, yet continues in mere abstraction and unexplained generalisations:

'He sat down, sulkily, without regard for his fine clothes, and astonished me as he pressed his elbows to his hips and his forehead in his interlaced fingertips.

'Well, I will tell you this, You know, I live a regular life, no-one could criticise me, I do whatever is necessary and generally recognised. The misfortune to which people are accustomed, in the society I frequent, has not spared me, as I and those near me saw with satisfaction, and even this general happiness did not hold back, and I myself was allowed to speak of it, within a limited circle. True, I had never yet been really in love. I regretted that from time to time, but used the expression when I needed it. But now I am obliged to say, yes, I am in love, I dare say excited with being in love. I am a passionate lover, the sort girls long for. But should I not have taken into account that this earlier absence of love gave to my circumstances an exceptional, and happy, a particularly happy twist?"'

There are some revealing things in this passage, especially the last sentence, with its confession (which might have been Kafka's own) of a pleasure in isolation. There was a part of Kafka which wanted nothing better than to be left alone, describing the misery of his condition and not remotely seeking to come out and love anyone. Yet there are also sentences that remain completely unintelligible, and which the context does nothing to make more intelligible. One may guess at some illicit sexual pleasure, but none of all this is 'placed' by Kafka: one is left blank at the lack of contact and explanation. And it is so from time to time in all Kafka's work, though very seldom in the work he passed for publication, and then never quite so obscurely as in this passage: in the torment of his mind, he is always capable of writing without fully conscious control, but usually achieves a certain minimal clarity.

Torment does not always seem the right word, or rather the torment is related in a tone so detached that the reality of the mood is recognised only with a shock. This is true of the last piece in *Meditation*, 'Unhappiness', in which a conversation takes place with a ghost who materialises in a corridor. The tone of conversation remains so normal, that it might pass for an exchange between two people of flesh and blood, though the ghost seemingly appears in answer to a shriek from the man who tells the story. The compulsive terror is underplayed, but without any sense of inverted bravado: that is the achievement of the story – the cleanness of tone, which avoids any attempt at arousing sympathy in the reader, even though the situation is desperate beyond all normal experience.

This playing down is also a feature of the short piece 'Reflections for Gentleman Jockeys', the theme of which is the absurdity of competition and the embarrassment caused by any designation of merit. Here Kafka uses a favourite device, the isolated gesture which lends an air of absurdity:

'The winner looks ridiculous to many of the ladies, puffing himself up and still not knowing how to cope with the everlasting handshakes, salutes, bows and distant hallooings, while the losers keep their mouths shut, and pat the necks of their usually neighing horses.

In the end, the dim sky begins to rain.'

Walter Benjamin has remarked on the way in which Kafka singles out gestures. One of the most frequent themes in this collection, which clearly leads on to the themes of *The Trial* and *The Castle*, is the satirical portrayal of an inflated sense of self-importance, whether it is the sense of utter desolation which reveals itself, too preciously, too consciously, and so inauthentically, in the passing of a little finger across the eyebrows, or whether it is the euphoric feeling of being in tune with everything, and overwhelmed with the consciousness of one's own merits, which ends with opening a window very wide, perhaps to avoid the constriction one is imposing on oneself, and hearing distant music. Kafka is delicate about such hints, and does little to bring out the extreme nostalgia (for solidarity with others? for things as they are before we see them?) which the gestures imply. He also takes for granted that in the spiritual battle in which his characters are sometimes involved the rules are well known on all sides, so that victory and other occasions for heroic stances are not to be thought of.

The possibility of an escape from the spirallings of self-regard is suggested by the very short piece, 'A Wish to Be a Red Indian': only evanescence into unreality will serve:

If only one were a Red Indian, always alert, and on the galloping horse, perched aloft, continually throbbing for brief moments over the throbbing earth, till one dropped the spurs, for there were no spurs, till one threw away the reins, for there were no reins, and then scarcely saw the country in front as a smooth mowed heath, with no horse's neck or head.

The abrupt surprise of the conclusion does much to bring it home as a felt reality, and this evanescence is the theme of a much later piece, 'Fürsprecher' ('Advocates' or 'Intercessors'), though here the restless forward movement is converted into an upward one. As in the Red Indian piece, the barest vestige of existence has to suffice, and in the end there is only so much ground as is needed to climb on:

So if you have begun to go a certain way, go on with it in all circumstances, you can only win, you run no danger, perhaps you will fall at the end, but if you had turned back after the first few steps and run down the stairs again you would have fallen right at the beginning, and no 'perhaps' about it. So if you find nothing here in the corridors, open the doors, if you find nothing behind these doors, there are more floors above, if you find nothing up there, never mind, clamber up more staircases. So long as you don't give up climbing, the steps won't stop, they will grow upwards under your climbing feet.

Except for the ironical humour in the tone, which takes away at the same time as it gives, this is quite close in meaning to Rilke's poem 'Autumn', in which the endless falling of all mankind is sustained, paradoxically, by a divine hand which holds men and falls with them. The sense of an existence, whether rising or falling, which has only so much to sustain it as will serve for its immediate purpose, without guarantee as to the future (one notices in the Kafka passage how an eventual fall is foreseen), is common to both. But the tone could as well be frantic as ironic, and the frantic tone is not heard in the later works.

On the other hand there are pieces in *Meditation* of a quite different character. Running through all Kafka's work, there is a sense from time to time that a super-real peace is possible, if only for others. The remark he is said to have made to Max Brod about a bourgeois family, quoting Flaubert – 'ils sont dans le vrai' – is well known, and expresses an approval of ordinary life such as one finds in some of Thomas Mann's characters too. Similarly K. in *The Castle* thinks of the officials in their offices as not hostile to him (for once), but tired in the midst of happy work; they have 'something which looked like tiredness from outside, and was actually indestructible quiet, indestructible peace'. ('The Indestructible', it will be seen, grows to be an important concept.) K. thinks of the Castle itself as a person, 'quietly sitting there gazing, not lost in thought and thereby shut off from everything, but free and untroubled, as though he were alone and observed by no one, but this did not disturb his quiet in the least . . .' In trying to reach the Castle, K. may be trying to achieve this kind of peacefulness, as Gregor Samsa in 'The Metamorphosis' longs for the peace heard in his sister's violin-playing. And this peacefulness is expressed perhaps best of all in another of the early pieces, entitled 'On the Tram':

I stand on the end platform of the tram and am completely unsure of my footing in this world, in this town, in my family. Not even casually could I indicate any claims that I might rightfully advance in any direction. I have not even any defence to offer for standing on this platform, holding on to this strap, letting myself be carried along by this tram, nor for the people who give way to the tram or walk quietly along or stand gazing into shop windows. Nobody asks me to put up a defence, indeed, but that is irrelevant.

The tram approaches a stopping-place and a girl takes up her position near the step, ready to alight. She is as distinct to me as if I had run my hands over her. She is dressed in black, the pleats of her skirt hang almost still, her blouse is tight and her collar of white fine-meshed lace, her left hand is braced flat against the side of the tram, the umbrella in her right hand rests on the second top step. Her face is brown, her nose, slightly pinched at the sides, has a broad round tip. She has a lot of brown hair and stray little tendrils on the right temple. Her small ear is close-set, but since I am near her I can see the whole ridge of the whorl of her right ear and the shadow at the root of it.

At that point I asked myself: How is it that she is not amazed at herself, that she keeps her lips closed and makes no such remark?

As in the story of the children on the highroad, the reality here is vivid and individual, sensuous and yet not sensuously attractive: the narrator gives a picture so precise as to evoke a desirable woman, yet desire remains absent, giving place to the sheer amazement at existence, and even this is phrased so as to remain impersonal. There is no simile or metaphor in the whole piece. The situation of the narrator, typical of Kafka's central characters, is that he is completely cut off from all human contact, and this is so because the requirement to justify his existence comes from no human source: as the narrator says, 'no-one requires it of me'. Yet the need to make such a justification was so powerful that Kafka wrote at least two novels in attempting to satisfy it. The girl on the tram-platform might get along perfectly well without this questioning. Kafka himself was unable to, yet through all the questioning the same sense continues, that there is a place of security either in the sense of the woman taking tea in the garden, or in the dynamic sense of the man climbing the never-ending stair.

The atmosphere produced by these stories is, then, not all in key with any inward groaning. The outside world is recognised in realistic detail, and its right to exist, regardless of Kafka's inner problems, is not questioned. As his writing progresses, this realism yields to the shifting world of his novels, playing between dream and reality, and even in the early prose there are presages of the change:

Today there is a southwest wind blowing. The air in the square is whirling about. The tip of the town hall steeple is going round in small circles. Why does no-one make peace in all this uproar? What a noise it is. Every windowpane rattling, and the lamp-posts bending like bamboos. The cloak of the Virgin on the column bellies out, and the stormy wind snatches at it. Does nobody see it then?

At this stage in Kafka's writing life, the final question is still a possibility. He is aware that nobody sees what he sees, and he even exaggerates its oddity. Later, it will be increasingly taken for granted that the strange world of his vision coincides or overlaps with the world seen by others. Gregor Samsa, in 'The

Metamorphosis', is transformed into an insect, but the rest of
his family acknowledge the fact without question. Joseph K. is
put on trial by a mysterious court which operates in the attics
of houses: it emerges that most people acknowledge the existence of the Court, whether or not they are on trial themselves –
they know how it operates, that it exists all over the town, that
to be tried by it is as good as being condemned, and thus they
make what might seem a private fantasy take on much more
reality. In the early stories, this tendency is already beginning to
show, the wider implications are beginning to appear, although
there is as yet no conceivable ground for seeing any religious
overtones in them. They are simply experiential. The broader
frame of reference in Kafka's later writing added both enigmatic
magnetism and occasionally, a questionable generalising. The
issue begins to present itself: did the situations of Kafka's
central characters remain on the whole fantastic or idiosyncratic, or did they acquire the links with traditional concepts
which Kafka himself and many others have seen?

Meditation was only some twenty pages long, and Kafka
was already thirty years old when it appeared, by which time
he had published in periodicals only the two 'Conversations',
'The Aeroplanes in Brescia' and 'A Great Noise', with three
short reviews, amounting to only a further dozen or so pages in
all. Even this had been gently wrested from him by the publisher
Rowohlt and Max Brod, who has related how he devised ways
of bringing Kafka's work to a wider circle. Brod was generous
in his praise. Reviewing *Meditation* in *März*, a Munich periodical, he admired not only the quality of the writing, but began
the mode of interpretation which came to seem peculiarly his
own when he edited the posthumous works:

I can very well imagine someone coming across this book and having
his whole life altered by it on the spot, becoming a new man. . . .
In this age of compromises there is here the silent working of a profound and powerful mediaeval inwardness, a new morality and
religious feeling . . . Love of the divine, the absolute, speaks out
of every line . . . here the mystic's engrossment in the ideal is at
last experienced – and therefore remains unspoken – and on its sur-

face there rises with seemingly playful ease a new solemnity, a new humour, a new melancholy.

The attempt at a traditional explanation was understandable enough, in the circumstances – how else was Kafka's meaning to be introduced? Yet 'humour' and 'mediaeval inwardness', placed alongside each other, must have made some readers blench. Was there any justification at all for speaking of the divine here? Was Brod reading these features into his friend's work? The striking quality of Kafka's writing was not best served by reducing it to clichés. His next work defied any such attempt.

It was at Brod's flat while Kafka was arranging the pieces in *Meditation* for publication that he met Felice Bauer. 'I was putting the pieces in order last evening under the influence of this young lady,' he wrote; 'it is quite possible that as a result I have made some blunder, some juxtaposition that will be comic, though perhaps only confidentially.'[3] Within a few weeks, during which he repeatedly wrote to her, they had begun a relationship which they were to continue, twice entering on an engagement to marry, and twice breaking it off, for several years. Kafka saw very little of Fräulein Bauer at this time (the autumn and winter of 1912), though he wrote her many letters. Throughout he was haunted by the thought that marriage, which he wished for and spoke of as the proper fulfilment of a man, was certain to make his writing impossible, the feeling 'that if I had ever been happy apart from writing and all that went with it, it was precisely then that I was incapable of writing'. All the same, it is from the meeting with Felice that the flood of Kafka's writing really begins. He met her first on 13 August 1912. On the night of 22 to 23 September of that year he wrote, at one sitting, 'The Judgement', the longest and most compelling story by far of any he had yet written, and though comparatively short, the most complete and most rounded, though also the first to end with the hero's death. How far Felice encouraged him, how far encouragement came from the publishers Ernst Rowohlt and Kurt Wolff, who now began to press him for publishable stories, is not determinable: all three, with Kafka's friends, acted simultaneously. The fact is that between September 1912 and early 1913 some six hundred sheets of *America* had been written, while the longest complete story Kafka ever wrote, 'The Metamorphosis', was written in November and December 1912. In comparison with what he had written so far, this was a very great amount, and the indebtedness he felt was indicated by his dedication of 'The Judgement' to Felice.

The story was Felice's in more than dedication. The initials of Frieda Brandenfeld, the fiancée of the central character, are hers, Kafka remarked, as are in a sense the initials of Fräulein Bürstner in *The Trial*. The autobiographical element in the story is clear enough, though Kafka's remark about the name of the young man Georg Bendemann is a further indication. ('Bende-', Kafka noted, has the same pattern of consonants and vowels as his own name; he was to allude to it again, later, in the name of Gregor Samsa, which is slightly closer to his own.) But more than a mere rewriting of his own experience was involved. He records in his diary his 'terrible exertions and happiness' in writing the whole story of some three thousand words in eight hours, finishing at six in the morning.[4] 'More than once, this night', he writes, 'I carried my weight on my own back. I realise that everything can be said, that there is a great fire prepared for even the strangest ideas, in which they vanish and rise again.' And, contrasting the progress of his novel (presumably *America*) with this rapid outpouring, he goes on, 'That is the *only* way to write, in a sequence like that, with body and soul completely open.' The implications are those of another diary entry, in which Kafka counsels himself: 'Open up. Let the man ('der Mensch') come forth.' It seems as though a total self-revelation were involved. The revelation was not purely conscious. Kafka though of Freud, as he completed the story, and like a good deal of Kafka's writing it is what he called 'a representation of my dreamlike inner life'.[5] That last phrase needs some definition. The story is clearly akin to dreams in its free associations, its strange logic, its acquiescence in fantastic happenings like the father's order to his son to kill himself, and its indirect relevance to Kafka's waking life. Yet it is also often lucid and precise in a way that dreams seldom are, and certainly much less dreamlike than 'A Country Doctor'. There is nothing magical, visionary, or exotic about most of Kafka's work – nothing like Nerval's, for instance. Presumably Kafka did not mean to say more than that his inner life proceeded as irrationally as dreams do, but the surveillance of his conscious mind is also apparent, at least some of the time.

As a story, 'The Judgement' can be as telling as a nightmare. Only when the conscious, rational mind goes back over the experience of reading it does its obscurity come home. What passes at first sight as intelligible enough – though there may be hesitation from the start about this – is the significance of the mysterious friend in Petersburg to whom Georg has just finished writing as the story begins. This friend, who lives in almost total isolation, is the thread linking the whole together. Because Georg has been doubtful about telling the friend of his engagement, he goes into his father's bedroom to seek advice. The father's doubts whether the friend exists carry the story further forward, as does his sudden denunciation of Georg, not only admitting the friend's existence but claiming him as 'a son after my own heart', with whom he has been in touch all along. And it is partly on account of Georg's supposed neglect of his friend that his father passes on him the sentence of death by drowning which, in the final moment, he executes on himself.

The story is clearly not dealing with any real world, unless the participants are supposed to be insane, which is in fact the interpretation made by Claude-Edmonde Magny.[6] On the other hand, while still remaining ultimately obscure, it has more logical sequence than dreams ever have, and is rounded off, working to a climax, in a way that suggests a more conscious effort than the mere setting out of a dream. The story is a cryptic account of the gaining of self-knowledge by Kafka through a waking dream: its relevance outside his own situation is secondary to that, though genuine enough.

The dream-world is sometimes the most dominant aspect, as in the incident where Georg's father says he has a certain document in his pocket. The humour of the absurd is present here, as so often:

"Pockets in his nightshirt too!" Georg said to himself, thinking with this one remark to ridicule him of existence. He thought like that only for a moment, for he was forgetting everything all the time.

This compliance of the dreamer with any incongruities that chance to present themselves in his dream are less immediately apparent in the opening pages, when Georg reflects on the reasons why his friend in Russia cannot be told of his engagement. The description of the friend's circumstances, in fact the whole of the opening, could belong to any story of a perfectly realistic kind. Only gradually does the reader see that Georg's reasons for not writing any news of importance to the friend are not of the kind that anyone would rationally consider, though they seem to be reasonably set forth. They are rather the reasons that a person might use who was attempting to block some other thought from his mind, or the kind of pseudo-reasons that serve well enough in a dream: one has the impression that an argument is being given, and does not inquire too closely, resting content with the mere show. (There may of course be the same laxity in day-dreaming too.) So it is with Georg, who then goes on to reflect that, when only trivial matters are really fit to be communicated to the friend, he really cannot tell him about the engagement. It is at this point that the strangeness of Georg himself begins to show, when it is related that he preferred to write about trifles rather than 'admit' he is engaged to Frieda Brandenfeld, or when Georg tells his fiancée that the friend would feel 'compelled, and hurt' if he were invited to the wedding, and would then return home alone, and everlastingly unsatisfied. These unlikely reasons for not inviting him are, however, accepted unquestioningly by the fiancée, who says – not very intelligibly by any realistic or rationalistic standard, though very intelligibly, once one sees the full inner meaning for Kafka – 'If you have friends like that, Georg, you ought never to have got engaged at all.'

None of this is ever commented on in the story, which thus remains mainly within the dream-world, despite the shaped climax. Taking it at face-value, the story is so impenetrable that one commentator finds in it 'a discovery of the profound significance of insanity as a paramount manifestation of the fundamental irreducibility of all points of view'.[7] A better suggestion is made by Kate Flores. It remains a suggestion, and there can be no proof of so esoteric a point, but if it is acceptable that Georg is to be identified with the outer Kafka, 'a normal enough young man, affable and debonair, suave, self-contained, decisive, the favoured son of a well-to-do merchant', while the friend bears a striking resemblance to the inner Kafka, 'a reserved, silent, unsocial, dissatisfied person', as he described himself, many otherwise obscure remarks become clear. The explanation seems at first sight to run against Kafka's remark in his diary that 'the friend is the link between father and son, he is their strongest common bond', but that difficulty can be met later. If Kate Flores' view is accepted, including the suggestion that the friend's business, now stagnating, is Kafka's writing, which had not been going well up to the time of writing 'The Judgement', much of the obscurity disappears:

Georg Bendemann's soliloquy [on whether to write to his friend about his engagement] is Kafka's soliloquy, an objectification of his inner debate. It is an analogy, and a remarkably apt analogy: his inner self, his writing self, is a friend who for years has been in exile where, and only where, he can pursue his business. However, his outer self, Georg, now wishes to marry . . . and Georg is concerned lest his marriage alienate his peculiar friend and cost him his friendship.[8]

(It does not contradict this notion of 'the writing self' when Max Brod observes that the friend has many traits of the Yiddish actor Löwy, a friend of Kafka's in real life to whom he did write of his engagement, and who was not only an artist, and thus close to Kafka as a writer, but also a man who lived in some desperation.[9]) In such terms, the fiancée's remark that if he has such friends as this he ought not to get engaged makes perfect sense. So does his reply, which is otherwise, on the rational level, a *non sequitur*: 'Yes, we are both to blame for that [being one and the same person]; but even now I wouldn't have it otherwise [I prefer to remain a writer, even if it means in the end not marrying you].' The friend's suggestion that Georg should join him in Russia becomes translatable as the idea that Kafka should devote himself entirely to writing. The father's doubts about the friend's existence become the father's disbelief in Kafka's talents as a writer.

The condemnation of Georg, however, gives a new twist to the relationship. The writing becomes particularly vivid here (with a characteristic exaggeration in the flying blanket, which gives an *elan* to the whole scene):

'Am I well covered up now?' asked his father, as though he could not see whether his feet were properly covered.

'There, you like it in bed already' said Georg, tucking the bed-clothes more closely round him.

'Am I well covered up?' asked his father again, seeming to await the answer very expectantly.

'Never you worry, you're well covered up.'

'No!' shouted his father, his answer almost clashing with his question, and flinging back the blanket with such strength that for a moment it straightened out in flight, he sprang erect on the bed. With one hand he held lightly to the ceiling. 'You wanted to cover me up, I know that, you young lecher, but I'm not covered up yet, by a long chalk. And if it's the last strength I have, it's enough for you, too much for you.'

It is with the condemnation of the intended marriage, however, that a new direction is taken. Though the writing remains vigorous, a new obscurity enters:

'Because she lifted up her skirts', his father began to twitter, 'because she lifted up her skirts, the stupid slut', and to demonstrate the point he lifted his nightshirt so high that you could see the scar at the top of his thigh, from his war-wound, 'because she lifted her skirts like this and this and this, you had a go at her, and so that you could get what you wanted from her undisturbed, you disgraced your mother's memory, betrayed your friend, and stuck your father in bed so that he wouldn't be able to move. But can he move, or can't he?'

And he stood up completely free of support, and kicked his legs out. He was beaming with joy at his own insight.

That this reflects not what Kafka's father would have said, but what Kafka 'unconsciously' (though here, momentarily, consciously) would have liked him to say, is very likely. But the strange point about this story is that the sexual condemnation is not the most important, nor is the Oedipal relation with the father. Georg is accused of having 'betrayed' his friend (a word which has no meaning in the given context, though it is quite intelligible in terms of Kafka's choice between marriage and writing), and shortly after, the father shouts that the friend is not betrayed: 'I have been his representative in this place.' It is this strange remark which suddenly reverses the role of the father, if the autobiographical suggestion is accepted. Kafka is realising that the condemnation of marriage, though it comes from the hateful father of his unconscious mind, is nevertheless a condemnation he himself wants to accept, for marriage will prevent, so he believes, that relentless self-examination for which his writing affords the opportunity: it will destroy the conditions in which his dread exists and thereby destroy his only hope of salvation (however paradoxical that salvation may be). If the friend is not told of the engagement, that is, if Kafka cancels his own engagement and devotes himself to writing, he will be able to achieve that quasi-infinite awareness which the Kierkegaardian in him wants, even though it is an awareness of infinite guilt, for such awareness will give him a quasi-divine position. Naturally the father, the representative of the divine on earth, will associate himself with that part of Kafka that seeks such awareness, although, paradoxically, he will also condemn him for it. In this way the friend is indeed the link between father and son, in so far as the son, Kafka, realises that devotion to the writer in himself is the only way to the Father, even that the Father and the writer in him are one. That Georg's father is the representative of the friend in this place means that Kafka's father's accusations are acceptable substitutes for the self-accusations which Kafka the writer was bound to make, the infinite trial which he was expecting to undergo. Or rather, not substitutes, but of the same substance, not ultimately different, the equivalent of the 'Angst' which he was constantly recreating in himself.

The father's words of condemnation may thus have also a latent sense:

'So now you know what has been existing outside, till now you have only known about your own self! You were an innocent child, actually, but even more actually you were a diabolical man! And therefore, know that I condemn you to death by drowning.'

Kafka knows, now, that his 'Angst' is not merely private, that it is the very thing his father stands for, the thing he must accept, even though it means his extinction. He is diabolical because he is infinitely guilty, but there is nothing his conscious self can do about this, except give up marriage, give up all self-maintaining instincts, and, like Gregor Samsa in Kafka's next story 'The Metamorphosis', calmly accept extinction. This Kafka, like Gregor, thinks of his parents with affection in his last moment. But by dying he releases the writer who has no human emotion (the friend was totally unmoved by Georg's mother's death), the self who will be able to go on recording his own infinite degradation. The hero is dead, but the writer, the one part of himself which Kafka believed to be indestructible, can continue.

An interpretation like this repeatedly makes sense when the reactions of the characters, taken normally, would be nonsense. This is true not only of the key expression 'betraying the friend', in connection with the intended marriage, which is the most revealing of Kafka's devices. When the father says that the friend 'knows everything' (because the father has written to tell him, though the phrase has overtones) the father adds 'He knows everything a thousand times better', whereupon:

'Ten thousand times', said Georg, to laugh his father out of court, but in his very mouth the word acquired a deadly serious sound.

– which is to say that Kafka is aware (though he will not make it quite plain) that the friend is in reality the fearful Inquisitor of Kierkegaard's vision, the revealer of truth which the writer in him can be, but one who is infinitely superior in knowledge to the surface self represented by Georg. Similarly the father's attack on Georg's sexual appetite corresponds to the words of the priest in *The Trial*, when he accuses K. of seeking too much help, especially from women. The thought is a constant one in Kafka, continually dividing him between the spiritual struggle represented for him by his writing, and the satisfaction he looked for but feared from the other sex.

The interpretation works, and gives more satisfaction than the mode of reading suggested by Mme Magny. Yet as Kate Flores says, this is assuming that there is a 'secret code which Kafka evidently wished to remain a mystery',[10] and the question must arise, whether in that case the story has more than an esoteric value. For Kafka it was important to realise that the image of a condemning father which he had learned to fear was also the representative, so far as he was concerned, of a mode of being which he could respect: that is, that he wanted nothing better than to condemn himself infinitely, and could now find support for that in the father he had always held in dread. But the reader who is not so closely informed about Kafka's life is certain to be left with a sense of frustration if he inquires more deeply without referring to biographical details. And so it must be asked whether this story is more than a very surprising one, a means by which Kafka found himself able to write for another twelve years, because it made him aware of the only condition under which he could write at all, namely acceptance of his infinite guilt, or whether it is a masterpiece of controlled form. Has Kafka done more than cater for himself; is there anything here for the reader, in so far as he is a 'common reader', someone who reads for pleasure and enlightenment rather than research? The quantity of biographical information needed for understanding the story suggests that it is essentially esoteric, that it has value for its position in Kafka's work, as a gateway, rather than as an accomplished achievement in itself. The achievement will come with 'The Metamorphosis'. Yet there is some representative significance in 'The Judgement' too. Granted that no man in a real world would take his life as Georg does, unless insane, the vivid portrayal of the condemning figure who exists in many men is real, and so is the crushed self who obeys him inwardly though not outwardly. Kafka in his neurosis could see with intense clarity what many would simply but wrongly want to deny on their own behalf. By accepting this truth about himself so emphatically he made an impact on the outside world which can still be felt.

4

'AMERICA'

One of Kafka's earliest novels, planned in childhood, concerned a quarrel between two brothers, one of whom went to America, while the other remained in prison in Europe.[1] It might have been a forecast of the dichotomy in his own future development, swaying uncertainly between the conviction of innocence and the conviction of guilt, the surface personality of confidence and calm, and the subliminal personality of desperation, Karl Rossmann in *America* and Joseph K. in *The Trial*. In 1911 he notes in his diary a remark of Edison's about the renewed energies discovered by Czech immigrants to the United States: perhaps he saw America still as a land of promise for his own countrymen, a symbol of release from the normal conditions of his existence.

If such a symbol was in his mind it gave no lasting hope. In 1915 he sees the end of the novel pessimistically:

'Rossmann and K., the guiltless and the guilty, both of them alike, in the end, punitively killed, the guiltless one more gently, rather pushed aside than beaten down.'[2]

Max Brod, it is true, speaks of an intended happy ending to the final, fragmentary chapter: 'Kafka used to hint enigmatically that his young hero would find in this (almost limitless) theatre [by which he is finally given a place in life], a job, freedom, a mainstay, and would, by a paradisal magic, even rediscover his homeland and his parents.' Kafka always referred to the book either by the title of the first chapter, 'The Stoker', or as *Der Verschollene* (*Lost without Trace*), which suggests what in fact is the ending of the last chapter as we have it, the disappearance of the hero from all the scenes he has known hitherto. (Perhaps, indeed, he might find his parents in the paradise of lost childhood which could only be reached if he were lost without trace to all mortal concerns – some ironical oscillation of viewpoint may still be intended.) It may be, nevertheless, that the attempt at reaching freedom is taken up again in *The Castle*, begun after *America* had long been given up. Certainly there is something of a polar contrast between the active quest in a new country, undertaken by Karl and K., and the passive defence put up by Joseph K. against the Court.

By 8 March 1913 all but the last chapter of *America* had been written for some time, as he told Felice Bauer.[3] Characteristically, he was extremely critical of what he had done earlier, but the way in which he expresses his criticism does not suggest the merely neurotic self-rejection which sometimes underlies his remarks. He was reading to his friends in Prague, he says:

> 'So, as the exercise books with my novel happened to be lying in front of me (by some chance or other the books which I hadn't used for so long had come to the top), I took up these books, read at first with an easy confidence, as if I knew from memory exactly where the good parts, and the semi-good, and the bad parts came, but grew more and more surprised and finally came to the irrefutable conviction that as a whole only the first chapter comes out of an inward truth, while everything else, apart from one or two larger or smaller passages, of course, seems to be written as it were in memory of a great feeling now completely absent, and is therefore to be rejected, that is, out of about 400 large exercise-book pages, only 56 (I think) remain. If you add to the 350 pages the roughly 200 pages of a version of the story written in the previous winter and spring, I have written for this story 550 useless pages.'[4]

True to this opinion, Kafka agreed to send for publication the first chapter, but told the publisher Kurt Wolff that the next 500 pages were 'a complete failure', and proposed not to add anything further to it. The chapter was not complete in itself, he admitted: 'It is a fragment and will remain one, such a future will give the chapter as much completeness as it can have.'[5] Apart from the final chapter, which was added in 1914, Kafka remained true to his word, and added no more to the novel, though he left the MS to Brod along with all the others.

This fairly wholesale condemnation of the novel must be borne in mind especially when reading studies of Kafka which treat all his work on an equal footing. Kafka's judgement is not always to be trusted: he allowed some pieces to be published which were not of his best work, but what he declined to publish or to take up into collections after earlier publication is usually of poorer quality. To treat *America* as though it were published with his full approval is to treat him unfairly, though to read it to gain a better understanding of what he accepted and what he rejected makes for better sense.

'The Stoker' appeared in May 1913, as part of a new magazine, *Der jüngste Tag*, and had several enthusiastic reviews. As a story it is straightforward: a simple account of how Karl Rossmann, an émigré from Hamburg, goes between decks after his liner arrives in New York, meets a giant stoker, defends him against a shipmate before a tribunal of the captain and his officers, and is finally recognised by a wealthy uncle who takes him ashore to his own lodging. The originality is in the mode of narration, which, like 'The Judgement', slips easily from the real world into one on the borderline between reality and dreams. There is barely a shock as the Statue of Liberty (the 'Goddess' rather) is seen, at the entrance to the harbour, holding her sword aloft in a sudden glare of sunlight, and the incongruity of the sword replacing the torch, as well as its possible implications, are swallowed up in the impartial flow of the narrative. This is already the mood of a dreamer, and the reader who suspends his disbelief willingly enters it. The sudden realisation by Karl that he has left his umbrella below deck is another device of the dream to isolate him from his companions, and by the time he has lost his way, stumbled upon the stoker, and been invited to sit on his bunk, all thought of normal behaviour is abandoned. For the time being neither Karl nor the reader thinks any more of the umbrella, or the luggage left on deck, or the intention to go ashore, and the heroic role of Karl in the trial-scene, undermined as it is by the sense of unreality, is fully in the mood of uninhibited dreams.

Even the opening sentence does not correspond to realities. In relating how Karl Rossmann, sixteen years old, was sent to America 'by his poor parents', because he had been seduced by a woman-servant and got her with child, it suggests a certain sympathy with the parents which the story does nothing to justify. Karl's parents are not poor financially: his father is a comparatively well-off businessman. Morally, they have behaved scandalously, refusing to pay any compensation to the woman-servant, saving themselves from trouble by sending Karl off to New York to earn his living as best he may, his education still incomplete, with no companion and no luggage except a suitcase, and no one to give him any attention when he arrives. Nothing related of them suggests that they deserve any sympathy: they have cut their son off like a dead limb, even though, as it appears, he was a helpless victim of a woman's determination to have a child by him. The story itself, on the other hand, makes no such point. The facts emerge piecemeal, and it is only by emerging from the dreamlike state that a reader observes that 'poor' was a very inappropriate word for them.

There is a kind of logic in all this, but it is a dream-logic or day-dream-logic in which morality and questionings take no part; it accepts first promptings as they happen to come. At each point there is an impetus, a prompting of some kind: Karl sees a friend with a stick, which reminds him of his umbrella, which sends him down below, which leads him to the stoker; but the controls of conscious life are gone. He does not remember the friend, or the luggage he left with him, even at the end when he leaves the ship, though it is returned to him much later without his having thought of it again till that moment. In the same equable but unreflecting state of mind he takes up the cudgels on behalf of the stoker in what becomes the centre-piece of the chapter, the trial before the captain. Here Karl behaves a little naively; he makes no further inquiry but embraces the cause wholeheartedly. It has to be admitted, though, that Karl is gullible to an unusual degree, and that he takes his campaign to lengths that only extreme wish-fulfilment could demand. The sole complaint of the stoker, when his words are sifted a little, amounts to an accusation that his immediate boss is a Rumanian with anti-German feelings, but this is enough to make Karl fly passionately to his defence, marching with him to no less a place than the captain's stateroom, there to deliver an oration on his behalf to the captain, the purser, and several other slightly astonished officials. Karl's self-identification with the stoker leads him not only to defend like a lion what he takes to be an innocent man, but to feel a remarkable vindictiveness, relishing the thought of holding the Rumanian in position so that the stoker might have 'smashed his hated skull in with his fists'. It is a combination of credulity, self-dramatisation and spite, all in the name of what Karl takes to be selfless heroism, and entirely suited to the kind of dream in which the ego has it all its own way.

It does emerge after a while that Karl's ready defence of the stoker was inspired partly by thoughts of self-congratulation. He does not need so much to fight for justice as to have a cause to fight for:

'If only his parents could see him now, in a foreign country, defending the good cause before highly-respected persons, and, even if he had not yet brought about a victory, making himself completely ready for the final conquest. Would they revise their opinion about him? Make him sit down between them and give him their praises? For once, for once look into his so devoted eyes? Uncertain questions, and a most unsuitable moment for putting them.'

It is clear from this that the word 'poor', applied to Karl's parents, was not incongruous in his eyes. Despite their treatment of him, he asks nothing better than to justify himself before them. Extreme injustice passes unnoticed, if he can only impress them with his crusading zeal, no matter for what cause. And so the stoker – a giant of a man, as Kafka's father was – substitutes for Karl's father. In defending him so vigorously, even if in such ignorance of the case, Karl is maintaining in his own mind the never-questioned purity and innocence of his parents, guarding himself from knowledge of their abominable treatment of him. And even the stoker is ambiguous, not merely an innocent party to be defended, but also, at a certain point in the proceedings, turning against Karl as much as any father might have done:

'"You are right, right, I have never doubted it." He would have gladly, for fear of blows, held fast his flailing hands, even more gladly have thrust him into a corner and whispered a few gentle, pacifying words, that nobody else would have needed to hear. But the stoker was beside himself with rage.'

Such feelings were surely often Kafka's own, as a child, and the thought is a moving one.

But the weakness of Karl's attachment to justice begins to show almost as soon as his uncle Jacob turns up to take him under his wing. Wealthy Uncle Jacob is a much better substitute for a father than the stoker was – not that Karl realises this – and within a short while Karl has forgotten his indignation and allowed the Rumanian and his recently detested cronies to do all the goodbye-waving. 'It was really as though there were no stoker left', Kafka ironically observes, and although Karl doubts whether the uncle can ever really replace him, he never does give the stoker another thought throughout the novel, despite his flood of tears as he leaves the ship. The incident with the stoker was a handy pretext by which to reassure himself of his parents' goodness, and the happy ending seems momentarily to confirm that.

Some years later, Kafka observed, while reading *David Copperfield*, that 'The Stoker', and even more the novel he had intended to follow it, was 'sheer imitation of Dickens'.[6] He mentions several incidents common to the two novels, whose heroes are clearly similar as young boys cast adrift in a heartless world. One sees, too, that the encounter with the stoker has something in common with Pip's encounter with Magwitch at the start of *Great Expectations*. Kafka's admiration of Dickens's 'opulence and carefree, powerful prodigality', is, however, tinged with criticism, to the effect that this leads to a meaningless or senseless whole, a fault which he believes himself to have avoided, 'thanks to my weakness, and taught by my coming so far after him'. Yet despite Kafka's modesty here, one cannot feel that he has judged these two novels well. As his own progresses, Karl meets a variety of people, most of them bent on exploiting him, just as David does. But it is a journey into nowhere, with no end in view. Where David moves from Yarmouth or Dover or Canterbury to London and back, as to a centre, Karl simply moves on. David has good angels to counter the evil ones, a

Betsy Trotwood for a Murdstone, a Peggotty for a Uriah Heep; Karl has only the cook at the Ramses Hotel to speak for him, and she gives him up in a crisis. Dickens moves up character after character to keep the reader of his serial agog, which results in the richness Kafka speaks of, and does have a disorienting effect; Dickens does, however, weave them into a far-flung plot, which they reappear to promote. Kafka's new characters are not only fewer and less idiosyncratic and less memorable than Micawber and Creakle, they appear only to be forgotten again. One looks in vain for any guiding thought in *America,* any balance of forces or intentional shaping, anything to match, say, the reflections on love and marriage aroused by David and Steerforth; there is simply the not highly inventive sequence of seedy figures.

The decision to publish only the first chapter was surely a right one. The ironical portrayal of the dream-ambitions, together with the play on paternal relationships, sustains itself for a short while. What was needed for a novel was some more conscious intention: a dream which continues aimlessly for several hundred pages is a kind of nightmare. Kafka had available almost nothing but reiterations of the same theme of Karl's youthfully assertive innocence (if an ego so inflated can be called innocent, in terms of conscious life) coupled with his powerful persecution-mania. Karl is convinced, even during the sea-passage, that he must be on the alert: a certain Slovak is determined to steal his suitcase at night with a long pole, and he stays up long hours to guard it. Sitting with the stoker in the stateroom, he begins to fear that 'the whole ship with its corridors full of enemies' may conspire against him. So much is in his character as Kafka wants to show it. Surprisingly, however, he finds himself repeatedly in situations which confirm his feeling of being persecuted, as though the dream or the author were intent on endorsing his worst suspicions. After a short stay with his uncle in New York, Karl is handed a letter (dramatically enough, at midnight), telling him that because he has gone to the house of the father of a certain girl, his uncle – a new, antipathetic father-figure with suddenly revealed sexual hostility – is no longer prepared to give him any help whatsoever so long as he lives. Shortly after this revelation of brutal unkindness, though he never thinks of it as that, Karl falls in with the two hoboes Robinson and Delamarche, who do almost nothing but reward his goodness with ingratitude. His dismissal from the job as lift-boy in the Hotel Occidental would have been relished by every reader of Victorian sentimental fiction: having repeatedly and unselfishly stood in for another lift-boy in exacting conditions of work, he chances to leave his own post for two minutes on an errand of mercy, is discovered by the head-porter, abandoned by the cook, who is overwhelmed by the spurious proofs of his depravity, discharged with ignominy, and denounced in front of a policeman by the very friend on whose account he had momentarily left the lift unattended. The policeman then refuses to believe a word Karl says, but is overwhelmed when one of the hoboes shows evidence of genteel respectability by producing a visiting-card. Such incidents continue to the penultimate chapter, and seem designed to confirm the sense Karl already has, that the world is thronged with personal enemies of his. The perennial 'I am Innocent' was never more piercingly implied.

Yet it is never more than implied. Karl never protests at his treatment; he is always attentive to his duty, compliant, eager to move on to his next task, as in this neat piece of caricature:

'Soon Karl learned to make the rapid, profound bows that people expect of liftboys, and he accepted his tips in a trice. They vanished into his waistcoat pocket, and no-one could have said from his looks whether they were large or small. For ladies he opened the door with a little touch of gallantry, and swung slowly after them into the lift, since in their anxiety about their skirts, hats, and other trappings, they entered more hesitantly than men. During the ascent or descent he stood close by the door, not to draw attention, with his back to the passengers, holding on to the handle of the lift-door so as to open it suddenly at the moment of arrival, without, however, causing a fright by pushing it to one side. Very rarely someone would tap him on the shoulder to ask for some piece of information, at which he would turn rapidly round, as if he were expecting this, and answer in a loud voice.'

The instinct to over-act the part, to placate almost to the point of buffoonery, is finely observed by Kafka. The Chaplinesque attentiveness, however, is nowhere ironical. Karl is never aware of the assiduous figure he cuts, and even when alone in the lift, hauls on a rope which gives added speed, 'with strong, rhythmic tugs, like a sailor'. There is no centre of self in him or in the novel, no place from which he can take a look at himself, none of the smirk of pleasure which Chaplin would have supplied at the thought of his passengers appreciating such compliance. And though this absence of a self may resemble innocence (it is certainly not that), it allows no genuine satire. The interest in the passage just quoted is entirely in Karl, who is less than a strong enough personality for satire, not in the passengers whom he sought to please. Many repetitions of such scenes put a question-mark against the book. The submissiveness of Karl having been established within a few pages, the piling-up of situations, which only reinforce the impression that his persecution-mania is justified, is merely repetitive.

This absence of direction is also part of the penalty Kafka paid, when it came to writing a novel, for his submissiveness to the dream or day-dreaming mood. It has been thought, for example, that a pattern of development can be found in Karl's progression from homosexuality and narcissism to heterosexuality, but if Kafka intended this he did nothing really to indicate it. Certainly Karl has had no joy of his first sexual experience with a woman, and his second ends in a jiu-jitsu fight. The stoker and one of the lift-boys may represent a homosexual attraction for him, but this is also a point which Kafka does not explore. Karl has more sympathy from the woman cook and from Therese than any he knew before, and in the final chapter he meets Fanny, whom he has evidently got to know affectionately at some point in the unwritten pages. But if this is development it is thinly sketched in, and nothing comes of it, since after meeting Fanny Karl leaves her again, almost at once, and is last seen in the company of another lift-boy, Giacomo. Love for either sex is never actually touched on, and if Kafka meant a development to be seen he left very few pointers.

One casts about for some sense of significance. Is the odd name of Brunelda meant to have Wagnerian overtones? She is fat, and lies on her back most of the time, but the parallels cannot be taken beyond that. What is the point of Karl's repeated association with a *pair* of men, first Pollunder and Green, then Robinson and Delamarche?* There seems to be an affinity here with the pairs in other novels of Kafka's: Franz and Willem in *The Trial*, Arthur and Jeremias in *The Castle*. Perhaps it is significant that Karl is no longer with the hoboes in the final chapter, just as K. severs the connection with the assistants in the later stages of *The Castle* and as Joseph K. loses contact with his two warders. But all speculation is lamed by the overriding impression that Kafka provides no clues, or if any, then esoteric ones of the kind met in 'The Judgement'.

The final chapter is a different matter, in almost every respect. (Strictly speaking the chapter as printed is not a final chapter, but, as the MS shows, joins a penultimate chapter with the beginning of what may be taken as the really final chapter, which breaks off.) Nor did Kafka supply for it the title 'The Oklahoma Nature-Theatre', which was supplied by Max Brod: the MS gives no title for the chapter, which is presumably the one written, according to the diary, late in 1914,[7] and 'Nature-Theatre' is an expression not found in the text. Still, it is clear that an entirely fresh start has been made, which may end happily with Karl's acceptance by the theatre, or may merely lead to his total disappearance from human society.

There is, it is true, almost no connection with what has gone before, apart from the presence of Karl himself, and the casual mention of Giacomo, who has played a brief part in the earlier chapters. The gap between these and the final chapter is otherwise complete. In addition, all the mood has changed, though without explanation. Up to this point, Karl has met almost nothing but hostility and injustice. The invitation to join the Theatre of Oklahoma suddenly provides a world where nothing is hostile and there is no injustice. The Oklahoma Theatre accepts everybody, no matter what his qualifications or background. It is not even interested in the veracity of the answers

* There are several such pairs in Lewis Carroll's books, and one in *Hamlet*.

given to its employment agency, with the result that Karl is admitted under the surname 'Negro', as a technical assistant. The other America of his earlier experiences is a long way off.

As a conclusion, all this might suggest that Karl had somehow won through, rather in accordance with what Max Brod believed the intended ending to have been. If one wanted to interpret in a religious sense – though the only justification for this is in the crude alternation of angels and devils outside the recruiting booth, and the curse uttered in the advertisement – one might say Karl had come to salvation, or that his acceptance by the theatre is a kind of religious conversion, which is what one interpreter does say.[8] 'Everything he had done up to now was forgotten, nobody was going to reproach him with it any more,' Kafka writes, and though Karl has not done anything very reproachable in the novel as it stands, his relief is understandable. It is still not a matter of forgiveness or sympathetic comprehension. Karl is still as eager to please as ever, he submits to authority with the same gratification, and though he has some brief doubts about how a theatre can guarantee to find jobs for all professions, the doubts do not last long. Kafka shows his ironical detachment from Karl through the manner in which he allows the recruiter to question Karl, making big eyes as he puts his questions, listening to the replies with his head reverently on his chest. These are typical Kafka-caricatures. Indeed the whole conclusion is ambiguous and ironical, not only in the absurdity of the acceptance, but also in the very name 'Oklahoma', for while the name may have been synonymous in Kafka's mind with the 'bad lands' – as Uyttersprot has argued – it may also have stood for a land of promise, since hundreds of thousands of settlers were pouring into the recently formed State just before the novel came to be written. Again, it is surely intended to be significant that what Karl joins is a theatre. As Walter Sokel argues, the whole of existence in Kafka's world is a kind of theatre: later, the men who execute Joseph K. in *The Trial* will appear to be second-rate actors, and K.'s end will be hideous; Karl, on the other hand, is accepted by the acting community, and so the theatre, welcoming and condemning, is as ambiguous as anything else in Kafka. Similarly, though Karl has evidently met Fanny before, perhaps intimately, and so seems to have better prospects, he does not stay with her, and his future on the last page, as he rides in the train through deep, dark ravines, the cool air making his face shiver, is nothing like as inviting as he at first expected. The last words of the fragmentary ending suggest that he will in fact be lost without trace.

But the ambiguity on this point, especially on the question of Karl's 'salvation', does not lend a mature interest to the ending; the ambiguity is of a trivial kind. When so much of the novel has reiterated, or seemed to reiterate, the inadequacy of Karl's black-and-white view of innocence and guilt, and even reinforced it by letting his dream-world seem to confirm him in it, it is disappointing to find at the end merely a white to the previous black. The alternative to a world where one is constantly persecuted is not one where everything is suddenly forgotten: that is only an alternative in the eyes of a man himself suffering from persecution-mania, and the pattern of the novel does not show Kafka sufficiently distanced from such a mania himself to be able to shape it in art. The novel breaks off after the seventh chapter, and starts afresh in the last, so far as one can see, simply because Kafka did not in all honesty see how the transition was to be made. He had met Felice since he began the novel, and the new spirit she engendered possibly introduced the figure of Fanny, together with the image of the theatre as a place which accepted as freely as a woman's love did. But Kafka was deeply sceptical; he saw no way of moving from Karl's position at the end of chapter 7, and the ending. A gap was inevitable.

America attempted to be more than a dream-novel, it sought to make a comment on the United States in general, and it sometimes achieved brilliant expressionistic caricatures, comparable to the exaggeratedly gesticulating characters. Kafka did not have Dickens's intense social concern, or the indignation against America expressed in *Martin Chuzzlewit* and apart from Therese's story of her mother's poverty and suicide, which leaps right out of the context of Karl's own narrative, there is scarcely any moving picture of conditions of work and life. At his best, however, Kafka presents the fantastic hustle of New York streets, with parallel frontages joining at some infinite distance, lorries rolling past in traffic-columns five abreast, masses of pedestrians, and an election campaign observed from the upper region of a skyscraper. The difficulty here is due again to the initial concept of a dream-story, or Kafka's submissiveness to a dreamlike mood, since this required the plot to continue at such an elementary level of wish-fulfilment that serious political or social comment was ruled out.

Taken as a whole, *America* will be seen to be the weakest of Kafka's three more or less completed novels, and the chief interest it offers, after the first chapter, is an insight into Kafka's progress towards *The Trial* and *The Castle*. The pull of the trial, as a dream-situation *par excellence* (it is prominent in *Alice*) had already begun to make itself felt, and there are two trials in *America,* if one reckons both the stoker's trial and Karl's trial before the head waiter at the Hotel Occidental. But in *America* there is still a minimal specific point: the stoker has a particular, defined grievance against the Rumanian, however trifling, and Karl has technically committed an offence by leaving his lift unattended, if only for two minutes, There is thus a rational basis, and rational counter-arguments can be applied. In *The Trial* rationality is removed; the charge against K. is never specified and so there can be no defence. This accords better with the situation Kafka was attempting, through the novelist's art, to deal with. The basis of the condition was an unreasoning fear, a nameless horror, coupled with a conviction at times that to feel such horror was to achieve a spiritual goal. All specific feelings of guilt for this or that misdemeanour were therefore masks over a faceless abyss. Once that was realised, the possibility of a compelling novel was available.

There is also in *America* a 'Castle', if one takes the castle as a goal which the hero is determined to reach. There is the continent into which Karl penetrates further and further, without knowing where he is going or what he is looking for, and there is the Theatre of Oklahoma, suddenly emerging as though it were what Karl had been seeking all along. But at this stage of realisation, the theatre is taken as an absolute goal. Karl over-comes his qualms, and expects nothing but good to come of his organisation, though Kafka and the reader are aware that he may be mistaken. In *The Castle* the organisation is not only the consciously envisaged goal from the outset, it is also ambiguously presented from the outset. There is no longer the hostility of the 'normal' world, represented by the hoboes and the hotel, contrasted with the unqualified welcome offered by the Theatre: the Castle is both a threat and a welcome simultaneously, and in this way a more apt representation of authority, paternal or otherwise, as Kafka knew it. The ambiguity is inherent in a single power, not separable into aspects that can be alternately placated and defied, and this single power, constantly confronted, gives a unity to the later novel which *America* lacks.

In *The Castle*, too, there is from the outset the suggestion of an authority immeasurably superior to K., which he could learn to dominate. There is thus an element of something like symbolism throughout, closely integrated, whereas in *America* it is only in the final chapter that symbolism, or rather allegory, becomes apparent, with the result that the Theatre-scenes seem tacked on to the rest rather loosely. Again, where Karl's acceptance as a technical worker is specific, though he has no idea what is involved, he does not have time to speculate on this before the novel ends; in *The Castle* this theme is more strongly developed – K. is told that he is taken on as surveyor, though he also has no idea of this profession, but his speculations about this apparently nonsensical action of the Castle's are an integral part of his whole situation from the beginning.

Above all, in *The Castle* as in *The Trial*, complete uncertainty reigns, and this is the condition in which they could best unfold. There were disadvantages, since the major novels appear, much more than was the case with *America*, to treat questions of general metaphysical or religious import, and the absence of particularity can therefore be misleading. When nothing definite is being said, the possible range and scope can seem to be much greater than the situation will really warrant, and generally valid truths will seem to be expressed when that is not really the case at all. But at all events Kafka had tracked down, in *The Trial* and *The Castle*, the featureless nature of his terror, and with this much realised he could go on to the peculiarly difficult task of shaping it.

Contemporary reviewers of 'The Stoker' did not observe the dreamlike quality of the events, nor did they see anything in Karl but pure simplicity. 'It is', said Robert Musil in *Die Neue Rundschau*, 'deliberate naivety, and yet has none of the unpleasantness of that kind of thing. For it is true naivety, which in literature (just like the false kind, *that* is not where the difference lies) is something indirect, complicated, acquired, a longing, an ideal. But it is something that has been pondered on, with solid foundations, a feeling with living roots, whereas the false, but so-called genuine variety, the simple variety that is so popular, is not so, and is therefore so valueless.'[9] The description of the really genuine variety is vague, one has to admit: it may happen that extreme sophistication and extreme naivety meet and become indistinguishable, but what does the difference between the true and the false amount to, and how do you really tell them apart? Musil did not say, but his tone is that of other critics of his day. The reviewer in the Viennese *Neue Freie Presse* spoke of the 'originality and purity of the feelings here expressed. The way in which this young lad,' he added, 'forgets both his past and his future, and out of an innocent human impulse makes friends with the strange, burly and unhappy stoker, the whole scene of his defence – this really is an art that is fed by the deep springs of unconfused, undeflected, naive feelings and attitudes.' The *National-Zeitung*, far from having any nightmarish sense of unreality, spoke of 'a glow of summer fullness', while the *Deutsche Montags-Zeitung* was taken in by the ending of that initial chapter, despite doubts – 'the whole thing is so suspiciously comforting and so moving in its mood of "All's well that ends well"'. A franker writer, the critic here (Heinrich Eduard Jakob) confessed, 'I have read the story three times, don't know what to make of it, and am glad that the power of a great writer will probably leave me for good in this state of suspended judgement.' What remains doubtful is the comfort the critic afforded himself: 'For the irony and the non-irony, the meaning and the non-meaning of this story – to begin with they seem to be two mutually exclusive lines, madly diverging – are really parallels which, as I think the highly magical science of mathematics affirms, meet at infinity.' That paradoxical claim, akin to others often made on Kafka's behalf, is one that can never be made except by faith, and the reader who is looking for a meaning rather than a non-meaning will not be helped by it.

5

'THE METAMORPHOSIS'

The other story written in the autumn of 1912, after the meeting with Felice Bauer, was written in circumstances quite different from those of 'The Judgement'. Earlier, Kafka had been delighted at the steady flow of creation throughout the night. 'The Metamorphosis' (originally translated as 'The Transformation'), by contrast, took almost three weeks, from 18 November to 6 December, with interruptions on several evenings. For the first time, Kafka was able to hold a conception of some length and complexity over a period of weeks, and maintain its composition through to the end. This is the longest by far of all his completed works, and the only one in which the formal achievement is really important. Unlike any other of his stories, it is divided into three equal sections, each headed by a Roman numeral like an Act of a play, each section ending with a climactic moment. In the first, Gregor Samsa awakens to the realisation that he has turned into an insect and emerges from his bedroom, to be driven back by his infuriated father. In the second, he tries to accommodate himself to his absurdly hideous predicament, while his sister offers him various foods, doing all she can to reconcile herself and the family to the monster he has become; again, a brief sally into the living-room is repulsed by the father, this time even more violently, as he pelts Gregor with apples. In the third, Gregor comes out while his sister is playing the violin, entranced by the music which seems to be the 'food' he has so long been unable to find, but a third attack drives him back to die alone and untended. The family (excepting the father) having done all they can with their varying limitations, to acclimatise themselves, or to offer comfort and love, finally recognise their failure. After Gregor's death they turn with relief to the happier life that now awaits them.

Kafka was usually reluctant to have anything he had written published, and this remained true of 'The Metamorphosis': he declined Kurt Wolff's invitation to send it to him in April 1913, perhaps because Kafka intended it for a book planned long before, to be entitled 'Sons'. He did, however, send it in 1914 to the novelist Robert Musil, who accepted it for the *Neue Rundschau*, where it would have appeared but for opposition from the conservative management. And in the following year he came as near as he ever did come to urging a publisher to print a work of his, saying he was 'particularly concerned' to see publication.[1] Considering Kafka's normal hesitancy, this suggests a strong feeling that the story came up to his expectations.

The formal excellence is striking enough in itself. Whereas very many of the stories are incomplete (including a large number of fragmentary beginnings in the diary, not normally printed in collections of the stories as such), or rambling and repetitive, 'The Metamorphosis' shows all the signs that Kafka was able both to portray his own situation and to achieve artistic mastery over it. That this is Kafka's situation, as he saw it, need not be doubted. He himself comments on the similarity between the name Samsa and his own, noting that this time he has come closer than he did in the case of Bendemann. The parents and the sister correspond closely to his view of his family, though only his sister Ottla seems to be included, and the sisters Elli and Vally are left out. It remains, of course, a projection from his own circumstances as much as any autobiographical subject in a novel does. The distinctive feature is the device by which Kafka omits all the repetitive doubts, the neurotic self-circlings, packing them all into the one image of the transformation, and viewing that as though from the outside. The transformation is at first sight incomprehensible, without some experience of it through Kafka's diaries. Yet it remains the obvious and most compelling image for his condition, as he saw it, and there is no symbolism about it, or rather the metaphorical element seems so slight, so ordinary, so much a matter of everyday speech that one scarcely wants to translate when Gregor discovers himself to be 'ein Ungeziefer' (a word which means 'vermin', rather than 'insect'). Gregor is, as one says, a louse. Nor does Kafka allow the comfort which might come from the expectation that the whole affair is a dream from which there will be an awakening. Exceptionally, there is no quality of dreams in this nightmare. Kafka insists on what the reader knows to be a physical impossibility, even though the general idea is common enough, because that is the only way that the full weight of his meaning can be conveyed, without overloading the story with the minutiae of self-recrimination. The conviction of being verminous is given full statement, once and for all, on the first page, and the rest becomes a matter of working out the practical details so that the truth comes home in concrete form.

This conviction is not the conviction of humanity at large, nor does the story ever make it out to be so; the implications exist for Gregor alone, and the rest of the characters are far from thinking themselves or being vermin. The notion that there is here what a recent school-edition described as 'an ultimately serious and universally human parable of man's fate'[2] though obscurely conveyed in those words, seems to rest on a preconception that all men find themselves utterly repulsive, or should do. A not very different idea is expressed by another commentator, who finds here an exposure of the 'persistent primitiveness of man'.[3] 'Shall we not say that the bug is better, more oneself', writes Paul Goodman, 'than the commercial traveller or the official in the insurance office?' and again, more emphatically, 'the animal-identity is deeper than the ordinary human being and his behaviour, it is nearer to the unknown deity . . .'[4] To deny this is not to remove all possible sympathy with Kafka's story, it is to maintain a sense of proportion. The cliché which says that every novelist worth his salt is normally describing Everyman is too persistent.

The really significant thing is the control which Kafka gains by stating his own condition, nobody else's, so simply. One of the principal advantages thus won is that, the interminable and inconclusive debates of later stories being excluded, he is able to take in the feelings and reactions of other people. The humanity which is lacking in some of the other stories, especially in 'In the Penal Colony', is more in evidence in 'The Metamorphosis'. The concentration on the *alter ego* who is the central character goes with a concentration on his relationship to the rest, simply because his condition is accepted without demur. What tenacity of will this acceptance implies needs little comment.

The whole story is worked out in terms of Gregor being an insect, and at no point does the reader have the sense of being slyly invited to see more than meets the eye. There are no enigmas in the dialogue, to be resolved (as in 'The Judgement') only by reference to Kafka's own life; though his life is latently present throughout, it is independent of the story and allows it to proceed without hindrance. At times in Kafka's writing he suggests compassion through some artificial device, as he does in 'A Hunger-Artist'.[5] In 'The Metamorphosis' there are no devices, and the compassion is felt in the writing. It is not simply that the sister, confronted with an impossible situation, attempts the impossible in caring for the insect her brother has become, though the implications of that are moving in themselves. The love Gregor feels for her is in the rhythm of the prose, as when he hears her play the violin in the presence of the three lodgers. It is even more clearly present in the passage where Gregor's father starts throwing apples at him. The emotion mounts to a climax in which the urgency of the mother's pleading is as strongly present as the desperation of Gregor himself.

The little red apples rolled around on the floor as though magnetised, cannoning into one another. An apple thrown without much force grazed Gregor's back, but slid off without harm. Another, following immediately after it, however, sank deep into Gregor's back. Gregor tried to drag himself forward, as if the astounding, unbelievable pain might change if he moved to another place, but he felt as though he were nailed down, and flattened himself out in complete derangement of all his senses. The last thing he saw was the door of his room being flung open and his mother, followed by his shrieking sister, rushing in in her slip, as his sister had undressed her to let her breathe freely after her swoon, and then rushing up to his father, her petticoats falling down one after another, stumbling over the petticoats and hurling herself on his father, embracing him, in complete union with him – here Gregor's sight was already failing – and with her hands clasped at the back of his father's head, pleading with him to spare Gregor's life.

Strangest of all passages in Kafka, this has his double edge in its most notable form. There is surely some human sympathy here, in the portrayal of the mother, one wants to say, yet the thought of Kafka's avowed detachment from the emotions his readers were likely to feel, the calculating element in him, gives cause for doubt. 'An apple thrown without much force . . .'? It sounds over-nonchalant when an insect is the target, and so does the interest in the behaviour of the apples on the floor. Is there a paradox present, or is the mood simply one of detachment? A touch of humour is noticeable even in the tragic situation. It is partly due to the petticoats falling down, partly something slightly stylised in the way the mother beseeches the father – 'beseeches' is the word, it has just that faint touch of the melo-dramatic, and the mother's hands grasping the back of the father's head also have a classic, and therefore stylised simplicity. Certain overtones also appear, especially in the reference to Gregor's being 'nailed down' ('festgenagelt')* and, differently, in the *coup de grâce* of his seeing his mother and father perfectly united – the one sight he would have preferred not to see – at the moment that his eyesight dims. But above all there is the breath-less rise to a climax, grotesque in the circumstances when one realises what kind of creature is being protected, and the urgency of 'Schonung' ('sparing'), uttered with the mother's own inten-sity. Yet the whole is shot through with that mystical dissocia-tion that actually allows a humorous note to accompany every moment.

A similar paradoxical mood characterises the moment of Gregor's death; not in itself, for the description here has nothing ironical or melodramatic, but in its context, in the events which

* The allusion to a crucifixion of the central character occurs also in 'In the Penal Colony', and perhaps, more cryptically, in the exclamation 'Jesus!' with which Georg Bendemann is greeted as he rushes to his death. The second suggestion is more tenuous, but Kafka seems at least to have had some general parallel with Christ in mind in the figure of the 'Hunger-Artist'.

follow immediately on it. Left alone in his room with the apple festering on him, he feels his strength ebb:

'And what now?' Gregor thought to himself, and looked round in the darkness. He quickly discovered that he was unable to move at all now. He was not surprised at that, it seemed unnatural to him that he should actually have been able to get about up to this moment on these frail little legs. And on the whole he did feel relatively comfortable. He had pains all over his body, it was true, but he felt they were gradually becoming weaker and weaker, and would in the end disappear completely. The rotting apple in his back and the inflammation round it, covered with dirty fluff, scarcely troubled him. He thought again of his family with affection and love. His feeling that he had to vanish from the face of the earth was, if possible, stronger than his sister's. In this state of vacant, peaceful contemplation he remained, until the tower clock struck three in the morning. He was just conscious of the first brightening of the sky outside his window. Then, without his willing it, his head sank to the floor, and his last breath passed faintly through his nostrils.

There is no such moment as this anywhere else in Kafka, no such calm recognition of what was a reality of his own condition. He is convinced here that Gregor must disappear from the face of the earth, and the conviction has no resentment in it, nor has it any expectation of Gregor's being rewarded by some dialectical reversal of fortunes. Unlike Leverkühn in Mann's *Doktor Faustus*, Gregor is not speculating on being a particularly attractive morsel for divine Grace to snap at; the story is basically humanistic, atheistic, unconcerned about divine sanction or resurrection. Considering the savagery with which 'In the Penal Colony' describes a death without prospect of benefit, the calm of 'The Metamorphosis' is surprising. On the other hand, it is not a passage to which one can do more than assent. There is no other way out for Gregor, it is true, so far as one can see from the story. Yet 'vacant, peaceful contemplation' is not particularly admirable, and the general sense is of a feeble rather than a serene calm.

It is not a calm proudly presented for inspection. As soon as

Gregor's death has passed, Kafka allows the charwoman, one of his best comic creations, to burst in. The reaction she shows is inhuman if one still regards Gregor as a human being. But that is the point: for the charwoman Gregor is not a human being; he is an insect and always has been. In allowing her to show such indifference Kafka does, it is true, indicate that the attempt of the sister at bridging the gap between herself and Gregor is vain. The story has this utterly pessimistic note, so far as Gregor is concerned, but the reader who finds this assertion of a human being's unloveableness unbearable may have to see that it is also ineluctable. Gregor must vanish, and the charwoman is chosen to say so:

When the charwoman came, early in the morning, – out of sheer energy and impatience she slammed every single door, for all that she had been continually asked not to, so that from the moment she arrived there was no possibility of sleeping anywhere in the whole flat – she at first found nothing special in her first customary, cursory visit to Gregor. She thought he was lying so motionless on purpose, playing at being insulted; she credited him with every conceivable kind of intelligence. Happening to have the long broom in her hand, she tried tickling Gregor from the door. Obtaining no success that way either, she became annoyed and shoved at Gregor a little, and only when she had pushed him from where he lay without the least resistance did she begin to take notice. Quickly seeing how things stood, she opened her eyes wide, whistled to herself, but did not take long before she had flung open the door of the bedroom and shouted into the darkness at the top of her voice, 'Come and have a look, it's done for, lying there done for it is!'

Kafka could only have written in that way out of an inner certainty which recognised the crude life of the charwoman as decidedly as he recognised his own nature, or the dominant aspect of his own nature. The charwoman sweeps back into the scene like something out of a comic postcard, a self-sufficient bull of a woman, although as she does so, a critical reservation in Kafka's mind begins to make itself felt. He is not writing here a story on the lines of Mann's *Tonio Kröger*, where there is such an abject surrender to the spirit of the triumphant 'Bürger'.

Gregor is dead, but the victory is not with the opposition. There is a certain comedy already in the slight hesitation shown by the charwoman about opening such a thing as a bedroom-door early in the morning, and this now develops into a further not wholly serious situation, as Herr and Frau Samsa, woken by her shouting, get out of bed symmetrically. This is kept up in the description of the three lodgers – a main source of comedy in the story (and perhaps derived from the four Buffers in *Our Mutual Friend*) – who act with the perfect uniformity of the decent, convention-respecting man. They take their hats from the hat-stand, their sticks from the umbrella-stand, all at the same moment, they bow, and go down the stairs; reappearing at regular intervals as the landings hide them or bring them into view. One sees here Kafka's ironical reserve, working from a point of view well behind the horrifying persona with which he had to live. The 'Bürger', to use Thomas Mann's term, may have vitality and robustness, but he has the absurdity of an automaton. The victory does not belong to him, and there is no talk of reconciliation between him and anything that Gregor stands for.

This is still not the end of Kafka's comment; amusing as these moments are (if one can see them from out of his wretched state), they offer more light relief than social criticism. They are not penetrating, and the 'Bürger' is not really to be so easily dismissed. There remains the final scene when, Gregor being dead, the family is at last free of him and decides, since it is springtime, to take a tram-ride for an excursion into the country. The last sentences have some of Kafka's best cadences as well as his fullest vision:

> While they were conversing like this, it occurred almost at the same moment to Herr and Frau Samsa, seeing their daughter's vitality return more and more strongly, that despite the sorrow which had brought a pallor to her cheeks she had recently blossomed into a pretty girl with an attractive figure.
>
> Falling silent, and almost unconsciously exchanging understanding glances, they reflected that it would soon be time to be finding a proper young man for her. And it was like a confirmation of their

fresh dreams and good intentions when, as they arrived at the end of their journey, their daughter rose to her feet first and stretched her young body.

This is Kafka most fully in possession of himself as a writer. The verminous self must go: it has no hold on life, and no destiny but extinction. On the other hand, the brave new world now emerges, not unsatirised: the parents are still slightly uniform and symmetrical, and such good intentions as they may have are coloured by the half-conscious, and presumably calculating glances they exchange, their minds half-fixed on what advantages a suitor may bring. But the story does end with that glimpse of a woman ready for love and marriage; there are subtleties and simplicities here of a human order.

The ending was the one part of the story Kafka could not approve. At the moment he finished it he wrote to Felice to tell her so, adding, 'only the ending as it is today doesn't make me feel glad, it could have been better, there's no doubt.'[6] Whether he had anything specific in mind is impossible to say; he very seldom did make specific criticisms of his work. Not much more than a year later, he again rejected the ending, and perhaps the whole story with it: 'Great dislike of "Metamorphosis". Unreadable ending. Imperfect almost to the very bottom. It would have been better if I had not been disturbed by the business trip.'[7] Unlike his objections to *America*, this did not prevent him from trying to get the story published. Did he dislike the momentary suggestion of an optimistic conclusion with its possible insincerity (as it probably was, for him)? What he had written was, all the same, more subtle than mere optimism would have been. And it was in any case a very brief escape. In 'The Metamorphosis' he had seen his own existence as though from outside, in its relation with other lives, and though there was always another self which watched this self, he had recognised the need for this self to die. It was a personal affair, and he made no more of it than that, in this story. Had he realised the implications, he might never have written in the same vein again.

Within a short while, however, the conviction that his own

state could represent a universal fact of existence entered his consciousness, and the stories he wrote after this are given a more general symbolic value. It seems very likely that his reading of Kierkegaard had something to do with this, for it was not until 21 August 1913, a year after the meeting with Felice, that he first read him, to judge by his diary-entry for that day:

'I received today Kierkegaard's "Book of the Judge". As I already sensed, despite essential differences his case is very like my own, at least he is on the same side of the world. He confirms me like a friend.'

This was an important moment in Kafka's life. The isolated state he had always been in now appeared to him mirrored in another man's existence, a man who had gone through much the same crisis in relation to the woman he had intended to marry (Kierkegaard deliberately sacrificed his love for Regine Olsen) and whose father had meant as much to him spiritually as Kafka's had to him. From Kierkegaard he could have taken the view that the condition of his own mind was that of all men who had experienced dread, in the sense of awareness of infinite guilt, and he could have gained the impression, or had his impression confirmed, that this was a proper state for all men to be in. The fact is that, though there is nothing directly to suggest religious or generalising tendencies in the stories and novels begun before 1913, the first to follow after the reading of Kierkegaard showed them very clearly.

6

'IN THE PENAL COLONY'

It was a year and a half after the conclusion of 'The Metamorphosis' in December 1912, before the mood for writing took Kafka again. For the whole of 1913, and the first half of 1914, there is no record of his having written any fiction at all. (This was his normal way of writing: after the group of stories written in late 1914 there was next to nothing for the whole of 1915 and 1916, and the stories of 1917 were followed again by an almost completely uncreative two years; in the remaining time before his death in 1922 Kafka was also prolific, with fairly barren years either side. Four bursts of from six months to a year account for the great bulk of his creative work.) As before, the writing seems to have been precipitated by external events, since in June he became engaged to Felice Bauer, only to break off the engagement in July. In August came the declaration of war, and in that same month, not inappropriately, Kafka began *The Trial*, though the initial subject-matter of the novel was obviously related to his difficulties with Felice.[1] The impact of the war itself is seen rather in the grim tale 'In the Penal Colony', written between 4 and 18 October 1914. Kafka thought of including it along with 'The Metamorphosis' and 'The Judgement' in a volume to be entitled *Punishments*, but nothing ever came of this.

The most telling aspect of the piece is its capacity to grip the reader relentlessly, and to stay in his mind even if it festers there. There is a truth in it, so far as it shows the senselessness of suffering in a world without values of any kind, or only inhuman ones. In origin it owes something to Schopenhauer's comparison of the world to a penal colony, though perhaps Kafka may have thought also of Captain Dreyfus on Devil's Island. In its general purport it suggests that the world is under the rule of a sadistic god who at least in former times allowed some reward to those who suffered the torments he imposed, but who today denies even so much. Here is an institution where the slightest infringement of rules by ordinary soldiers (there are no prisoners as such) is visited with barbaric punishment: a machine is at hand, constructed to tattoo on the naked bodies of offenders the precise commandment they have unwittingly transgressed; the end, even for trivial offences, is execution. The only offence mentioned is a refusal by a soldier to salute outside his officer's door every hour – Kafka is careful to make the discrepancy between crime and punishment as outrageously absurd as possible. For his crime, the soldier is to be placed under the so-called harrow, to be killed at the end of twelve hours. There is this shred of consolation, an officer explains to an explorer who happens to call in, that after six hours the prisoner usually becomes aware of the law he has transgressed, which he is able to read in the tattooed marks, and is wonderfully transfigured. But in the present instance nothing of the kind happens. The offending soldier escapes scot-free. The officer, on the other hand, after describing the machine to the explorer, finds him mildly objecting, whereupon, believing for his own part absolutely in the justice of the procedure, he sets the machine to inscribe the commandment 'Be just', and lays himself under the harrow. At this the machine miraculously starts into motion of its own accord, before the officer can reach for the starting-lever, but instead of inscribing the words for which it has been programmed it transfixes him, and instead of being transfigured as prisoners formerly were, and still are, according to his own account, he remains just as he was in life, though with a spike of the machine sticking through his head. The machine itself breaks in pieces, apparently unable to deal with the paradoxical situation presented to it. And the explorer, after reading a prophecy that the former commandant who invented the machine will one day come back to life, to reinstate his former rule, escapes as fast as he can to his ocean-liner, and no doubt, to the comforts of modern civilisation.

Poe's 'The Pit and the Pendulum', which may also have suggested at least the idea of the machine of torture, is in comparison with this a mere tale of horror, and its whole tone is shriekingly melodramatic, while the rescue at the end is something that Kafka was very unlikely to reproduce. Kafka's sober, neutral note, and the overtones he employed, give a more ambitious touch than Poe's, and interpretations have on the whole been confident that the story is a thinly disguised allegory of the Crucifixion. This was certainly in Kafka's mind. The hints dropped about the old commandant and the young officer give them a relationship as between Jehovah and Christ, up to a point. As Austin Warren says:

The earth is a penal colony, and we are all under sentence of judgement for sin. There was once a very elaborate machine, of scholastic theology, for the pronouncement of sentence, and an elaborate ecclesiastical system for its administration. Now it is in process of disappearance: the old commander (God) has died, though there is a legend which you can believe or not, that he will come again.[2]

But although it is to that region of meaning that Kafka is alluding, he is not so systematic as that helpful account might suggest. The machine, for instance, is not so likely to be an allusion to scholastic theology as to the Cross itself, and its divinely ordained torture, and the idea has been put forward, not unreasonably, that the marks made by the harrow were suggested originally by the numerous small wounds covering the body of Christ in the painting by Matthias Grünewald in the Isenheim altar-piece (there are also faint suggestions of a cruel sexual intercourse). The miraculous self-starting of the machine when the officer lays himself on it then hints at a supernatural purpose which becomes convulsed at the paradox of teaching Justice to the most just of men, and destroys itself in the process. Nor need the absence of any resurrection be an obstacle to this kind of interpretation. By Kafka's day, the Resurrection had become virtually an impossibility for many theologians. In fact he not only found a Christ in contemporary theology who was not resurrected, he derived a vital moment in his story from it. Albert Schweitzer describes, in the concluding paragraphs of *The Quest for the Historical Jesus*, the scene before and after the death of Christ in terms so similar to Kafka's that Kafka must surely have read the passage and deliberately alluded to it:

There is silence all round [Schweitzer writes]. The Baptist appears and cries 'Repent, for the Kingdom of Heaven is at hand.' Soon after that comes Jesus, and in the knowledge that He is the coming Son of Man lays hold of the wheel of the world to set it moving on that last revolution which is to bring all ordinary history to a close. It refuses to turn, and He throws himself upon it. Then it does turn; and crushes Him. Instead of bringing in the eschatological conditions, He has destroyed them. The wheel rolls onward, and the mangled body of the one immeasurably great Man, who was strong enough to think of Himself as the spiritual ruler of mankind and to bend history to His purpose, is hanging upon it still. That is His victory and His reign.[4]

The parallels are close enough to establish the general direction in which Kafka meant to point, which is not to say that his meaning was bound at all closely to Schweitzer's. An allusion is not an adoption, and it is easily enough seen that in the terms of the story as Kafka wrote it the officer dies in attempting to prove himself right, rather than out of love for men, while the guilt of the prisoner bears no relation to any Christian belief in reward and punishment, being clearly absurd. Kafka makes the soldier's offence such a peccadillo that he must have intended the punishment to appear indefensible on any moral grounds. Guilt, says the officer, is always beyond doubt: that is the principle on which he works. It is the principle on which the Court in *The Trial* seems to operate, and it is the overriding experience of Kafka's life, but it is characteristic of neurosis and is neither the common experience of mankind, nor the basis of the Christian religion, despite the doctrine of Original Sin. If Kafka intended a general allegory of Christianity, he left some unaccountable discrepancies.

More probably, Kafka intended thoughts of the Crucifixion, the Second Coming, and so on, to be planted in the reader's mind without fitting them into any definite theological view or scheme of history. His real concern is not to offer a reinterpretation in either of these fields, but to arouse certain thoughts and emotions about the idea of redemptive suffering, partly thinking of the chances of his own suffering leading to any redemption.

To some extent he expresses scorn, through the story, for the easy ways of modern civilisation, represented by the ladies of the officers' mess who send sweets and other comforts to the prisoners, but are never at hand when the executions take place. The officer, relating this, reflects nostalgically on the old days when suffering was respected and people would come in thousands to see the transfiguration take place in the dying prisoner's face. In this, as Dr Pasley points out, Kafka must have had in mind the passage from Nietzsche's *Genealogy of Morals* in which ambiguous praise is given to the idea that pain is one of the great teachers of mankind:

There was never any lack of blood, torment, sacrifice, when Man considered it necessary to imprint anything in his memory: the most painful sacrifices and pledges (including sacrifice of the first-born) and the most repulsive mutilations (for example castrations) – the most cruel rituals of all religious cults (and all religions are at bottom systems of cruelties) – all this had its origin in that instinct which divined pain to be the most powerful aid to memory.[5]*

What Nietzsche intends in this passage is not certain. In the context he seems half to be decrying the barbarity of Man, half lamenting his fall into soft decadence and humanitarian reforms. But there is the same ambiguity about Kafka's story. He may begin with Kierkegaard, and Kierkegaard's words, already quoted,[6] about the inquisitorial torments devised by the Almighty as he saw him, he may have continued to form his view of himself in his recognition of infinite guilt, but a certain sadistic or masochistic pleasure is involved in the very idea, which Nietzsche then develops in his own way. Part of the sense to be had from this story of Kafka's, then, and this ought not to be blinked, is the feeling that modern times are decadent in their rejection of pain and cruelty, since in rejecting them they reject also the very means by which knowledge of the abyss of human guilt is to be obtained. And unlike Kierkegaard, Kafka

---

* That Nietzsche was right about the pleasures of public torture is amply shown by Huizinga's *Waning of the Middle Ages*. Huizinga also makes clear, however, what Nietzsche omits, that the impulse to mercy and sympathy was equally strong.

seems to insist here that there is no rising again from the abyss. Though prisoners in the past were transfigured, the officer remains just as he was in life, with the spike sticking out of his forehead.

The personal experience which could have driven Kafka towards such a view was intense enough for him to have actually held it. Yet he is, after all, not writing a philosophy of history or a religious tract, but writing a story, in which he does not necessarily side with any particular character: he includes the explorer as well as the officer, when all is said and done, and we should look rather for the sense of the whole, which comes not so much from what is said, as from the tone, and from the balance of one aspect against another. Here, for instance, is the passage in which the officer describes to the explorer the effect of the transfiguration as it used to be in former days, when large crowds used to attend the executions:

'Well, and then came the sixth hour. It was quite impossible to grant permission to everybody who asked to be allowed to watch from close at hand. The commandant in his wisdom ordered that the children should be given the first consideration – I was, myself, of course, allowed to stand by at all times, by virtue of my profession, and I would often squat there with a small child right and left in each arm. How we all absorbed the look of transfiguration in the face of the tortured man, how we used to bathe our cheeks in the glow of this justice, attained at last, and already so quickly vanishing! Those were the days, comrade.' The officer had obviously forgotten who was facing him. He had embraced the explorer and lain his head on his shoulder. The explorer was in great embarrassment, impatiently looking past the officer . . .

There is something insane about the officer here, since he cannot possibly be thought ironical. (Supposing that satire of Christian education of children through contemplation of the Cross were intended, it would misfire in that such education cannot rightly have been directed to pleasure at the justice being done to Christ through his Crucifixion.) The embrace of the explorer by the officer is equally grotesque. But Kafka allows for no common humanity here; he shows no sign of expecting that the reader

will detest what is being offered. On the contrary, an equally
grotesque element is present in the reactions of all the others. The
explorer is merely embarrassed by the embrace. A little later,
the prisoner, though about to be tortured to death, takes a
detached interest in the machine, leaning over the glass cover of
the harrow, trying to see what it is that others have seen, and
he has missed. Later still, when he is actually on the machine,
the needles touching his flesh, he makes signals to the soldier,
whispering to him, and seeming to be on friendly terms, as
though the whole thing were a charade. He takes a childish
pleasure in the gift of ladies' handkerchiefs, and spends some
time trying to snatch them back from the soldier, who playfully
snatches them back again. When the officer himself lies on the
machine the prisoner laughs noiselessly for a long time, in
pleasure at the thought of what he takes to be revenge. In all
this there is an absence of humanity so complete that it can
perhaps only be explained in terms of the position beyond
humanity which Kafka sometimes fancied himself to have
reached. From the point of view of the God who ordained such
tortures, it might appear that they could be described and even
experienced with such callous amusement. The humour here
becomes nauseous.

The only human standard provided in the story is that of the
explorer, a somewhat detached figure himself, who objects to
the injustice of the machine up to a certain point, but evidently
has no strong feelings. Kafka needed the explorer for technical
reasons, in any case, partly so that the machine could be
explained to someone totally ignorant of it, partly so that someone could remain at the end of the story to provide a comment,
explicitly or otherwise. But in allowing the explorer to make off
for his ship, Kafka lent all the weight of the story to the officer.
In the balance of the whole, the impression is created that the
alternative to the officer's conviction is merely the pusillanimity
of the explorer, and this gives a certain grim majesty to the
officer's dead face.

To create that balance, Kafka was obliged, however, to
accept an ending with which he was not entirely satisfied.

Several drafts of the ending exist in the diary, and he wrote to his publisher on 4 September 1917, nearly three years after writing the story, of his extreme dissatisfaction. He is fairly specific this time: 'Two or three pages before the end', he wrote, 'are fudged [sind Machwerk], their presence hints at a deeper fault, there is a worm there, that makes even the full roundness of the story hollow.' Two or three pages from the end is just about the point where the officer meets his death, and where the machine destroys itself. The part with which Kafka was dissatisfied was thus the passage in which the explorer leaves the scene and goes back to his liner. Now the machine does not so much destroy itself as vomit out its cogs and wheels as though retching at the contradiction imposed on it, of punishing for injustice one who had, in its own terms, been entirely just. There is something of a Hegelian 'Selbstaufhebung' here, a 'self-annulment', well brought out by Professor Emrich: when the recognition of extreme, infinite guilt comes dialectically into play with the extreme, infinite innocence of the officer (one recalls the combination of innocence and devilishness attributed to Georg Bendemann by his father, in 'The Judgement') the system cannot survive in its existing form. The machine being destroyed, however, the explorer and the prisoner might be expected to show some sign of relief, even of exultation. What follows instead is a series of inconsequentialities: from being a fantastic story told with every mark of realism, apart from the destruction of the machine itself, the tale begins to show signs of dream-logic, and there are unintelligible moments such as occur from time to time when Kafka has lost control of his terrifying material. That loss is almost revealed at once, by the passage which follows, after a short typographical space, on the image of the dead officer:

When the explorer, with the soldier and the condemned man behind him, came to the first houses of the settlement, the soldier pointed to one of them and said 'Here is the tea-house.'

The sudden reference to this hitherto unmentioned place is needed on account of what is about to come: it is still a re-

markably irrelevant observation at this point. Kafka is attempting to lead the reader towards a scene which he is determined to
include, however little it may spring from the conditions of the
story up till now. Shortly afterwards, he relates that the atmosphere of the tea-house suggests to the explorer a historical
memory: 'he felt the power of earlier times' in some unexplained way, from the sheer presence of this building. Kafka's
intention is clearly to inform the reader that the more or less
humane explorer is awed after all by the ancient cruelties and
suffering imposed by the old commandant, but he has not found
the means to do this impressively; the tea-house is an inadequate
invention and does not arise from the 'inward truth' which
Kafka prized. Then comes the revelation that the old commandant has been buried under one of the café-tables – a typically
dream-like thought, especially when it appears that there is
actually a little tombstone, low enough to be under the table.
But at this point the need for a tea-house becomes apparent,
and one sees how much of a contrivance it is. On the stone is an
inscription prophesying that the old commandant will one day
arise from his grave and call on his followers to reconquer
the penal colony – in other words, there will either be a Day of
Judgement or the religious rites described by Nietzsche will be
restored. To read this, the explorer is obliged to kneel down,
and thus assumes a posture of reverence. A normal tombstone
would not require such a posture in order to be read: only a very
small one, with 'very small letters' as this one has, could make
the kneeling look natural. And so one sees how Kafka's intention in the whole of this passage – not necessarily an explicitly realised intention – has been to lead up to this moment
of, as it were, defeat for the explorer. The little tombstone
suggests a covering table, the table suggests a tea-house, and the
first thought after the machine has been destroyed is to go
straight to it. Kafka's generalising intention produces the
awkwardness of this sequence: he wishes to insist that the destruction of the machine does not mean the end of all it stood
for, and that those who oppose the view of suffering he had
come on the whole to adopt should be made to look small. It

is meanly done. The physical gesture of obeisance is made, but there is nothing morally compelling in the circumstances, and the explorer is not really impressed, only made to appear so.

In 'The Metamorphosis' Kafka had also written a story which ended with the extinction of the central character – Gregor Samsa is thrown out with the morning's rubbish. There he had ended with a positive moment which displeased him, so far as one can guess, because of its reassertion of life, because that reassertion was not possible for him with sincerity. In 'In the Penal Colony' he now writes an ending which is negative in so far as it asserts the values of self-torment and acceptance of extinction over against a sentimentally humane world. This too displeases him, perhaps for the reason suggested. The most significant point here, however, may be that it is the endings which dissatisfy him. In both stories extinction is the real end, as it is the real, and not merely the virtual end, of *The Trial*. This was the point towards which Kafka was inexorably driving himself. Despite the destruction of the machine the final pages must not be allowed to make any further comment: not only was there no resurrection from the abyss, no end, however paradoxical, to infinite guilt, one must not allow anything to follow, not even a tribute to the power which ordained these things. The life in him had to be still more deadened. *The Trial* was the next step in that direction.

7

'THE TRIAL'

'The anguish that pervades this book', André Gide wrote of
The Trial, 'is at some moments almost intolerable, for how
should one not say, this hounded creature is myself?'[1] Anyone
who has submitted to the experience of the novel knows that to
be true. Within those confines one is stifled along with Joseph
K., baffled by the same endless arguments, confused by the
inscrutability of the Court, and relieved when execution is
carried out and the claustrophobia ends. It seems to be not
merely Joseph K.'s world, either. *The Trial* takes place for the
most part in a perfectly ordinary setting, in a modern *pension*,
in a bank, in tenement buildings, in offices where there are files
and safes; only occasionally does it move to stranger places, the
cathedral in complete darkness, the attic with its court officials,
the magistrates' court off a remote staircase. So the suggestion
often is that this is a commonly accepted world, the world as
conventionally seen, but seen through to its depths. There is a
Court under every roof, and K.'s uncle as well as his landlady,
Frau Grubach, are aware of it although they rarely talk about
it. The effect is more telling than a more romantic setting would
have been, in pressing upon the reader Kafka's own experience
of dread.

Not only Kafka's. Martin Greenberg quotes with surprising
appositeness lines from Wordsworth:

> Then suddenly the scene
> Changed, and the unbroken dream entangled me
> In long orations, which I strove to plead
> Before unjust tribunals – with a voice
> Labouring, a brain confounded, and a sense,
> Death-like, of treacherous desertion, felt
> In the last place of refuge – my own soul.[2]

And one might be excused for thinking some words of Luther's,
from his lecture on the *Epistle to the Romans*, equally relevant,
though the context is not the same:

'For God does not wish to make us blessed through our own, but through an alien justice [or righteousness: 'Gerechtigkeit' – Luther goes on to say in effect that we may make ourselves vain of what we take to be our righteousness], through a justice which does not come out of us, and have its origin in us, but which comes to us from elsewhere. And thus there must be taught a justice which comes completely from outside and is completely alien. Therefore our own justice, native to us, must first be uprooted.'

Certainly, the idea of justice in Kafka's novel is as far removed from all human and humane notions as Luther's is. The difference lies in the idea that the ultimate purpose is to bless men. Of this there is no trace in *The Trial*, whatever Kafka's own views were: the point about the trial in the novel is that there is no specific accusation. When K. asks, at his arrest, what he is charged with, he is told that while there is no possibility of error, the Court is 'attracted' by guilt, which can thus, evidently, not be in doubt. But there is never any definition even of the kind of guilt that might be in question. Perhaps, as Martin Greenberg says, 'Joseph K.'s wrongdoing consists in the complaint, which he never ceases making until just before the end, that a wrong has been done to him.'³ But if we, the readers, are able to see that, when K. cannot, we are placed in an embarrassingly superior position. To know the answer to K.'s problems in such a way is to remove oneself from the experience of the novel. Similarly, the explanation sometimes offered, that K. is at fault because he visits a woman once a week 'for hygienic reasons', is conventional in its disapprobation: such visits may have been valuable to K. for the reason given, and that is literally all we know about them. To suggest that the whole mechanism of the Court was brought into play for so minor a sin (it is true that K. presumably had no love for this woman), is almost as absurd as the fact which is insisted on all through the book, that K. is never charged with anything.

Yet another explanation that has been put forward is of a political kind. It is noticeable, for instance, that the First Interrogation takes place in a poor quarter of the town, quite unlike K.'s own quarter, and since the assembly of people there

is compared with a 'political meeting', it has been suggested that
K. is on trial for his political beliefs or perhaps for his lack of
political activity. (Max Brod's list of variant readings states that
Kafka had originally written 'Socialist meeting'.) This interpretation was given some additional weight by Klaus Wagenbach's revelation that Kafka had been interested in anarchist
movements of his time, and had attended meetings of the 'Klub
mladijch', which was under police supervision. However, more
recent investigation shows that Kafka was not listed among the
members of the club, and that 'his name does not figure in the
police reports of its meetings or the judicial interrogations of its
officials, thorough as they were.'4 If Kafka attended, it can only
have been in an unobtrusive way, and in fact for the whole of
his life he had a clean police record. But the evidence lies not so
much in that as in the novel. It is true that there is some reference
to the various attitudes towards K. of the crowd on the right
and the crowd on the left, but if this has political meaning it is
extremely slight, and Kafka never develops any political theme.
Possibly some pricking of social conscience in himself gave rise
to the placing of the first courtroom in a poor quarter. One
cannot go on from that to imply, as Wilhelm Emrich does, that
K. is a typical bourgeois on trial for antisocial behaviour. The
political aspect barely emerges at all, and when the chapter ends
the reader is left with the same sense of indeterminate accusation. The 'infinite guilt' of Kierkegaard comes nearest to a
correspondence with K.'s guilt.

Yet there is still a distinctive quality, the humour. Max Brod
relates that when Kafka read the first chapter of *The Trial* aloud
to a group of friends, he and they were doubled up with laughter. That is hard to credit, but there are some slightly comic
elements, expecially in the opening scene, as when K. thinks of
presenting his bicycle-rider's licence as evidence of identity, or
in the vulgar importunacy and indifference of the warders:

'How can I be under arrest? And in circumstances like these?'
'There you go again', said the warder, dipping a piece of bread and
butter into the honey-jar. 'We don't answer that sort of question.'
'You will have to answer', said K. 'Here are my papers, now you

show me yours, particularly the warrant.' 'Bless my soul', said the warder. 'Why can't you take what's coming to you instead of going all out to annoy us, the two people probably nearest of anybody to you now, for no reason at all?' 'He's quite right, believe you me', said Franz, lifting the coffee-cup in his hand not quite up to his mouth, and giving K. a long look that was probably significant, though unintelligible.

That translation slightly overdoes the humour, but it is certainly there, unemphatically but persistently all through the scene of the arrest. The strangest thing about K.'s 'accursed trial', as they call it, is that although it is a matter of life and death it is presented as something trivial and faintly ridiculous (at his death, K. thinks it appropriate that second-rate opera-singers are sent to kill him). Luther had no such note as that in his writing, nor did Kierkegaard. Not since Villon, perhaps, had death and execution been treated in European literature so flippantly, and the fact that Kafka could conceive of the warders in such a mood is indication enough that he was not projecting the whole of himself into the character to whom he gave his own initial.

Despite broad similarities with other men's experience, then, there is a characteristic note, and as with many of Kafka's works, there are concealed personal references which it is useful to know about, since they sometimes make intelligible what must otherwise remain esoteric. That he began writing *The Trial* in August 1914 is significant in itself, for his diary entry for 23 July of that year records the breaking-off of his engagement to Felice Bauer, at what he calls 'The Court (Gerichtshof) in the Hotel' (that is, the 'Askanischer Hof' in Berlin, where he had gone on purpose to tell Felice that he could not marry her). The execution of Joseph K. is closely connected with this event, for, as Klaus Wagenbach relates, the death of K. on the eve of his thirty-first birthday is paralleled by Kafka's own decision just before his own thirty-first birthday (3 July 1914) to go to Berlin and announce his intention to Felice. Thus the verdict on K. seems to be linked with Kafka's own determination to go on alone, without Felice. The execution of K. is not unlike the death of George Bendemann in that it allows the writer in Kafka to go on with his writing, with his self-analysis.

The novel itself, which advanced quickly for several chapters, hanging fire afterwards, and being dropped in 1916, begins in a dream-world rather like that of 'The Judgement'. It is a waking dream, both a real world experienced as a dream, and a dream experienced as a real world. Nothing physically impossible happens in it – there are no flights through the air – yet people come and go with the same insouciance and inconsequentiality as in dreams. It seems a matter of course to K., after his arrest, when he sees three clerks from his own office sitting in the background (though the incident may derive not from a dream but from a similar encounter in the first chapter of Dostoevsky's novel, *The Double*): he knows, just as one does know in a dream, that they have been there all along, however surprising it would be to see them in waking life. There is a similar recognition of the businessman Block, in the room of the lawyer Huld, who has also been sitting unnoticed in the darkness.

This quality has its disadvantages in a work of fiction. As in *America*, almost all the characters except the central one make their single appearance and then vanish, never to be referred to again. What seem to be irrational blockages occur, as happens in the first chapter, and this can have damaging effects in the long run. It must strike every reader that the extraordinary opening soon gives way to a much less compelling series of events, first the conversation with Frau Grubach, then the waylaying of Fräulein Bürstner. The mystery of the unexplained arrest is followed by the confrontation with this young woman in the next room (referred to in the MS as F.B.), in such a way that it seems as though the arrest had something to do with K.'s feelings for her, of which he is ashamed. The likelihood of this, given the background of Kafka's own life, and his use of these particular initials, becomes a virtual certainty. The difficulty is that the point is never allowed to develop. One might hazard a guess that Kafka was writing about the conflict in himself between the desire to maintain the possibility of infinite guilt (and infinite uncertainty about both guilt and innocence), as a precondition of his writing, and the desire for Felice. But the novel does not actually say that, and when K. goes later to see Fräulein Bürstner again, he is obliged to speak for a whole wearisome chapter to a certain Fräulein Montag, who does nothing but obstruct him in an irritatingly inconsequential way. It is as though the initial impetus in the writing of the novel had faded. K. is not to see Fräulein Bürstner again, but Kafka as a conscious artist has not so much decided this, as permitted the substitution of a woman in whom K. takes no interest whatsoever. A kind of censorship has operated, which it is the artist's business, as a rule, to circumvent, whereas Kafka here is more in the position of a psychiatric patient whose analysis needs to be undertaken by someone else.

But although Fräulein Bürstner disappears from the narrative, the feelings she arouses in K. ensure that a number of women take her place, while at the same time K. begins to realise that all the officials of the Court are women-chasers, in other words that they are like himself. If often happens, in this novel, that K.'s own inward expectations are reflected by the Court (he is reproved for turning up late at his first interrogation, though no time has been appointed for it, and he is late only by reference to the time he had privately decided on). So the impression is formed that the whole Court is corrupt, as perhaps it really is, though no such positive affirmation is made. Everything proceeds unquestioningly, as in a dream, and K.'s discovery of the venality of the Court is all part of the same acquiescence in first impressions. The reader too, if he goes where the book guides him, will form the same impression, and, when the woman in the courtroom shows K. the law-books commonly in use there, will see them, with K.'s eyes, as obscene. Here, however, a point of some importance for the whole reading of Kafka emerges. The description of the picture in the law-book that offends K. reveals that he was mistaken:

K. opened the top book, and an indecent picture was revealed. A man and a woman were sitting naked on a sofa, the filthy intention of the draughtsman being quite clear, though his clumsiness had been such that in the end only a man and a woman were to be seen, jutting out too three-dimensionally, sitting much too upright, and, because the perspective was wrong, finding difficulty even in turning towards each other.

Within the dream-consciousness, this passes well enough as a confirmation of K.'s disgust. Yet the indecency is not apparent to a conscious eye, and all the faults in the picture seem to be a matter of drawing technique rather than moral guilt or perversity. K. is so obsessed with guilt about sexual matters that it is natural for him to interpret obscenity in the picture, just as he interprets and accepts the hitherto unobserved bank clerks at the time of his arrest. That is a dream-judgement, but not a rational judgement on the Court as it is actually revealed, in the dream, to K.*

With this, the question of art as distinct from self-revelation arises. The business of a novelist is to expose himself to experience without reserve: the remaining part of his work is to see what

---

* Possibly Kafka had not come to terms with his own vision here. Malcolm Pasley argues convincingly[5] that he had in mind, in this passage, a Jewish legend in a book he is known to have read, according to which a picture of a man and woman in the act of making love was discovered by heathens who had invaded the Ark of the Covenant, and crudely misinterpreted by them. The invaders failed to understand that the picture represented the union of the Jewish nation with God, and similarly Joseph K. fails to interpret the drawing correctly. It seems very likely that Kafka did have this legend in mind. Yet he cannot have imagined that his readers would know or discover the obscure legend and interpret it as Dr Pasley does, as a sign of Joseph K.'s failure to understand the real (benevolent?) nature of the Court. They, after all, have no such contrast in front of them, only the strange failure to describe anything that corresponds to the 'filthy intention'. Here is a fair example of the pitfalls of scholarship. Dr Pasley has had access to information which most readers will never come across in their lives, and seems to be in a superior position. The critic's business, on the other hand, is to read so much as the author was willing or able to put on paper, and form his impressions from that. Here, it has to be admitted, Kafka seems not to have been as clear about his intention as a novelist usually needs to be. Was he aware that the description of the man and woman which he gave was contrary to K.'s impression of it? Did he recall the picture, as it was described in the legend, without himself seeing it very clearly, and so seem to attribute a certain prudishness to K.? Was he using an allusion which meant more to him than it possibly could to his reader, without becoming aware of its real significance for himself?

that experience looks like with the most lively consciousness he can bring to bear. The distinction of Kafka is that he was able to strip himself to the bare skin, when his whole cast of mind, inherited or acquired, was past most men's bearing. It is still proper, all the same, to ask of him the most difficult feat of all, that of bringing his conscious, shaping mind to bear, even although that may have been a feat he was less able to accomplish.

Conscious shaping was less within Kafka's power on this occasion than in the case of any other of his larger works (and much less than with his stories). All his novels are incomplete, but whereas *The Castle* continues in unbroken sequence, lacking, apparently, only the last few pages, while *America* also tells a continuous story for seven chapters, after which it breaks off and resumes after a gap, only to break off once more, *The Trial* is unfinished in a more complex way. There is no obvious sequence of chapters, and the proper order of some of them is disputed. Between some of the chapters there are gaps, which may be partially filled with the fragments printed at the end of the main sequence. Some of the chapters are known to be incomplete, or appear to be so. Yet the ending, unlike that of the other two principal novels, is definite and incisive, being the final murder of K. by the court authorities. Kafka had no hesitation about that part of the book. That is the most significant point about the state of the text.

Some further account is needed, however, if the novel is to be read in anything like the form Kafka intended for it. The universal practice of printing the final chapter as though it followed immediately upon the scene in the cathedral, without indicating that there is a gap between them, is the most misleading feature of the published versions, but it has also been argued convincingly that chapter 4 should be renumbered chapter 2, and though other suggestions have less to be said for them, there is a need for a schematic presentation of what has so far been established. It should be borne in mind that Kafka handed the MS to Max Brod in June 1920, four years before his death, without putting it in order and without numbering the chapters, though

Brod had some knowledge of the sequence from having heard the novel read aloud, and from other evidence he has given.[6] Arguments about the editing concentrate on the indications of the seasons – since the whole time-span covers exactly one year – and on certain obvious groupings, chapters 1 to 5 and 6 to 8 seeming to belong together.[7] The best general picture available, then, is as given in the table.

'THE TRIAL'

Chapter	Contents	Additional fragments
		'State Attorney' (apparently a rejected draft for a first chapter).
1.	Arrest of K. Frau Grubach and Fräulein Bürstner.	
4.	Fräulein Montag (unfinished?)	
2.	First interrogation.	
3.	Second visit to the Court. The student. K. enters the chancelry offices.	
		'To Elsa'? (belongs after chap. 3 or chap. 5?)
5.	The Whipper.	
6.	Lawyer Huld. Leni.	
7.	K. in his office. Titorelli.	
8.	Second visit to Huld. Block (unfinished according to Brod).	
9.	The Cathedral (unfinished?) (placed by Uyttersprot after chap. 6).	
		'Fight with the Deputy Manager'? 'The House'? 'Journey to his Mother'?
Last	Execution of K.	Variants of the execution in the diary? (See 19 July and 22 July 1916.)
		There is also a piece about a Joseph K. entitled 'A Dream', published by Kafka in his own lifetime, which according to Brod was meant for this novel.

Some patterning is of course apparent here. It is natural for the courtroom scenes to follow the arrest, and for the visits to the lawyer to come after the interrogation, but this does not amount to a design, and the discrete nature of each block of chapters consorts with K.'s own baffled movement from one disconnected series of happenings to another. Only in such a way could his frustration be conveyed.

Yet there are startlingly vivid passages, most of all in the scene with the Whipper, which is so gripping a narrative as to stand out in memory from almost all the rest. Suddenly, and rather unexpectedly, it begins to appear in this chapter that something of the reasons for K.'s predicament is about to be revealed. The flogging of the warders is only carried out, so it is explained to K., because he complained to the magistrates that the warders had tried to take his clothes. As on other occasions, the Court meets K.'s expectations. In calling the warders 'corrupt riff-raff' he had certainly used some venom, and though he did not actually call for punishment, let alone a flogging, he had, as it were, already flogged them in his own mind. (One recalls too, from the 'First Interrogation', how K. complained of the presence of 'low-ranked employees' at his arrest, how absurdly inflated he became in defending himself, how meanly suspicious, and how the Court played up to him by huddling together in fright when he struck the table with his fist. The grotesque complaisance of the Court is a continual parody on K.'s pretensions, comparable to the hushed attentiveness of the captain as Karl Rossmann defends the stoker, or the deferential courtesy of the employment agent in the Oklahoma Theatre. The outside world is constantly playing K.'s game.) Now, when he opens the cupboard at the bank and finds the warders about to strip for punishment, his wary self-regard is in evidence again. Hearing sobs or groans behind the door to what he had always supposed to be a lumber-room, his first instinct is not to open the door but to find a servant – 'it might be necessary to have a witness' – and when he does open it, he does so from nothing more than 'insatiable curiosity'. K. does not know, at this stage, that the Court is involved, though he may suspect it.

But all through the scene, his only thought is for his own safety and secrecy. When the cane first descends on Franz, and he lets out an inhuman scream, K.'s only thought is to tell him not to scream, and to push the man hard enough to make him fall over. (The standard English translation, which has simply 'Don't', for 'Schrei nicht', might be thought to be addressed to the Whipper, but it is not.) The whole scene seems to be devised to show how the trial has already so engrossed K.'s attention that he can give no thought to others. The idea of freeing the warder by offering to substitute himself is quickly dismissed, perhaps properly, on the grounds that the Whipper would not accept the substitution, though K. cannot know that for certain. After leaving the two warders to take what is coming to them, K. still carefully observes every passer-by in the street to check up on Franz's story that his girl-friend is waiting for him, and the discovery of the lie, rather than any compassionate feeling, is his last reaction to the incident. When he returns next day, and finds the flogging still going on, he slams the door shut and beats with his fists against it, running away 'almost in tears'. It hurts him, then, to turn his back on the warders, and the whole scene may well appear to be an illustration to a saying of Kafka's that 'you can shut yourself off from the suffering of the world . . . that is the one suffering you might spare yourself.' But the totally pessimistic note in that aphorism should not go unnoticed. If one does withdraw, one will suffer all the same, as K. shows when he is close to tears; there is only suffering in one form or another, no relief. Even Franz, though complaining of his own beating, had hopes of rising to Whipper-status himself one day. So the episode is not presented so as to suggest a possible remedy, as though by learning to show a little charity K. could escape his dilemma. The lesson he has to learn is that the Court not only mirrors him, but that it only mirrors suffering and evil, nothing else is ever possible.

The lesson is reiterated in K.'s encounters with the lawyer Huld and the painter Titorelli, though less in terms of action, more in terms of theory and comment. Huld is finely drawn, his dry legalisms spun out to the point of elegant satire. The fact that his name means 'grace' – not exactly the theological term, which is 'Gnade', but still close enough to it in meaning – is an irony in itself. Similarly Titorelli provides a parody on every neurotic straining after impossible escape-routes, with his explanation of the various forms of trial and sentence. The two characters are not very different from one another, and the change from the apartment of one to the room of the other may be no more than a rough device for introducing variety: Titorelli is made to apologise at one point for speaking like a lawyer, and his being a painter seems to have little point in itself. There also enters into Titorelli's speech, though this is not yet the place to go into detail, an element of the compulsive style, full of qualifications and ramifications, which was to emerge more damagingly in the later chapters of *The Castle* and the last stories. More significant, perhaps, as indicating how Kafka's creative mind worked, is the episode in which Titorelli shows K. a painting of one of the judges. It is described in some detail near the beginning of the conversation with Titorelli, and as Malcolm Pasley has shown, though Kafka does not say so, and perhaps did not expect the allusion to be caught, the posture and features of the judge follow very closely indeed those of Michelangelo's sculpture of Moses.[8] This is an interesting point, in that it may suggest Kafka had something like the Mosaic Law in mind, when he spoke of the Law administered by the Court. That can scarcely be so, since the Mosaic Law is specific, and a man charged under it would in most cases know whether or not he was guilty, whereas K. is always completely ignorant. It may be, rather, that the half-rising figure of Moses in the sculpture, showing a man on the point of delivering a crushing verdict, seemed to Kafka peculiarly apt for the kind of judge he had in mind.

But at this point in the novel the action has become desultory. The impossibility of arriving at any satisfactory conclusion is apparent, but it becomes so with all due oppressiveness, and disconnection is the key note. What holds the novel together is the theme of K.'s relationship with women. After Fräulein Bürstner comes Fräulein Montag, then the woman in the

Chancelry, then Leni, and though none of them has much to do with the trial, it is to this point that the priest returns in the last chapter but one, as though taking up the threads and tying them afresh. The accusation brought by the priest is of seeking help too much, and especially from women. It is from women that K. most expects to find relief or comfort or explanation of the nameless arraignment that hangs over him all the time, much as Kafka himself must have felt that women played too large a part in his life. The priest's warning is reminiscent of Kafka's words to Milena Jesenská, that it was presumptuous of him to expect so much from her. Yet the accusation brought by the chaplain is not simply concerned with women. It is that K. seeks too much help, in other words he is required to face his predicament in total isolation. There is a Nietzschean ring to this – it is from Nietzsche, above all, in modern times, that the idea of a completely self-reliant mode of existence derives. Yet the meeting with the chaplain does not really confront this demand for self-reliance.

Of all the people K. meets, the chaplain is the most sympathetic to him. As K. says: 'You are an exception among all the others who belong to the Court. I have more confidence in you than in any of them, and I know quite a few. With you I can speak openly.' But this very possibility of contact is something which the chaplain rejects. 'Don't be deceived about the Court', says the Chaplain. 'In the introductory scriptures about the Law, it says about this deception . . .' And then follows the parable 'Before the Law', which Kafka had already published separately, as a short story.

The chaplain is, in effect, telling K. he must stand entirely on his own feet. At the same time, he offers K., not explicitly but by his mere presence, the comfort of knowing that there is another human being who cares for him. And it is this comfort which the chaplain tries, by his parable and the interpretation of it which follows, to remove out of reach:

Before the Law stands a door-keeper. To this door-keeper there comes a man from the country who begs for admittance to the Law. But the door-keeper says that he cannot admit the man at the moment. The man, on reflection, asks if he will be allowed, then, to enter later. 'It is possible,' answers the door-keeper, 'but not at this moment.' Since the door leading into the Law stands open as usual and the door-keeper steps to one side, the man bends down to peer through the entrance. When the door-keeper sees that, he laughs and says: 'If you are so strongly tempted, try to get in without my permission. But note that I am powerful. And I am only the lowest door-keeper. From hall to hall, keepers stand at every door, one more powerful than the other. And the sight of the third man is already more than even I can stand.' These are difficulties which the man from the country has not expected to meet, the Law, he thinks, should be accessible to every man and at all times, but when he looks more closely at the door-keeper in his furred robe, with his huge pointed nose and long thin, Tartar beard, he decides that he had better wait until he gets permission to enter. The door-keeper gives him a stool and lets him sit down at the side of the door. There he sits waiting for days and years. He makes many attempts to be allowed in and wearies the door-keeper with his importunity. The door-keeper often engages him in brief conversation, asking him about his home and about other matters, but the questions are put quite impersonally, as great men put questions, and always conclude with the statement that the man cannot be allowed to enter yet. The man, who has equipped himself with many things for his journey, parts with all he has, however valuable, in the hope of bribing the door-keeper. The door-keeper accepts it all, saying, however, as he takes each gift: 'I take this only to keep you from feeling that you have left something undone.' During all these long years the man watches the door-keeper almost incessantly. He forgets about the other door-keepers, and this one seems to him the only barrier between himself and the Law. In the first years he curses his evil fate aloud; later, as he grows old, he only mutters to himself. He grows childish, and since in his prolonged study of the door-keeper he has learned to know even the fleas in his fur collar, he begs the very fleas to help him and to persuade the door-keeper to change his mind. Finally his eyes grow dim and he does not know whether the world is really darkening around him or whether his eyes are only deceiving him. But in the darkness he can now perceive a radiance that streams inextinguishably from the door of the Law. Now his life is drawing to a close. Before he dies, all that he has experienced during the whole time of his sojourn condenses in his mind into one question, which he has never yet put to the door-keeper. He beckons the door-keeper, since he can no longer raise his stiffening body. The door-keeper has to bend far down to hear him, for the difference in size between them has increased very much to the man's disadvantage. 'What do you want to know now?' asks the door-keeper, 'you are insatiable.' 'Everyone strives to attain the Law,' answers the man, 'how does it come about, then, that in all these years no one has come seeking admittance but me?' The door-keeper perceives that the man is nearing his end and his hearing is failing, so he bellows in his ear: 'No one but you could gain admittance through this door, since this door was intended only for you. I am now going to shut it.'

On the face of it, this is a simple story, if grim. The man is over-awed by the door-keeper and cannot summon up the courage to push past him to the even more awful portals that lie beyond. Or, to reduce the amount of interpreting in that paraphrase, the man accepts the door-keeper's assurance that he cannot enter, and makes no attempt to push past.

As the priest comments on the story, it becomes much more complicated. It was he who told the story in the first place, to illustrate to K. his own particular delusion about the Court. Yet when K. concludes that the door-keeper has deceived the man, the priest at once denies that there is any mention of delusion in it, and begins a commentary of such length and complexity that it might be thought of as a satire on all the commentators on Kafka who have ever written about him. There are arguments about whether the door-keeper was fulfilling his duty, whether he has sympathy for the man, whether he is simple-minded, whether he has any knowledge at all of what the inner regions behind his gate are like, whether he is subordinated to the man, and whether he is inferior since he does not himself see the glory of the Law which the man sees in his dying moments. In the end, the priest seems to be taking the view that the integrity of the door-keeper is not to be doubted, since to doubt him is to doubt the Law itself, which the Court exists to administer. Yet as K. points out, the priest has already doubted the door-keeper, and cannot accept as true everything the door-keeper says. To which the priest replies that it is not necessary to accept everything as true, one must only accept it as necessary – a conclusion which K. will not accept readily because it implies the requirement to accept as necessary what one knows to be in the deepest sense untrue. '"A melancholy conclusion", said K. "It turns lying into a universal principle."' In short, the interpretation has veered towards the view that the story illustrates delusion or deception, yet at once Kafka adds that though K. said this with finality it was not his final judgement. The story brought in by the priest leaves everything in as much confusion as before.

The priest recalls to mind here those rabbis who sit down to discuss the Pentateuch in the mediaeval cabbalistic work, *The Zohar*, who examine page after page, syllable by syllable, the first word in the first chapter of the book of Genesis. 'Be–re–shith' – 'In the beginning' – What emerges is a system of theology which the writer of that simple expression never had in mind, and to which his expression bears the same relation as does the subject's reaction to an ink-blot in a psychological test. Similarly the priest, in raising questions of whether the door-keeper was doing his duty, whether he had any knowledge of the interior, and so on, is raising doubts which the story has no means of answering, these matters not being within its scope. It is as though one were to ask whether the credentials of the narrator in Goethe's *Werther* are really acceptable, Goethe not having troubled to authenticate them, or whether Hamlet is really killed by the scratch of Laertes' allegedly poisoned sword, or is only pretending. Unlike reality, a story can only answer questions addressed to its own limited situation: there is no more evidence to be unearthed later on. K., however, becomes involved in the priests' speculations to the point of total confusion.

It is not the conscious conclusion of a waking man to which K. comes. As is well known, in hypnosis it is possible to persuade a subject to do a number of things, though not everything, which he is normally inhibited from doing, merely by providing him with the semblance of a reason. Anything that looks like a reason will serve, so long as the opposition to the action is not too strongly developed. So here, K. accepts pseudo-reasons, just as in the passage about the 'obscene' law-books, he accepted pseudo-evidence, perhaps because in the dream he was inclined to believe in the Court's corruptness. What the priest offers is the muffled show of argument that might throb in the head of a man experiencing a nightmare.

The contrast with the not dissimilar passage in *Pilgrim's Progress* is striking; it is almost as though Kafka had had this in mind, and deliberately written in a contrary sense. Here Christian comes as it were to the gate of the Law, and meets opposition:

'Who bid thee go this way to be rid of thy burden?'
'A man that appeared to me to be a very great and honourable person: his name, as I remember, is Evangelist.'
'I beshrew him for his counsel!' said Worldly Wiseman, 'there is not a more dangerous and troublesome way in the world than is that onto which he hath directed thee; and that thou shalt find, if thou wilt be ruled by his counsel. Thou hast met with something, as I perceive, already; for I see the dirt of the Slough of Despond is upon thee; but that slough is the beginning of the sorrows that do attend those who go on in that way. Hear me; I am older than thou: thou art like to meet with, in the way which thou goest, wearisomeness, painfulness, hunger, perils, nakedness, sword, lions, dragons, dark-ness, and in a word, death, and what not. These things are certainly true, having been confirmed by many testimonies. And should a man so carelessly cast away himself, by giving heed to a stranger?'
'Why, sir,' said Christian, 'this burden upon my back is more terrible to me than all these things which you have mentioned: nay, methinks I care not what I meet with in the way, if so be I can also meet with deliverance from my burden.'

Kafka's mode of writing is too closely identified with the helplessness of dreams to allow of such boldness. K. remains within the compass of the nightmare.

The nightmare was also Kafka's own. As he said, in a passage of his diary where he recalls criticising this parable, the diffi-culties he had in making contact with others were due to the

fact that 'my thought, or rather the contents of my consciousness are quite misty, that I can rest in it, so far as I alone am
concerned, undisturbed and even self-content, but that a human
conversation needs precision, solidity, and permanent connections, things which I do not have. No one will ever want to
lie down with me in clouds of mist, and even if anyone did, I
cannot produce the mist out of my forehead; between two
people it disperses and is reduced to nothing.'9 This was true,
but there was a rational being capable of control, as Kafka liked
to think at other times, a part of him that could confront his
phantoms 'with quiet critical ability'. It was such a confrontation that Kafka seems at times to have envisaged in writing
The Trial, a deliberate submission to his phantom, which
should be more than a mere outpouring of his terror at it.

Thus the most delicate part of his whole operation still
remains to be considered. The mind below the surface, which
feels itself threatened by nameless accusations, is not totally
detached from the conscious mind, and Kafka took care to
interweave the episodes dealing with the Court with episodes
of K.'s daily routine at the office. At the same time, there are
features in all this talk of a trial which lend some colour to Max
Brod's observation, that Kafka was writing in *The Castle* an
account of the operation of divine Grace, while here, in *The
Trial*, he was describing the workings of divine Justice.

With this the vital issue is raised, whether Kafka was intending to write simply about a condition like his own – as he had
done in 'The Metamorphosis' – with such reserves of humour,
irony, detachment, as he had available, or whether he was also
intending to portray something more universal in its import.
Even when he himself provides the clues, however, the way in
which he does so deserves attention. This is particularly true in
the passage in *The Trial* in which, the connection of the Court
with a Cathedral, at least, having been made, K. is seen –
abruptly, without explanation – accompanying his executioners
to the desolate spot where the knife is to be thrust into him. It is
at this moment that it becomes clear, though still only dimly
clear, that the trial has overtones in K.'s mind of a religious

character. It is the obliqueness of the reference, as much as anything, that concerns us now:

K. knew very well that it was his duty to snatch the knife passing from hand to hand above his head, and thrust it into himself. But he did not do so; he turned his neck, which was still free, and looked about him. He could not completely rise to the occasion, he could not relieve the officials completely of their work; the responsibility for this last failure lay with him who had denied him the remnant of strength with which to do so.

The being that plays this cat-and-mouse game with K., tempting him to rise to the occasion by committing suicide and then denying him the strength with which to do it can only be some divinity. But the interpretation is not the main thing here – after all, K. could prove to be wrong; the only certain fact is that that is how K. sees it. What matters is, rather, the indirectness of the reference, through a single, unexplained personal pronoun, nearly at the end of a novel in which there has hitherto been no hint that a being who actually gives K. vitality is connected with the Court at all. As an attempt by Kafka at giving a further sphere of relevance to K.'s position, as a way of suggesting a very wide scope, extending to the whole of life perhaps, this is a weak part of the structure of his novel. Admittedly it is in any case an incomplete novel, which he did not mean to be published, yet if this wider relevance was in fact in his mind, it needed more emphasis than this. The idea slips out almost as an afterthought, with no reference to the far-ranging ramifications it implies. If some god is involved, his responsibility for the injustices inflicted on K. would seem to need attention, whereas K. is too weary now to face that. A bolder man than Kafka might have taken de Sade's view of the world as ruled by a malevolent deity, 'most vindictive, wicked and unjust', creating and sustaining the world by and for evil, requiring his creatures to exist in evil and to return to evil at their death:[10] that is half-implied by the episode of the Whipper, the most sadistic passage in the novel. But Kafka, involved in the dream-technique, and exhausted in his own battles, allows such possibilities without giving them serious, rational consideration. He is all submission and passivity here.

The point is sometimes made in K.'s defence that at any rate he refuses to stab himself; this is seen as a sign of paradoxical grace or original goodness in him. But K. does not do anything so willed as to refuse. Like his namesake in *The Castle* at another vital moment,[11] he simply has not the strength or will to do anything but lie helpless, waiting for the others to decide his fate. And by leaving the responsibility to the unnamed 'him', K. at the same time confesses that suicide was the proper course. By contrast with Georg Bendemann, who is still defending himself (asserting his love for his parents as though in self-justification) even at the moment that he drops from the bridge, K. sees himself as totally resigned, totally without responsibility, though still in the wrong. The resignation is more complete even than that of Gregor Samsa, who dies simply because his vitality fails. What happens to K. is much closer to what happens to the officer in 'In the Penal Colony': it is in that line of progression that K.'s death should be seen. And whereas the officer is taken unawares by the sudden operation of the machine he had so confidently expected to justify him, K. actually sees that the machine of the Court requires him to pull the lever himself. The thought in K.'s mind is more annihilating than any that had appeared in Kafka's work before. That Kafka should have allowed it to stand without further comment is a mark of his own closeness to K.'s mood at this time. That he did not publish the novel, on the other hand, and thought it should be destroyed, is a mark of his lack of confidence in what he had said at the time he wrote 'The Judgement'. It was not true, he must have felt, that 'everything could be said',[12] that there was a great fire prepared in which even the strangest ideas could vanish and rise again. For the idea of the end of *The Trial* could only lead to annihilation of everything human, without hope of renewal.

The writing is at its best, on the other hand, in scenes like the arrest, the search for the court in the various tenement flats, the first interrogation, the scene with the whipper, and the cathe-

dral scene. Here, not being concerned to bring universal implications into the warp of his story, Kafka most achieves the
oppressive atmosphere of ruthless enmity coupled with comic
pliability, the claustrophobia, the dark labyrinth of inward
tunnels which formed his mind, and because of the concrete-
ness of his detail he draws the reader in to share it. The situation
of the final chapter, as K. is led to execution, has most of these
features: the simplicity is near to Bunyan's:

So they came quickly out of the town, which at this point merged
almost without transition into the open fields. A small stone quarry,
deserted and bleak, lay quite near to a still completely urban house.
Here the two men came to a standstill, whether because this place
had been their goal from the very beginning, or because they were
too exhausted to go further. Now they loosened their hold of K.,
who stood waiting dumbly, took off their top-hats and wiped the
sweat from their brows with pocket handkerchiefs, meanwhile
surveying the quarry. The moon shone down on everything with
that simplicity and serenity which no other light possesses.

The quiet tone of that, a certain calm in the simplicity of the
utterance; and the rare reference to the natural scene, do not
make the whole story: the top-hats, and the wiping off of sweat
with handkerchiefs, give a humorous note even at such a
moment. It is not a particularly significant humour: the point
made by it is that Kafka is presenting K.'s situation in a detached
mood, and there is no suggestion, for instance, that the top-hats
represent big business, or 'respectable' opinion. Yet the detachment is important.

There is peace of a kind in the final chapter of *The Trial*,
though there is despair as well, a peace conveyed by the presence of the moon, not only at this moment, but also a little
later. It is seldom enough that Kafka describes such a scene in
his later work, and its occurrence at this moment of his progress
to execution is moving in its own way:

The water, gleaming and trembling in the moonlight, divided on
either side of a small island, on which, as if pressing against one
another, clumps of trees and bushes rose thickly. Below them, but

invisible now, ran gravel paths with comfortable benches, on which K. had stretched himself and eased his limbs many a summer. 'I didn't mean to stop', he said to his companions, shamed by their compliance. One of them seemed to reproach the other gently behind K.'s back, for the wrongly interpretable stop they had made, and then they went on.

But it is largely the peace of indifference. The easy brushing aside of Fräulein Bürstner in these final moments is a mark of the inhumanity which went with Kafka's total resignation to his lot, or curse, to the situation he was in almost all his life. It is not really a matter of much concern to K., whether or not the distant figure he sees is Fräulein Bürstner; when he guides his executioners to follow her it is not because he wants to see her but 'in order not to forget the warning she represented for him' – a warning, presumably (but why doesn't Kafka say?) like the chaplain's, not to depend on women. He deceives himself, too, when he resolves that the one thing he can do from now on is to maintain his calm, analytical reason to the very end, for he has shown little sign of such a frame of mind in the course of the novel, least of all in the most recent chapter, when he accepted the priest's analysis of the parable with so little demur. Ultimately, K. is listless in everything, without even the activity that would be involved in 'acceptance'. Even the figure who appears at the window at the last moment does little to change him: within the pattern of the novel this figure, appearing 'as a light darts up', corresponds to the sudden gleam of the Law in the chaplain's parable, but it means nothing to K. beyond an occasion for putting many questions to himself as to who it may be. Only his last gesture, stretching his fingers in a way that again recalls Grünewald's Isenheim crucifixion, is really emphatic and purposeful.

One is reminded by this peace of K.'s of such entries in Kafka's diary as this: 'Early this morning, for the first time for a long while, the joy of imagining a knife being turned in my heart.'[13] The kind of joy that this would be has nothing to connect it with the normal meaning of the word. Similarly, when Kafka said he could find happiness only if he could raise the world into 'the pure, the true, and unchangeable', he meant by this nothing in a traditional sense, rather a total willingness to be in his deathlike situation: this was what was true and unchangeable. The 'perfect' cry of Kafka's earlier ambition has already been mentioned.[14] This is the sense in which the last cry in *The Trial* is to be understood. 'Like a dog' – the continuing shame of K.'s death is removed from all earthly or human meaning, and by outliving him, it suggests an unchangeable, pure state of perfected degradation. The cry of the artist who gives permanence to his condition, so long as his words continue to be read, is actually superior to the cry of the man or woman who is not an artist – so Kafka's claim here runs. And the final chapter, the final words of *The Trial* are Kafka's fulfilment even more than they are K.'s, since he has the conscious enjoyment of them. But it is a fulfilment intended to satisfy only himself, not the reader, and this should be held in mind, too, when the whole effect of the novel is considered.

The universal applicability some readers find was not put there by Kafka. That most men undergo a trial is not a sufficiently close parallel to justify seeing in his novel a parable of the human condition. On the other hand, the false trial to which many submit at one time or another, substituting imagined guilt for real guilt, supplies enough affinities to give this novel a telling power. The rest of us do know what this trial of K.'s is; what is required is that we should not confuse it with a more generally significant one.

8

'A COUNTRY DOCTOR' AND
OTHER STORIES

Kafka gave a good deal of attention to the arrangement of the stories in the collection he was persuaded to send for publication to Kurt Wolff in 1917, and insisted on the particular order in which they now appear.[1] For the most part they had been written early in that same year, together with half a dozen others not published till after Kafka had died. They were, he said, 'far from what I really want',[2] but he believed he was already near to death, and that this was likely to be his last book, and so perhaps persuaded himself on those grounds to let it be published.[3] It was also a last offering to his father – the dedication to his father was as important to him as the arrangement and the publication itself, and even though, he felt, it offered no means of reconcilement he would at least have done something in that direction. The terms in which Kafka put this are helpful towards seeing what his writing meant to him, even when it was not completely satisfactory:

'Since I decided to dedicate the book to my father, I am anxious for it to appear soon. Not as though I could thereby conciliate Father, the roots of that enmity are ineradicable here, but I would have done something at least, and even though I hadn't emigrated to Palestine I would have travelled there with my finger on the map.'[4]

The combination of political, personal and literary ambitions seldom comes through so clearly. Kafka was interested in Zionism, and some Jews had already begun in his day to return to the Promised Land, though at this stage the Balfour Declaration had not been made, and there was no separate Jewish State in Palestine. It appears from this letter, however, that to emigrate there would for Kafka have been close to becoming reconciled with his father, rather as the return to Jerusalem was for Jews, after the Dispersal, at least a first reconciliation with God. And to write and publish stories would be a similar achievement. Kafka puts all this with his usual devastating reservations, but the intention, or the bare hope, comes through. He often talked in his diaries about the coming of the Messiah (as a future event) in much the same way, and just as equivocally. The Jew in him could only be satisfied by a complete reconciliation in every form, personal and supra-personal, while the sceptic was continually confronting the frustrations of reality.

To take the letter as a key to all fourteen stories in *A Country Doctor* would be to misuse it. They are varied, and while some are clearly symbolical, others are evocations of mood. One, 'Eleven Sons', is a complete enigma. It has been suggested that the eleven sons who are introduced one after another, and whose characteristics are minutely detailed – the story consists of nothing but these details – are allegorical representations of eleven of Kafka's own stories,[5] but the suggestion, if true, does little honour to Kafka, and attributes to him a mode of writing found nowhere else. Almost as baffling is 'A Visit to a Mine', which has also been seen as an allegory of the subjects of stories, and which certainly does seem to amount to nothing more than a series of portrayals. But though the story is nowhere near one of the best, it seems to have an intention deserving respect. It is told, apparently, by one of the miners, and his awestruck tone in relating the visit of ten mining experts with their liveried servant (this livery is the one obvious touch of unreality in the whole piece) is akin to the tone of the superstitious villagers living at the foot of the Castle. One catches a glimpse of the strangeness underlying all Kafka's world here. The 'supreme engineers', as they are called, could be persons of everyday life, yet the features noted about them seem oddly impressive, though perhaps it is merely the fact that they are noted that makes them so:

One, black-haired, lively, moves his eyes rapidly in all directions.
A second, with a note-pad, does sketches as he walks, looks round, compares, makes notes.
A third, hands in his coat-pockets, so that everything about him is taut, walks erect, keeps his dignity, only in the continual biting of his lips is his impatient, irrepressible youth revealed.

That last feature is the kind of thing one associates with Kafka's writing – partly because of the apparent contradiction between what looks like a mark of anxiety and the explanation given of it. The narrator seems over-respectful, and there is more of the same note in a later passage:

A ninth pushes a sort of pram with surveying instruments in it. Extremely expensive instruments, bedded deep in the softest cotton-wool. The pram ought really to be pushed by the servingman, but it is not entrusted to him, an engineer had to volunteer, and he does it gladly, as one sees. He is no doubt the youngest, perhaps he does not understand all the instruments as yet by any means, yet his eyes are continually fixed on them, he almost runs a risk thereby of hitting the pram against the wall.

The officials of the Castle are said to have just such an exaggerated devotion to their work, and their admirers breathe a similar reverence for them; both in the novel and in this story the reference can be purely terrestrial. Yet as the small procession fades into the darkness down the seam, a bare suggestion of some inexplicable quality in them occurs.

This inexplicable quality is the subject of the much stranger piece 'A Worry to the Caretaker',* describing a being known as Odradek, which looks like a flat, star-shaped cotton-reel ('Zwirnspule' – perhaps one of those saw-edged discs used for twine is meant), wound round with old bits of cotton, and propped up by a right-angled rod. The notable point about Odradek, which one grasps at, probably too thankfully, in the search for a meaning, is that he has no purpose, and consequently (though one doesn't see the connection) cannot die. Perhaps more important for understanding Kafka here is a conversation recorded by Gustav Janouch.

Kafka suddenly stopped and stretched out his hand.
'Look! Here, here! Do you see it?'
Out of a house in the Jakobsgasse we had reached during our conversation leapt a small dog like a ball of wool, crossed our path and vanished round the corner of the Tempelgasse.

* Mistranslated as 'The Cares of a Family Man'.

'Nice little dog', I said.

'A dog?' Kafka asked distrustfully, slowly setting off.

'A small dog, young. Didn't you see it?'

'I saw it all right. But was it a dog?'

'A small poodle'.

'A poodle. That may be a dog, or it may be a sign. [In Goethe's *Faust* the devil first appears in the guise of a poodle.] We Jews sometimes make tragic mistakes.'

'It was only a dog', I said.

'Good, if it was', Kafka nodded. 'But the "only" is valid for the person who says it. What is a bundle of rags or a dog for one, is a sign for another.'

'Odradek, from your story.'

Kafka did not respond, but went on in the same direction he had begun with the concluding words 'There is always something more than you bargained for.'[6]

However fanciful that particular incident looks (can Kafka have spoken so pretentiously?),* it is typical of Kafka's world: Kafka meets Odradeks on staircases, and gets into conversation with them; the visit of engineers to a mine can have equally strange implications. The world as it is before he sees it is continually threatening to appear.

A similar thought is present in the story 'The New Advocate', which Kafka insisted on printing as the first in the collection. If he intended by his insistence to give the reader any kind of lead-in to the rest of the stories, it was perhaps a hint that the rules of normal life might be broken at any time, though scarcely any difference was detectable. For the fact that the new advocate climbing the steps of the Palace of Justice was once Bucephalus, Alexander's war-horse, can only just be perceived, and even an expert racegoer is surprised to hear the clink of steel as the horse puts his feet down on the marble. The matter-of-fact tone which takes all this for granted is part of Kafka's frame of mind, it seems, and saves the fantasy from being merely curious or pretentiously whimsical. It is as though the story were not

---

* Janouch's conversations, written up long after they had taken place, are sometimes inherently improbable, especially those in the additional material of the second edition.

meant to surprise, and this remains true when it is remarked that 'the office' takes a very considerate view of the whole affair, making allowance for Bucephalus' unusual situation. At the same time the satire on the modern world's forbearance and absence of regard for miracles is meant to be sharp: Bucephalus, though a lawyer, still does remain a horse after all, and the office apparently knows this.

This contrast between past ages and the present continues in the thoughts about Alexander himself. As in 'In the Penal Colony', the time when there were great men – the old commandant for instance – has vanished, though Alexander's deeds were no more inspired by love and kindness than the commandant's. People can still kill their friends across a banquet-table (as Alexander once did, hurling a javelin at his friend Clitus), and many find Macedonia too narrow, so that 'they curse Philip, their father' – a personal note enters here, with the dedication to Kafka's father so close – but though such enmity and cruelty remain, there is no-one to point the way to the unattainable, represented here by the gates to India, though in Kafka's mind no doubt thoughts of the gates to Palestine were also present. With this, the theme of many of Kafka's works is reached. The American continent, the secret Law, the Castle, the dreamt-of nourishment that Gregor Samsa thinks he has found in music, these are all related to the world that Alexander went to conquer. Kafka at once selects that meaning from the legends of Alexander, and uses it to contrast with the present day, which he sees as having no spiritual concern. (His rejection of all modern idealists as mere brandishers of weapons is too easy and sweeping.)

The ending, when Bucephalus is said to be perhaps doing the best thing by steeping himself in his law-books, is a trifle on the smug side; it has a touch of the 'Biedermeier';

Free, his flanks unpressed by his horseman's loins, in the still light of a lamp, far from the thud and shock of Alexander's battles, he reads and turns the pages of our ancient tomes.

This is an ending to accept lyrically, if one can, though it is not

clear that Bucephalus is 'free' in any sense that would be meaningful to Kafka – he has merely outlived the kind of hero who
points to a great goal. As a beginning to the collection, though,
this gives clues both to the mood and the tendency of what
follows.

A similar note ends the story 'A Message from the Emperor',
whose symbolical meaning is much more definable than the
meaning of 'The New Advocate'. Here again, the great event –
the sending of a personal message to the 'miserable subject' –
took place many years ago, thousand of years ago, it appears,
and though there was greatness and splendour then, there is not
much of that left now. The Emperor is dead, as Alexander is
(though this Emperor sounds more Chinese, and the story may
have been meant for the work to be entitled *Building the Great
Wall of China*), and the messenger is all that remains of his
presence on earth, just as Bucephalus is all that remains of
Alexander's. But again the ending is half-consolatory, in a way
that, by its resignation, disappoints as much as it comforts:

Nobody can get through here, even with a message from a dead
man – But you sit by your window and dream it to yourself when
evening comes.

It is a gentle, elegiac note, though one observes the implication
that a message from a dead man may stand a better chance of
getting through than one from a live one, a thought which only
deathlike resignation might justify. What other resolution can
there be for a longing so desperately felt and so infinitely un-
requitable? Kafka's father could never have felt how much the
last sentence was a consolation to Kafka in his own banishment;
if he had, he would never have afforded Kafka the occasion to
write. Yet the consolation seems to be as much as Kafka wants,
at this moment. Possibly it was in the awareness that such consolation was not enough, even a shade sentimental, that Kafka
believed his work was still less than what he wanted it to be.

There is still such a note even in such a fine piece of prose as
'In the Gallery'. Again, a certain overtone of meaning is evident,
as in 'A Message from the Emperor'. Perhaps the circus

represents here the activity of the world–certainly nothing more definite than that – while the audience represent unperceptive mankind. Whereas it would be a grand and fulfilling thing to intervene on behalf of the weak and oppressed, as the young man in the gallery does on behalf of the bareback rider, the fact is that the oppression is not at all apparent to the vast majority, and there is nothing the young man can do but lay his head on the parapet and weep, 'without knowing it'. It is a helpless ending, and sadder than the two just mentioned, yet there is truth in the insight that inspires it: the general run of things does conceal the spuriousness of normal success, even when one knows that the world is run on confidence tricks, and the brilliantly satirical portrayal of the ringmaster can be applied to politicians, journalists, academics, businessmen, at will. Only the conclusion – so far as it is taken to have any normative value, and it does have some – is questionable. Is weeping the only course open to a man in the gallery, even if it is unconscious weeping? Is his protest in the first paragraph so obviously futile? To say so in a poem is not to be disallowed: it is a moment that may have to be known. That is why this story matters as much as any in Kafka's work. But taken together with the other stories 'In the Gallery' only repeats the note of acquiescent sadness: the great times are past, and one can only study the ancient laws, only dream the message one would like to hear, glimpse the passage of superior beings through one's dark tunnel.

The story placed last in the collection, 'Report for an Academy', seems in that context like a more bitter comment. Most of the tales involve some aspiration, even if it is only nostalgia. This final story, taking the form of a report by an ape on its capture in an African jungle, its voyage to Europe and gradual acquirement of human characteristics, can be read, if one so wishes, as a parable on aspiration. 'Man is something that is to be overcome,' Nietzsche had written. The ape might have substituted 'ape' for 'man' in that sentence, and the astounding thing is, speaking fictionally, that he does give almost every sign of having overcome his apehood: he writes accomplished German, formulates his thoughts and orders his account with all the skill of an educated man. It is, of course, the situation of 'The Metamorphosis' in reverse, opposing an ascent to Samsa's descent, and it succeeds only by the same bold stroke of not allowing a moment's doubt about the main fact. The ape speaks in person, and thereby establishes his claim. But from time to time he lets fall some remark that reveals his still untransformed animal nature:

The second shot hit me below the hip. It was a hard hit, and was responsible for my still limping to this very day. Recently I read, in an article by one of the ten thousand tattlers who talk about me to their heart's content in the newspapers, that my ape-nature was not yet entirely suppressed, as evidence of which was cited the fact that when visitors come I like to take off my trousers to show the position where the bullet went in. That fellow should have every single finger of his writing hand shot off, one by one.

One may say, of course, that it is equally a kind of human nature that the ape reveals in that last sentence. But the implication within the story is rather that such sudden self-betrayals are likely in passing from any one level of existence to another. The aspirations in the other stories might have their masks removed in much the same way, one may reflect.

That outburst of malicious fury has its counterpart in several of the stories, most of all in the piece of *grand guignol*, 'A Brother's Murder', but also in the reminder of Alexander the Great's murder of Clitus, and in the scene in 'An Old Manuscript' where the nomad warriors tear a living ox to pieces with their teeth. A fascination with such moments runs right through the collection, as it does through most of Kafka's work. It is a chief feature of the story 'Jackals and Arabs', in which the narrator, a European traveller, meets a pack of jackals in the desert and witnesses the hostility between them and an Arab camel-driver. The description of their gluttony in battening on the arteries of a dead camel is matched by the hatred in their account of Arab character:

'Their white is filth, their black is filth, their beards are an abomination, at the sight of the corner of their eyes we are compelled to spit, and when they raise their arms hell itself shows in their armpits.

133

Therefore, sir, therefore, O dear sir, with the aid of thy all-powerful hands, with the aid of thy all-powerful hands cut their throats through with these scissors!'

Yet this story leaves even more of a mystery behind it than most of the others; the ending merely relates how the jackals are finally driven off by the Arab, and the reader is left puzzling why his attention has been aroused. Perhaps no interpretation or other connecting link is really needed; perhaps Kafka was interested, as he apparently was in 'A Brother's Murder', simply in the evocation of hatred and obscene murderousness. Yet the fact that Kafka was still keenly interested in Zionism at the time he wrote, and that the story was first published in a periodical called *Der Jude*, edited by the leading Zionist, Martin Buber, makes one half inclined to accept a suggestion that Kafka may have read a meaning of his own into it. Such passages as this take on a different colour, in the light of that knowledge.

'We know', began the eldest jackal, 'that you are from the North, that is the very basis of our hopes. In those parts one finds that reasonableness which is not to be found among the Arabs. From such cold arrogance as theirs, you know, no spark of reason can be struck. They kill animals to eat them, and carrion they despise.'
'Don't talk so loud', I said, 'there are Arabs sleeping nearby.'
'You really are a stranger', said the jackal, 'or you would know that never in the whole history of the world has a jackal feared an Arab. Why should we fear them? Is it not misfortune enough that we are obliged to live among such people?'

It has to be said that the clues, if any, are no more definite than that, though the case for an allegory of this kind has been argued at some length.[7] Clearly, if Kafka had such a reading in mind at all – and could it have escaped him, in presenting the story to such a journal as *Der Jude*? – he would not provide many clues, unless he wanted to give unmistakable offence. Yet it is not altogether incredible that he meant to be understood in this way. Kafka mentions, in a list of interests he drew up for a survey of his life, not only Zionism, but also 'anti-Zionism'[8] – a curious mark of the dual tendency found in his writing generally, as in

his ambivalent relation to his father.* At times, as in the letter
about the whole *Country Doctor* collection, he seems almost to
identify his father with Zionism: no wonder, then, if he could
speak of that too in a hostile sense. In Kafka's letters to Milena
Jesenská he often speaks slightingly of Jews, and at one point
even seems to lend credence to anti-Semitic statements in a
newspaper.[9] One passage in the diaries, taken alone and out of
context, would seem at first sight to be the least likely remark
to come from such a man as him. He is speaking of two actors
in their roles in a play and sees them as

'people who are Jews in a particularly pure form, since they live only
in religion, but without toil, understanding or misery. They seem
to think everybody a fool, laugh at the murder of a noble Jew, sell
themselves to a renegade, dance, holding their hands along their
sideburns with delight, when the unmasked murderer poisons himself . . .'[10]

The ascription of vindictiveness, treachery, arrogance in this
'pure' form of Jewishness might have come from the worst
enemies of Jews, though it has to be remembered that these
same actors belonged to a Yiddish troupe about whose performance Kafka was enthusiastic, and that his admiration for
Jewishness could be equally great. At all events, the likelihood of
an ambivalent allegory in 'Jackals and Arabs' is slightly increased
by such knowledge of Kafka's own ambivalence.

Stranger still is the possibility that 'Report for an Academy'
also has a Jewish sense. That it has other senses, and cannot be
pinned exactly to any of them, is already apparent. That it is
really a story about the conversion of a Jew to Christianity, that
the spirits the ape learns to drink are the equivalent of the wine
of Holy Communion, and that the ape's lapse into barbarity is a
lapse into the savagery represented by Kafka's two actor-friends,
and by the jackals, is unlikely to be accepted as the whole truth.
Yet again the interpretation has so much to be said for it, that
the 'Report' appeared along with the story about the jackals

* The reference to 'anti-Zionism' occurs in a list of 'radii' Kafka pursued from
the centre of his personality. It could mean that he had studied it rather than
embraced it, but the other possibility is also present.

in the same periodical, the two being published as 'Animal Stories' (a misleading title if ever there was one) in consecutive numbers of *Der Jude* in 1917.[11] It is not at all impossible that Kafka had it in mind along with other potential readings, and this is worth keeping in mind when similar ambivalence occurs, for example, in *The Castle*.[12]

Also present in 'Jackals and Arabs', however, is another theme common to a number of these stories, the theme of the outsider called upon to help in some fantastically difficult situation. The narrator of 'Jackals and Arabs' is seen by the beasts as a saviour. The young man in the gallery feels called upon to rush into the circus-ring and save the damsel in distress. The narrator in 'An Old Manuscript' feels called upon to do something to prevent the savagery of the nomad warriors. Similarly K. in *The Castle* has almost a sense of mission, at times, as though he were the champion of his fellow-mortals against the official organisation. This is a theme of Kafka's with no specific meaning, no allegorical sense, yet a significant part to play in the total sense of his stories. It is also perhaps the main theme of the title-story in the *Country Doctor* collection, in which a doctor is called out during the night to a patient far away, but is unable to cure him of his terrible wound and is finally left abandoned in the snow, miles from home and without prospect of rescue. The frustration of Kafka's own position as a writer who sometimes had pretensions to lead his nation (pretensions satirised mercilessly in the story 'Josephine the Singer') is relevant here, though again no single interpretation will serve.

'A Country Doctor' is the most dreamlike of all Kafka's stories, in the sense that physical impossibilities frequently happen. Nowhere else, for instance, does a man travel several miles in a few instants. It is also much more crammed with incident and has less of a story-line than his other works; here Kafka is at his most baffling, for the temptation to make some sense of a dream is generally strong. Ultimately, the story will not yield rational sense. Yet since it is, like any other account of a dream, closely connected with the dreamer, some biographical pointers are helpful.

Kafka knew one country doctor well, his uncle Siegfried Löwy, a photograph of whom, riding on horseback, exists. It would be natural for Kafka to think of his uncle in connection with his own illness, and thus to conceive a story in which the doctor's mission to a patient with a wound in his side ended in failure. Though the wound as he describes it is a fantastic one, symbolical in meaning, Kafka did refer to his tuberculosis in his diary as 'my lung-wound', and drew Max Brod's attention to this connection between himself and the story in a letter.[13] The general purport of the story is that to answer the call of charity as the doctor does is mistaken, and leads to disaster. (Kafka referred in a letter to doctors' pretensions as 'ridiculous'.) But no alternative is offered, indeed the story may suggest that the alternatives are all bad: the sudden awakening of the doctor, and the emergence of the two new horses from the pigsty could suggest that the charitable impulse is sexual in origin, and therefore filthy, for not only the horses emerge, being the dynamic power which will transport the doctor to his patient as though by magic, but also the groom, who has only the satisfaction of savage lust in mind, and who is left behind by the doctor, battering down the door to get at the serving-maid. Out of the place of filth come both agape and eros, and neither of them can rise above their origin: that may be what Kafka intended.

At the same time, the doctor may also stand for Kafka himself, in his decision, or attempted decision, not to yield to the sexual desires which he had felt as shameful, but to devote himself to his calling as a writer. Such an association would account for the doctor speaking of this one snow-driven night as 'an endless winter' – a phrase which Rilke also used as a metaphor for a spiritual condition. It would also help to explain the passage at the end in which the doctor speaks of himself as 'naked, exposed to the frost of this most miserable epoch, with an earthly carriage and unearthly horses'. A common theme of Kafka's stories is the decision to abandon sexual love for an isolation which proves infinitely unfruitful, though this interpretation is partly contradicted by the charitable, rather than inward-looking concern of the doctor.

But like the symbols in several of the stories in this collection, the wound which the doctor discovers is ambiguous, this time in a contrived way. It is not simply a wound: as it is described it is clearly at the same time a rose, though a hideous one, its stamens formed of maggots battening on the open flesh:

Rose (or, strictly, 'pink'; the German is 'Rosa', which is also the name of the maid),* in many shades, dark in the depths, growing lighter towards the edges, with blotches of blood, open as an open-surface mine. So it looks from a distance. From close at hand a complication is revealed. Who can look at it without a low whistle? Maggots, as thick and long as my small finger, rosy with their own blood and splashed with other blood as well, writhe about, held fast in the inside of the wound, struggling with their white heads and many legs to reach the light. Poor boy, there is no help for you. I have found out your great wound; you will die of this flower in your side.

The sense uppermost in Kafka's mind could have been that his own disease (physical or spiritual was all the same) was his salvation, beautiful and repulsive at once. But to convey that sense, or any ambiguity of this kind in the rose at all, he is forced to invent a rose of his own rather than take one from the natural world. His mind has taken a rose and converted its features into the features of a wound, and an unnatural-looking wound at that. And his attitude to it is shown by the repellently incommensurate suggestion that one might give a low whistle at seeing it, as though appreciative of the absolute destruction it portends. A low whistle is not the most natural response to such a monstrosity. Kafka employs here a straightforwardly systematic conversion of ideas into things;† there is nothing of the imagination about the symbol, nothing so elusive as the Castle or even the advocate Bucephalus.

Lastly, the episode of the naked doctor lying alongside the boy recalls the moving scene in Flaubert's *Trois Contes*, where St Julian the Hospitaller lies naked to embrace a leper, who

---

* It is not impossible to find hints of her sexual parts in what follows.

† Compare the angels with worms in their noses in Mann's *Doktor Faustus*, an instance of the same perversity.

reveals himself as Christ and carries the saint with him up to heaven. In Kafka, there is no such apotheosis, just as in 'In the Penal Colony' there is no resurrection. As the doctor reflects, a priestly function is expected of him by those waiting for the patient to be healed, but he has only medical knowledge. Kafka might well have had similar self-critical thoughts regarding his own vocation as a writer, and the expectation that it might somehow benefit himself and others.

'A Country Doctor' is remarkable among Kafka's stories for its vividly nightmarish quality. Whether all the suggestions just made about it are relevant is hard to decide: a dream is often what the dreamer makes of it, or what some outside person persuades him to make of it. One can only supply such bits of information as may not be generally shared; only Kafka himself had all the experiences out of which the dream came; and only he could say with real authority what it suggested to him. Yet so far as one thinks one does understand it, it seems to circle indefinitely round the same pairs of opposites, the wound that is salvation, the love and the lust, the charitable and the savage impulse, and to remain caught up in them as no other work of Kafka's does. Despite the dreamlike quality, there is something more systematic – in the tradition of dialectical philosophising – in 'A Country Doctor' than in any other of Kafka's works.

That being so, could Kafka have ever fulfilled his ambition of 'going to Palestine'? 'Going' is definite, not ambiguous: you are either in Prague or in Jerusalem, you are either reconciled with your father or not (though that may be a subtler matter than mere location). The chief weakness in Kafka's position, which is also a weakness in the stories in this collection, is that he prefers the ambivalent loving–hating relationship to a possible cure. A cure would remove the sole topic of his writing, and he is too engrossed with that to want to give it up. Even the writing of 'The Metamorphosis', which had said all there was to say on that score, had not afforded him any relief, and he was still circling among the mutually reflecting contraries. There was still nothing in prospect but the deciphering of the inscription on his own body.

9

'THE CASTLE'

In September 1917 tuberculosis was diagnosed. Kafka knew he had not long to live; he moved to the village of Zürau, to join his sister Ottla, and remained there till the following summer. Meanwhile his second engagement to Felice, made in July, was broken off in December 1917. Little was written during this extremely difficult time. Kafka was broken with grief, as Brod relates, after seeing Felice to the train for the last time: 'His face was pale, hard, severe. But suddenly he began to weep. I shall never forget the scene, one of the most terrible I have ever witnessed. . . . Kafka had come straight to me in my office, at the busiest time of day, and sat next to my desk in the armchair that stood there for petitioners, pensioners, and people under prosecution. And here he wept, asking with sobs: "Isn't it terrible that this sort of thing has to happen?" The tears were running down his cheeks. I have never seen him, except on this one occasion, distraught and without composure.'

The decision had been a deliberate choice: it was either marriage or writing, although the same choice had to be faced later more than once, with other women. For a time, however, his creative writing did not benefit directly, though more philosophical work, especially aphorisms, was produced. It was not until 1920 that a flow came such as he had experienced in 1912, 1914 and 1917. Meanwhile, Zürau had possibly supplied an impetus to the novel he was to begin a few years later: certainly he spoke of a new novel, and the study of peasant-life at Zürau could well have contributed to some scenes in *The Castle*, though a tale begun in 1914 ('Temptation in the Village') had first embodied the general idea. (Other geographical possibilities, especially Wossek, a village about 60 miles south of Prague, are discussed by Wagenbach.[1]) By 1922, his life had altered considerably. Though still in theory employed at the insurance office, he had spent a great deal of time in sanatoria. He had also fallen deeply in love with a young Czech woman, the translator of some of his works, Milena Jesenská, with whom his relationship was easier than any he had known hitherto, perhaps just because she was both unhappily married and unwilling to leave her husband, so that Kafka and she saw little of each other and yet felt most tenderly. These were almost ideal circumstances, for a man placed as he was: here was a woman he could love, yet to whom he could not be married and who would thus not impede his writing. The new situation is reflected in *The Castle*, begun in January 1922, but abandoned, unfinished, in the autumn of the same year. For all that, the atmosphere of *The Castle* is often as oppressive as that in any of Kafka's works. Though the action moves from place to place within the village, the streets are always deserted, the rooms are cramped, there is frustration and confusion at almost every turn, the Castle itself looms over the houses yet is always inaccessibly remote. It seems to be always night, with snow falling, and the novel breaks off at a moment when K. appears about to be going to narrow quarters below ground rather than pressing on to his first goal, the most interior recesses of the Castle organisation. Yet out of this darkness and chaos Kafka makes a novel with more moving humanity, greater strength and subtlety of writing, more complexity of structure, more comprehensive scope than any he had written so far. It remains, like *The Trial*, partly a dream-novel: there are scenes which have all the incongruities, the obsessive acceptance of improbabilities, that belong to dreams. But the conscious mind has had more control in the writing, and the movement of the imagination has been more steady than it was in the fragmentary *Trial*. There are no stoppings and startings in *The Castle*, characters do not appear only to disappear, but are interrelated from the first moment, and the threads of action are distinct from the first pages: the attempt to gain an interview with the supreme official Klamm, with its ramifications into interviews with lesser officials, Momus, Bürgel and Erlanger, interweaves with K.'s attachment to Klamm's mistress Frieda, and this in turn interweaves with Frieda's hostility to Amalia as the woman who has rejected the love of a Castle official. *The Trial* resembles *The Great Wall of China* in the isolation and incompleteness of its chapters. *The Castle*, like 'The Metamorphosis', shows by its chapter-divisions, each chapter being complete in itself, yet leading on to the next, how much on this occasion Kafka's conscious mind is active, while at the same time the subconscious flow, the absence of any predetermined purpose, leads the novel forward in a mysterious way that holds the reader's attention because he himself is as much involved in the bafflement as K. is, and looks in the same way for a solution.*

The conscious mind within the dream shows up, in contrast to *The Trial*, in the greater determination K. now shows. It would not have been like Joseph K. to have answered, as K. does in *The Castle*, 'That's enough of that nonsense', certainly not to have used words like those 'surprisingly gently'. It would have been equally unlike Joseph K. to have said, as K. does after the Superintendent has explained official procedures, 'So the upshot is that it's all very unclear and insoluble except that they throw you out.'[2] That kind of directness is something new, and it fits with the general behaviour of K., which is active where Joseph K.'s is passive, critical where his is acquiescent, positive where his is negative. The contrast can be taken too far, but there is little doubt that in making K. come to the village and so to the Castle organisation, rather than letting it come to him, Kafka was deliberately reversing the situation of *The Trial*. The new K. is a man who would have at least attempted to pass the guard at the gate of the Law in the Court-chaplain's parable. Whether this amounts to a polarity, on a Hegelian model, as Emrich suggests, is a different matter. The reversal has been made, that much is true, but the conscious mind does not take over as it does, say, in the novels of Hermann Hesse, where dialectics play a schematic part. K. and Kafka remain largely ignorant or unknowing, the movement of the novel is not predetermined and can be sometimes painfully halting; that is the price that has to be paid. 'It's true', K. says, 'ignorant is what I am, that's a truth that remains, whatever you say, and it's sad for me; but

---

* See also Malcolm Pasley's account of the manuscript, according to which Kafka may have intended an even more regulated organisation, none of the chapters running to the excessive length of the present chapter 18.[3]

there is the advantage that an ignorant man will dare more, and that is why I am willing to put up gladly with ignorance and its no doubt bad consequences at least for a short while, so long as strength lasts.'[4] Kafka does dare more, and the result is not only more stimulating, it is sometimes deeply moving. Nowhere else in Kafka's literary work, for one thing, is there any character who speaks as Frieda does, in the genuine accents of love:

'If only', Frieda said, slowly, quietly, almost relaxedly, as if she knew she could have only a very short spell of peace resting on K.'s shoulder, but wanted to enjoy it to the full, 'if only we had emigrated somewhere that first night, we could be in safety somewhere, always together, your hand always close enough to take hold of; how I need you near me, how desolate I have been, ever since I have known you, when you are not near; believe me, having you near me is the only dream I ever dream, no other.'[5]

More is at stake in *The Castle* than in *The Trial*, or rather there is more to be gained for K. Leaving aside for a moment what the Castle stands for, and why K. wants to enter it, it seems towards the end that if K. were to play his cards right he could 'control everything'[6] (not that that is ever his own stated ambition) whereas in *The Trial* his only prospect was at the very best acquittal, at worst execution. Again, whereas in *The Trial* the judges were represented as mean and vindictive men, trivially vain about their quite unimportant positions, yet never actually met with, K. both sees Klamm quite early in the story, and conceives of him before long as a being far superior to himself:

The landlady had once compared Klamm to an eagle, and that had seemed ridiculous to K., but not now: he thought of his remoteness, his impregnable dwelling-place, his silences, broken perhaps only by cries such as K. had never heard, of his downward piercing gaze that could never be verified, never be refuted, of those circlings in the air that could never be destroyed from out of K.'s depths, and in which he wheeled about up there in accordance with incomprehensible laws, visible only for moments at a time: all that was in common between Klamm and the eagle.[7]

Klamm is never represented as the judges are in *The Trial*, and although some aspects of the comparison with the eagle make him no more attractive than they – one notes too that K. seems to have some hope of destroying Klamm – this presentation of the adversary has a more stimulating effect than the wearisome accounts provided by Titorelli, not least in the vigour of the writing. Similarly the Castle, though K. never reaches it, is portrayed almost as a living being, seen before revealing itself,[8] with qualities that it would be positively good to have:

When K. looked at the castle it used to seem to him at times as though he were observing someone quietly sitting there gazing, not lost in thought and thereby shut off from everything, but free and untroubled, as though he were alone and observed by no one, but this did not disturb his quiet in the least. And sure enough – you couldn't tell whether as a cause or a consequence – an observer could not maintain his gaze, and let it slip aside.[9]

These are definite statements about things seen, with meanings that can be ascertained, not vagueness piled on uncertainty, as the accounts of the invisible Court are, and the novel benefits from the change.

The Castle is altogether clearer, though the word is still relative to the clarity to be expected in Kafka. In choosing to write of a castle at all, Kafka may have thought to provide a general clue, though since some readers have found the theological interpretations 'totally unsupported by internal evidence', the position needs to be spelled out a little. The notion of a castle as a spiritual goal is of some antiquity, and one need go no further than the work by Kafka's seventeenth-century fellowcountryman, Komensky (or Comenius), *The Labyrinth of the World and the Paradise of the Heart*, to find an analogy. It is true that Komensky's castle proves to be a false lure, though Kafka must certainly thought of him at the town of Brandys, not far from Prague, where he is commemorated, and the mysticism of Komensky must have had some attraction for him. The only reference to him in Kafka's letters suggests, at the least, respect.[10] Again, Kafka did not write a straightforward allegory in the

sense of Komensky's pilgrimage or Bunyan's; his Castle remains
mysterious even when some of the outlines have been seen. It
may also be that Kafka was very slightly influenced by the
realistic nineteenth-century Czech novel, *The Grandmother*, by
Božena Němcová.[11] But there is good reason for saying that
Kafka's general drift is more easily understood in the terms
which St Teresa of Avila used in her well-known work on the
mystic's path to God:

While I was beseeching our Lord today that he would speak through
me . . . a thought occurred to me which I will now set down, in
order to have some foundation on which to build. I began to think
of the soul as if it were a castle made of a single diamond or of very
clear crystal, in which there are many rooms, just as in Heaven there
are many mansions.[12]

In St Teresa's terms, the soul that reaches the innermost mansion
of her castle 'is made one with God', but there is no need to
suppose that Kafka meant exactly the same as St Teresa. Unlike
her, Kafka gives no explanation, and some features of the Castle
make it impossible to reconcile with any Christian conception
of God, though people in the novel do speak of the Castle in the
way that people generally do speak of God. Still, there are
sufficient similarities for certain overtones to be unmistakably
heard. In the long passage on the inadequate telephone connections with the Castle there is a play on the idea of prayer. It is
largely ironical, unless it is taken as showing prayer to be as
apparently ineffective as it is often said by mystics to be. There
is also, however, a reference to sounds heard in the village on
the Castle telephone which suggests a more important function.
In the words of the Superintendent, there is no trusting any
verbal message that comes through from the Castle: on the
other hand there is a continual telephoning going on in the
Castle, which is heard in the village as humming and singing.
This, according to the Superintendent, is the only accurate and
trustworthy communication to be had, everything else is
deceptive. And as he says this, one cannot help being reminded
(though Kafka's modern setting gives a quite different tone)

of Rilke's words from the *Duino Elegies*, written at about the same time:

> Hearken, my heart, as only
> saints have done: till it seemed the gigantic call
> must lift them aloft . . . Not that you could endure
> the voice of God – far from it. But heark to the suspiration,
> the uninterrupted news that grows out of silence.

The difference is that Kafka does not vouch for his message, as Rilke seems to do: for Kafka it is merely one more feature of the Castle, that this is said about it. But the implication he intends cannot be ignored. Similarly, the role of Barnabas, K.'s appointed messenger to and from the Castle, seems to be that of an inefficient angel, and the long disquisition by the Superintendent on the infallibility of the Castle organisation, in chapter 5, has the same kind of obvious allegorical significance, with the same kind of ironical reserve, at least so far as Kafka is concerned. ('Are there inspectorates?' says the Superintendent. 'There are nothing but inspectorates. Of course they are not there to detect errors in the crude sense of the word, because errors never occur, and even if an error were to occur, as in your own case, who is to say in the last analysis that it actually is an error.' The satire on arguments about infallibility is obvious enough.)

Less obvious, but still striking as the pattern of the novel begins to unfold, is the curious hierarchy within the village, which seems to operate only among the women working in the two inns. It is a natural enough progression to move as Pepi does from chambermaid to barmaid, and it seems that a further step can be taken from there to the rank of landlady. But in the strange world of this novel these promotions seem to have spiritual or moral connections. When K. first meets Frieda, as a barmaid, he is struck by something in her eyes, a look of 'remarkable superiority'.

When she happened to look at K., it seemed to him that there was something about her eyes that had already accomplished things that had to do with him, things he as yet did not so much as suspect, yet which must exist, the eyes convinced him of that.[13]

The landlady at the Bridge Inn, however, is even more imposing, despite her fits of bad temper. When she first appears to K., he sees her knitting in a chair, a gigantic figure, 'almost darkening the room', and there are many suggestions that she is a woman of great spiritual power. Much the same is true of Klamm, who is talked about by the landlady in terms that sound fantastic or melodramatic: she asks how K. could withstand the look in Klamm's eyes, and admits that she herself could not withstand it without a door in between, so that again one is reminded (though a note of irony is presumably present in Kafka) of Rilke's at that time still unpublished *Elegies*, and the Angels who are terrifying in their sheer presence:

> And even if one of them suddenly
> pressed me against his heart, I should fade in the strength of his
> stronger existence . . . Each single angel is terrible.

This is not to say that Klamm has anything angelic about him. In so far as the name suggests anything – and names do occasionally have significance in Kafka's work – it is a normal German word for a narrow ravine, and suggests the verb 'klammern': to clutch, cling, or hang on. As an adjective it means numb, stiff with cold, or damp, and beginning with a *k* it may have vague suggestions of being appropriate to K.'s case. In short, it is ambiguous, partly suggesting an embrace (but a convulsive or desperate one), partly remoteness or constriction. Yet Klamm has extraordinary powers, as not only the landlady but also Frieda says: it is Frieda who believes that it was 'Klamm's work' that brought her and K. together in the bar, and Frieda's view, according to the landlady, that 'everything that has happened is the will of Klamm'. These are hints obvious and irrefutable enough, though they are not obtrusive within the novel, coming rarely and in a setting where the impression of ordinariness predominates. Klamm, as K. actually sees him, is a fat, thick-set, slightly ageing man with a long black moustache and a pince-nez set awry on his nose, who sits with a glass of beer smoking a cigar. The physical description would suit well the photographs of Kafka's father, and Kafka certainly had an earthly father in his mind, though he cannot have expected his readers to know that. Yet the fact that he places the suggestive phrases in the mouths of the two women, not in K.'s own, implies that Kafka did not wish them to be thought of simply as K.'s or his own subjective and absurd magnifications of his father's importance.

But it is not Klamm that K. wants to meet, or rather Klamm is only a stage on the journey. Somewhere beyond, though only briefly mentioned, is the owner of the Castle, the oddly-named Count West-West (Heinz Politzer surmises that an intensified decline of the sun may be implied, but it is anybody's guess.) Is it the Count whom K. expects to meet? We are never actually told, and here one of the questionable elements in the novel begins to show itself: the reader is never told why K. wants to meet Klamm, whether he regards him as a final authority, or why he should think of destroying him. Part of K.'s purpose is clear – he wants confirmation of his appointment by the Castle as a surveyor, and in this a certain human indecision on the value of activity in general can be understood. K. has been summoned as a surveyor, or so he says, yet there is no knowledge of his appointment when he first arrives, and in this a quite usual doubt about the authenticity of one's vocation may be reflected. For Kafka it may well have been a doubt about his value as a writer (and 'surveyor' is not a bad metaphor for 'novelist'), strong though his conviction was that there was no other career open to him. Doubts about writing, at all events, are the gist of his story 'Josephine the Singer', in which he presents an 'artist' about whom there are considerable doubts whether her art deserves the name at all. In the same way, there are extreme doubts about whether or not K. is 'called' to be a surveyor: the question is never remotely near to being solved from beginning to end. That in itself, of course, is no criticism of the novel. It is some criticism, though, to say that from beginning to end K. shows no sign of ever having had any smattering of knowledge of surveying, never shows any wish to survey, or any hint of what surveying might be done. It may be, as Erich Heller once suggested,[14] that the word 'Landvermesser', 'land-surveyor', is a pun involving the verb 'sich vermessen', 'to have false pretensions', but the hint could very properly have been developed, had Kafka wanted to do so. As it is, there is the bare statement that he is appointed as surveyor, and no clue whether he could carry out the work if he were asked to do so.* He accepts the assistants appointed by the Castle although they confess that they themselves have no knowledge of the subject, and he apparently realises very well that they are not what they claim to be, not the assistants who he originally engaged. And thus an element of uncertainty is present that could quite simply have been removed, and which seems merely meant to mystify. Is K. a surveyor, has he any right to expect recognition at all? The fact that absolutely no clue is given makes it possible for endless speculation to go on, but it is speculation about nothing, rather like the priest's comments on his own parable in *The Trial*, and it is just this kind of speculation that gives rise to tedium. K.'s vocation is as groundless as Joseph K.'s guilt.

The mystery does seem to lift a little near the beginning of chapter 5, when K. reflects on the difference between himself and the officials. They, he observes, are defending distant and invisible things on behalf of distant and invisible masters,

whereas K. was fighting for something living and close, for himself, and moreover, at least at the outset, by his own will, for he was the attacker; and not only he was fighting for himself, but evidently other powers also, which he knew nothing of, but in whom he could believe in view of the measures taken by the authorities.[15]

That K. is fighting for his living ('meine Existenz', as he puts it – the overtones are more positively audible in the German[16]) is intelligible. Yet here again, there is promise of more than is offered. What are the measures which lead him to believe that other powers are fighting for him (or for themselves; the German is not wholly unambiguous)? Again there is no clue, so that the

* Since Kafka's writing seldom reached beyond the confines of his inner self, it is often the case that his novels and stories do no more than set out the interminable problem of his own writing; it was writing about the possibility of preserving himself as a writer. In this sense, Kafka is a potential writer as K. is a potential surveyor.

writing begins to attract the suspicion of being merely mystifying, in a way that is really not impressive when the author seems either to be withholding information or to be putting down words which he is not concerned to back up. It is one thing to be 'unknowing', and another not to let the reader know.

Part of Kafka's intention must certainly be to cast doubt on whether K.'s experience has anything more than a subjective validity. The Castle itself is explicitly said to be not a castle in the sense of a fortress or a chateau, but 'an extensive contruction consisting of a few double-storeyed buildings and a large number of lower buildings huddled together'.[17] If one had not known it was a castle, Kafka goes on, one might have thought it was a small town, and the important thing is that it corresponds to K.'s expectations. Just as, in *The Trial*, the Court-room is in a place which K. almost stumbles into by accident, and the Court reproves him for coming an hour later than he had privately intended, though no particular time had been appointed, so the Castle lives up to K.'s idea of what it is to be. Since he insists that he is the surveyor, the Castle agrees, and even sends him a letter telling him that, 'as he knows', he has been appointed. Since he claims to have assistants, the Castle sends him two, and in accepting them K. seems to enter into the spirit of the game. All these incidents could imply that K.'s quest is solipsistic. The impressiveness of some of the allusive remarks about Klamm and the others loses some of its weight if that too was merely a reflection of K.'s expectations. He cannot be fighting for himself or for his existence if the opposition is no more than a mirage conjured up by his own wishes; there would be nothing to fight in that case.

Yet there is a good deal that does not simply correspond to what K. expects. K. is not an easily likeable man, at any rate for the greater part of the novel: he can be surprisingly, even childishly vindictive at times, when he throws a snowball at Gerstäcker's ear in a fit of pique, or goes looking for his assistants with a willow-rod in his hand, swishing it against his side in gleeful expectation. He may be in love with Frieda, as she certainly is with him, but he never does her any loving service or kindness, and he has an arrogant way with people in general. On the other hand, the Castle organisation, in the early chapters at least, seems intent on showing itself at its most benevolent, and the villagers, with a few exceptions, are very willing to offer help and advice, even if it is not always what K. wants. It is not stretching things to say that Kafka seems to have reversed the situation of *The Trial* not only by making K. active not passive, but also by making the organisation confronting him more sympathetic. But in doing this, Kafka lets fall an observation that offers a valuable clue perhaps to the whole of his work. Having conceived of the Castle (at all events at this early stage of the novel) as a mainly benevolent institution, even though an unattainable one, Kafka writes of the moment when K. withdraws after his first attempt at reaching it:

But as if to give him a sign of parting, for the time being, a bell began to ring gaily up there, a bell which at least for a moment made his heart leap, as if it were threatening him – for the sound was melancholy too – with the fulfilment of his uncertain desire.[18]

Apart from the difficulty of imagining the sound itself, being both gay and painful or melancholy, this passage presents the reader with the revealing information that K.'s desire is not only uncertain, he would actually prefer not to realise it, not to have it fulfilled. The suggestion of a deliberate, perhaps systematic commitment to frustration ought not to pass without comment. It may help to explain some of the developments later in the novel.

For there are quite strong suggestions that the Castle is well disposed, and that in looking for help from the women in closest touch with it – the mistresses of Klamm, that is – K. is not going wrong as Josef K. was said to do in *The Trial*, where women were merely a hindrance. The picture of Frieda is quite different from that of Fräulein Bürstner: she is a warm-hearted, sympathetic woman with a ready kiss for K., a willingness to get on with household jobs and to sacrifice her own interests for his, which distinguish her totally from any other woman in Kafka's work. Her first encounter, when she tears so savagely and desperately at him, is out of keeping with the picture given of her later, and the expression 'a mistress of Klamm's' ('Geliebte' – 'Love' or 'beloved') gains some honour from its connection with her. There may well be an autobiographical element here. Kafka wrote to Milena of his hesitation in putting so much hope as he did in another human being like herself, a hope which he spoke of even as blasphemous. Yet he also spoke in the same letter of something divine in her human face, and the bridge she provided for him, at least for a while, is reflected in several moving passages in *The Castle* about the relation between women and Castle officials. At times the relation suggests a mystical love. When the landlady at the Bridge Inn puts round her head the shawl which is one of her mementoes of Klamm, she lies quite peacefully, and all suffering seems to be lifted from her. The love she felt, as K. sees it, was a blessing which she was unable to draw down for her own and her husband's benefit,[19] it was not in the least like the purely self-seeking love shown by Leni in *The Trial*. But it is not only the women who have been in love with Klamm who are impressive. Olga, who belongs to the family of Barnabas, ostracised because her sister Amalia refused to give in to an official, is more companionable than the landlady by far, she shows a peaceful happiness in being able to sit by the stove with K., no trace of jealousy visible: 'and this very absence of jealousy and consequently of severity of any kind, did K. good. He was glad to look into these blue eyes, not tempting him, not ordering him about, but shyly resting, shyly holding their own.'[20] Barnabas himself has much the same gentleness, with a kind of humility in his smile which would be completely refreshing to K. if he were only better at delivering K.'s messages.

Yet the pattern of the novel can only have been intended to overturn the mainly benevolent picture built up in the early chapters. The first twelve chapters are comparatively full of incident – the arrival, the first attempt at reaching the Castle, the receipt of Klamm's letter, the settling-in with Frieda at the Bridge Inn, the attempt to waylay Klamm, give a movement to the novel which is not much halted by tedious speculations and explanations such as those of the mayor (or elder), who has too close a resemblance to Titorelli in this respect. By the twelfth chapter, it is true, some evidence of hostility to K. has begun to emerge, especially in the behaviour of Gisa the school-mistress, and the schoolmaster. But it is not until chapter 15 that anything amounting to a possible indictment of the Castle is seen, and when this does come there is not only an element of contrivance, the writing becomes almost totally obsessive. It is in this chapter, of course, that Olga begins to relate the story of how Amalia was seen by the official Sortini (suggesting perhaps the Italian for 'fate') and summoned to satisfy his lust, how Amalia refused, and how since that day the whole family has sunk into disrepute throughout the village. (Similarly, K. fears in *The Trial* that the accusation against him will ruin his family.) The purpose of this within the framework of the whole novel – or at any rate the function – is clear enough. The benevolence of Klamm, and the genuine attachment felt for him by Frieda and the landlady, with all that that implies, is to be shown as only one aspect of an ambiguous organisation, which occasion-ally treats village women with nothing but contempt. It is not impossible to see religious analogies here, if one wants to do so, for although Jehovah is shown mainly in a benevolently loving relation to women – for instance in Ezekiel 16 – the relations of Zeus with women were often more analogous to Sortini's, and if Kafka's intention was to comment on the ambivalent feelings of some women in relation to the divine, he had ample oppor-tunity here.

He may also have intended to introduce, as Brod suggests, a parallel with the situation analysed at such length in Kierke-gaard's *Fear and Trembling*, that is, the 'teleological suspension of the ethical' implied by God's command to Abraham to kill his son Isaac. In other words, where the divinity requires of men what normally seems to them iniquitous, it is the duty of a truly religious man to obey with a glad heart. But if that was part of Kafka's intention, the point is only obscurely dealt with, and nothing challenging either way is said.

Clearly, Kafka had the Sortini incident in mind from quite early on, since Frieda's animosity towards Amalia is shown at their very first meeting, and that animosity expresses the difference between a woman who has gladly accepted love from a Castle official, and one who has rejected it. The difficulty about the whole of this very long sequence, however, is not at all that an element of ambivalence and conflict is introduced. On the contrary, these could heighten the interest. It is rather that the doubts expressed are so total as to seem parodistic of doubt, and that the writing goes completely to pieces. Olga attempts – and here the contrivance shows all too clearly – to persuade K. that there is really no essential difference between the way that Frieda was treated and the way Amalia was, although it is quite clear that the insulting letter sent by Sortini to Amalia had no parallel in any letter from Klamm. The underlying purpose seems to be to show that nothing definite can be predicated of the Castle or its officials at all. 'The letter to Amalia', Olga argues, 'may have been thrown on to the paper in thoughts, completely regardless of what was really being written. What do we know about the thoughts of Castle gentlemen?' This kind of argument is of course very close once again to the style of the Court chaplain. If the words in the letter do not represent the thoughts of Sortini, there is no need to pay any attention to them, Amalia did not refuse any order of his, and the whole affair is blown up out of all proportion, however irresponsible Sortini was. But this is typical of Olga's way of talking in this chapter, and not insignificant for the novel as a whole. Olga goes on, not long after this, to express doubts of the same all-embracing kind, quite out of keeping with the earlier description of her serenity. It is not only that she again throws all notion of meaning arbitrarily to the winds, she speaks as nobody could who was 'resting', and 'holding her own'. For Olga as she is now represented, the idea of a village-girl not loving a Castle official is unthinkable: all girls do, if opportunity offers:

'But you object that Amalia did not love Sortini. Well, yes, she did not love him, but perhaps she did love him all the same, who can decide on that? Not even she herself. How can she imagine she did not love him when she rejected him more forcefully than any official, probably, has ever been rejected before.'[21]

This is either irritating the reader, who must object that people in love know very well whether they are in love or not, or it is making Olga share the absurd position of the Superintendent, in an earlier chapter, who seems to be offered merely as an object of irony. But if no one in his right senses could be impressed by the kind of argument about the impossibility of error put forward by him, what is it doing in the mouth of Olga, who to all appearances was a rational woman with a strong reserve of good sense? The most likely explanation is that Kafka himself, in obsessed moments, was prone to think in this way – there are passages of this kind often enough to justify the supposition, especially since they are not confined to one character or type of character, but distributed as though at random. Kafka's characters are scarcely ever distinguished by their habits of speech or processes of thought: all of them are capable of spinning on in the same indeterminate way, and though one or another may object more concretely from time to time, there is no consistency in the objections either: they are momentary flashes, not seriously weighed-up counterbalances. Olga, like the Superintendent, talks interminably for the reason that neither of them take words seriously. Words are for her often ciphers with no particular meaning, so that to say that a person is or is not in love is a matter of indifference.

This shows itself also in the writing, where a certain habitual tendency of Kafka's to use concessionary words shows itself here in the excessive use of 'gewissermaßen' ('to a certain extent'), a word which he can scarcely have used often with a convinced sense of its appropriateness. One finds Olga saying that certain kinds of villager are 'to a certain extent extremely'[22] appetising for Castle officials; one finds Bürgel saying that some opportunities are 'to a certain extent too large'[23] to be used, and the landlady saying that Klamm 'to a certain extent did not at all' ('gewissermaßen gar nicht') summon Frieda to him a second time.[24] These are uses which reveal the same kind of permanent and ungrounded indecision as Olga shows about Amalia's love.* Yet this ungrounded and impossible indecision, the characteristic of neurotic hesitation, is the ground bass of page after page, especially after chapter 15 has begun, and the attempt is being made to show the benevolence of the Castle as essentially ambivalent. To have shown Klamm and Sortini existing side by side as representatives of the Castle would have been perfectly reasonable and not without allegorical point, from a religious point of view. In trying to make them appear indistinguishable, Kafka is obliged to abandon the rational use of words, which is as much as to say, to abandon words at times altogether.

This is the reason, too, for the increasing obsessive use of certain words as the novel goes on.

All his life, Kafka was prone to write in a ruminative but inconclusive way, and a small number of words increasingly force themselves on the attention. 'Gewissermaßen' ('to a certain extent') with its retreat from definite assertion, is found surprisingly often even in early writings; its habitual use in *The Castle* has just been seen. 'Perhaps' and 'probably' come much more frequently, and there is a constant sense of possibilities being tentatively weighed up and just as tentatively either deprecated or approved: 'indeed . . . yet' ('zwar . . . aber'), 'for that matter' ('übrigens'), 'naturally', or 'it must be confessed' ('freilich'), 'at all events' and several others recur with such frequency as to be uncomfortably noticeable. At times in the later writings, as in 'The Burrow', or 'Josephine the Singer', the whole structure of a story depends on such a flow of half-assertions, concessions, renewed assertions and renewed yieldings to contrary promptings, and at times these amount to no more than an inconsequential rambling. When Titorelli or Huld, in *The Trial*, confuse themselves in this way, it is understandable as the natural utterance of characters who have little

* Compare this sentence from 'The Burrow': '. . . I know that my time is limited, that I shall not have to hunt here endlessly, but that to a certain extent, when I want to, and am tired of life here, someone will call me to him whose invitation I shall not be able to resist'.[25]

notion of what they are talking about; it amounts to satire. There are comparatively few instances of such words in stories like 'In the Penal Colony' and 'The Metamorphosis'. In the later stories, and particularly in the later stages of *The Castle*, they occur so often and so improbably as to raise the question whether Kafka was always in a condition to direct them.

With time, literally nothing can be said without a concession to a possible different point of view, whether such a view is reasonable or not, and the concessions can increase to the point where Kafka does lose control:

'So my plan had actually failed', says Olga, 'and yet did not fail completely, for while indeed we did not find the messenger, and my father's continual journeys to the Herrenhof inn and staying the night there, and perhaps even his sympathy, so far as he is capable of that, unfortunately finished him off – he has been in the condition you saw him for two years now, and yet perhaps he is better off than my mother, whose death we expect every day, and which is only delayed by Amalia's excessive exertions. But what I did achieve at the Herrenhof was a certain connection with the Castle . . .'[26]

Writing like this cannot be defended on the grounds that the novel recounts a dream, or that the need for indeterminacy dictates it. It is simply inchoate, tedious, and only to be understood on the grounds that Kafka himself did not wish it to be published, had not revised it, and thought (however ambiguously) that it deserved only to be burned. For there is page after page, not quite of this quality, but nevertheless of such lengthy and involved sentences, such repetitions of 'zwar . . . aber, allerdings, übrigens, freilich', as no serious writer could allow himself.

The style has set in well before Olga's narrative about the Sortini episode. Long passages of monologue reported in indirect speech, involving the subjunctive, are a wearisome feature as early as chapter 13, and they continue sporadically for the remainder of the novel. Here is the child Hans Brunswick, recalling how K. addressed a question to his mother shortly after his first arrival – the absence of the subjunctive in the English makes it appear a little lighter than it really is:

Hans's father had been very annoyed at the time about K., and would certainly never allow K. to visit his mother; indeed, he had wanted to seek K. out at the time, to punish him for his behaviour, and only his mother had prevented that. But above all his mother herself in general wanted to speak to nobody, and her question about K. was no exception to the rule, on the contrary, just on the very occasion of his being mentioned she would have been able to express a wish to see him, but she had not done so, and thereby clearly expressed her will.[27]

If it were not a child whose words were being reported (by Kafka, not by any intermediary character) one might suppose this to be a parody, humorously intended, of the official jargon likely to be heard at the Castle. But since a small boy is the supposed speaker one can only conclude that Kafka has succumbed himself to the weakness.

Only a man imbued with officialese and occasionally unable to shake free of it in his creative writing could write so often such sentences as these:

But with regard to the most serious deficiencies, the inadequate provision for sleeping and heating, she promised without fail some relief for the following day . . .[28]

The teacher would gladly have let the cat stay there, but an allusion relating to this was decisively rejected by the schoolmistress with a reference to the cruelty of K. . . .[29]

The frequency of words like 'somewhere', 'somehow', 'somebody', reinforce the general feeling of indeterminacy.

The writing in the second half of the book is inferior to that in the first half, and this may be partly due (if my presumption is right) to a determination to make the figures of Klamm and Sortini, in their symbolical functions, coalesce. Yet it would be quite wrong to conclude that the second half fulfilled none of the promise of the first. Some dogged reading is needed, to get through the Hans Brunswick and Amalia episodes, but in the final chapters (omitted by Max Brod from the earliest edition, and so not included in the first English translation) remarkable developments take place. I am thinking of the episode with the official Bürgel, and of the scenes which follow before the final pages peter out.

The meeting with Bürgel is not unlike the meeting with the prison-chaplain in *The Trial*. It comes at a climactic moment fairly near the end. K.'s whole situation is outlined to him by a person in authority, and he is for the first time given some assurance, however slight, about his position. As in so many cases, however, *The Castle* reverses the situation of *The Trial*. Where the chaplain seems concerned first to show K. that he has no chance of ever getting anywhere, then to confuse him completely, Bürgel seems to offer a real chance of success, which only K.'s somnolence prevents him from taking. All the confusion seems to have led, by virtue of the very fact that it is confusion, stumblingly, blindly, with no proper awareness of how it has come about, to a solution which, if accepted, would give K. all he ever looked for. It is a paradoxical solution, to be sure, yet a solution for all that. And all K. does is to fall asleep at the crucial moment. So the question that must arise, considering the vagueness of a good deal of what has gone before, is whether the climactic offer has any significance, or whether it is advanced merely to be dismissed as easily as other things are in the novel, on no particular grounds except a general readiness to be frustrated.

One striking thing about the Bürgel interview is that there is almost direct communication between two characters. In many parts of the novel there are monologues, and in this one also the main purpose is to expound a situation, indicating doubts and hesitations, and the usual obsessive words occur frequently here also. The difference is that Bürgel seems himself to be genuinely involved, and that he is offering a course of action which K. may at any moment adopt, so that the whole scene gains in dramatic tension. Bürgel is telling K., of course, that the situation he finds himself in at this instant is the only one that can really lead to success. K. has stumbled at night and by accident – not taking any advantage, then – into the room of an official not allocated to his particular case, and it is only in such an event that an official feels compelled to grant any request that the applicant may make. He does not tell K. this directly, but only obliquely, outlining a situation exactly like K.'s at this present moment, yet never saying openly that he, Bürgel, will grant any request K. makes, so that the whole interview begins to feel like a game of chess in which many pieces are *en prise*, and a single move will suddenly unfold incalculable possibilities. In fact Bürgel describes the situation in terms suggesting a kind of Hegelian intensification on both sides. (In Hegel's philosophy man is seen as 'alienated' ('entfremdet') from the Spirit that moves all things by virtue of the fact that he is a mere individual, whereas the Spirit is 'the All', or at least manifests itself as the All, even though essentially it is nothing. The greater this alienation becomes, and the more it is intensified, the greater is the tendency for it to suffer a reversal and to reassume a total identity with the Spirit. Thus the man in whom alienation is complete – one thinks, if one is Hegel, of Christ's words of forsakenness on the Cross – is the man most nearly at one with the Whole.) The more weary, disappointed and indifferent the applicant is, the greater is the desire of the official to help him, and for the official, at any rate, there are overtones suggesting that he acquires supreme power at such a moment: the official, Bürgel says, violently seizes 'a promotion in rank exceeding all conception'. There is a strong suggestion here that the official takes on quasi-divine powers at such a moment, while the applicant in his dejection seems at least to resemble such a man as de Caussade describes in his treatise on mystical prayer: 'This soul [in whom God lives] often enough, is abandoned in a corner, like a bit of broken pottery which no one imagines to be of any use. Thus abandoned by creatures, but experiencing Godly and very real, true and active love, though it is a love infused in repose, this soul does not apply itself to anything by its own movement; all it can do is to abandon itself and surrender itself into God's hands, to serve him in ways known to him.'[30]

It is quite common in treatises on mysticism to associate the ultimate dereliction of the soul, the moment when it feels itself completely abandoned, with the highest state to which that soul can attain – in fact it is one of the potential evils of mysticism, that it holds out such enormous promise as the reward of such total loss. But Bürgel is not represented as divine in any Christian sense, nor does he seem to feel any love for K., nor does K. seem to feel any love for him or anyone else. The whole scene is inverted, in comparison with orthodox Christian mysticism. Bürgel is only telling K. all this because he himself wants to go to sleep, and thinks he can talk himself into that state. He can scarcely be using a loving irony – that is, deliberately refraining from putting K. into a too knowing position out of care lest K. succumb to a 'temptation on the mountain-top' – judging by the way he exuberantly stretches himself as soon as the interview has to stop (there is something almost devilish in his glee here), and as K. goes he is really more concerned to assure him that nothing could have been done after all, than to lament his lack of success. There is something evil about Bürgel altogether, not so much in the way he speaks of normal interviews as ending more or less automatically in the defeat of the applicant – this is the first official confirmation K. has had, that the Castle is more bent on procrastination than anything else – as in the way he speaks of wanting to resist the temptation to do the applicant some good. 'When the applicant is in the room, it's already pretty bad, it's true. It presses on your heart. "How long will you be able to resist?" you ask yourself. But there simply will not be any resistance, you know that.'[31] There is passion in his desire to meet the applicant, 'a real thirst', he says, to suffer the applicant's useless demands along with him. And there is desperation, because one knows that the applicant's request will have to be granted, even though 'at least so far as one can see, it will well and truly tear down the whole official organisation'. Close though this situation is to that of some traditional mysticism, Bürgel is claiming to speak on behalf of an organisation that is opposed to the granting of any request, and which, so far as he (or the reader) knows, can even be destroyed by an action of its own inspired by an act of charitable sympathy. Hence the obliqueness, the sly presenting of K.'s own situation without actually pointing to the obvious parallel, the failure actually to make the offer which Bürgel says he is unable to resist making. Bürgel sees the whole position not as an opportunity for love, but as one in which he would undergo something like murder or rape:

'The applicant, like a robber in a forest, forces sacrifices from us that we should never be capable of otherwise; very well, so it feels at the moment, while the applicant is before us, strengthening us and forcing us and encouraging us, and while everything is going on half unreflectively; but what will it be like afterwards, when it is all over, and the applicant, satiated and unworried, leaves us, and we stand there, alone, defenceless at the misuse of our office – the whole thing is past thinking of! And nevertheless we are happy. How suicidal happiness can be.'[32]

It is as though K. had penetrated to the Will itself (in Schopenhauer's sense), to the very quick of life, and found it as ruthlessly bent on destruction as ever the Court was in *The Trial*, even to the point of deeply desiring its own death through the means of doing what is normally accounted good. Bürgel is offering K., however obliquely, the means of destroying him, and it is, presumably, a destruction he would welcome, as Joseph K. welcomed his execution. That *is* the way of the world, as Bürgel would have it: a kind of sexual relationship in which one partner is misused – and likes it – rather than a free giving and taking on each side.

Yet, such is the uncertainty about values in the whole work, it is not completely clear that Bürgel is wrong, or evil, in his unwillingness to grant a request made by an applicant such as K. If he sees that being in a cosmically dominant position is of no benefit to a man, he may be in the right to show such unwillingness. The trouble is, one does not know where Bürgel stands or what he makes of all this. The uncertainty is ingrained in the novel: it is not a quality for admiration, though attempts at interpretation lead one into subtleties; it is rather that the novel has no guiding centre, nothing by which to see how it may be read with a real sense of meeting the author.

And K. is too tired to do anything about Bürgel's offer. There is no virtue here. K. has made no progress in virtue since the beginning of the novel: despite apparent parallels there is no reason for thinking of him in terms of a Christian mystic who has arrived in a comparable state of dereliction after constant prayer and exercise. And in failing to take advantage of Bürgel's offer K. is not sizing it up, declining to do anything for this reason or that, he is simply very tired, and has 'a great disinclination for things that concerned him'. The sense of this extraordinary spiritual climax – that really is what it amounts to, however strange to tradition it may be – is not contained in any moral progress, but in the words of Bürgel just before K. leaves:

'Go then, what do you want here? No, don't excuse yourself on account of your sleepiness, whatever for? The vital spark only reaches certain limits, who can help it if this limit is significant in a different way too? No, nobody can. That is how the world corrects itself and maintains its balance. It is an excellent, an unimaginably excellent arrangement, though in another respect it is comfortless.

. . . Go then; who knows what awaits you over there [in Erlanger's room], there's no end of opportunities in this place. The only thing is, of course, that there are some opportunities that in a certain sense are too big to be made use of, there are things that collapse on account of nothing else but themselves.'[33]

The inference is that Bürgel was perfectly safe in making his oblique offer to K. Precisely because K. was so over-tired, disappointed and indifferent, he could not take up the offer: only by pursuing his goal with such energy that he became weary and indifferent could he ever have reached a position where he could put the vital question (whatever that might be), and so the one thing cancels out the other, the supreme command is at the mercy of the one man who cannot use it. That is how the world (Bürgel surprisingly says, but one sees his drift) goes on existing, because, as I interpret, it is an evil world in which the desire for destruction, the Schopenhauerian Will to extinction, is always predominant and even manages to incorporate 'the good' in its destructive process, even manages to survive when its whole nature is bent on vanishing out of existence.

If it were possible to speak of a fallen angel, in the context of this novel, Bürgel would fit the case very well. There is in him all the remaining desire to do good which one would imagine a former spirit in heaven to have, and it amounts to a passion, even now. Yet there is nothing in him that will actively seek to realise this good, he is acquiescent in the frustration which the whole organisation imposes, and shows every sign of delight when Erlanger's summons breaks off the interview before K. is able to put the situation to his own use.

'We are digging the pit of Babel,' Kafka observed in his diaries. Not the tower which challenged heaven and brought destruction on itself *that* way, but the pit which moves further and further down into dereliction and hopelessness, without the saving grace of the traditional mystic's continuing love, and which ultimately wants nothing but a destructive union with the all-annihilating Will.

But this strange climax, or, in a special sense, anti-climax, is not the end of the novel. There remains K.'s brief encounter with Erlanger and his witnessing of the distribution of the documents, and finally his return to the barmaid Pepi in the inn, and all this seems to prolong the moment in which a paradoxical achievement is being celebrated. K. has got nowhere, of course, in the terms outlined by Bürgel, and the futility of it all seems to be stressed by Erlanger's injunction to K. to see that Frieda returns to the service of Klamm, an injunction which K. has no means of fulfilling since Frieda has abandoned him for Jeremias. (Milena similarly broke off the relation with Kafka after some time.) But the terms outlined by Bürgel need not necessarily be admirable. When he tells K. that he could 'control everything' he may very well recall the temptation of Christ by Satan with the offer of dominion over all the world. There is no need to assume that Bürgel or indeed the Castle itself stands for anything good, despite the hints at divinity in Klamm: gods are not necessarily good. If K. had made a positive rejection of Bürgel's offer, instead of falling asleep, he would have made for an unambiguous conclusion.

There is no such unambiguity, at least in the last chapter but one (chapter 19). After meeting Erlanger, K. is left alone in the corridor while various documents are being handed out, and for the whole of the chapter a series of suggestions and counter-suggestions is made. K. reflects first on the officials behind the office-doors, and surmises that, though no doubt tired, they are enjoying 'indestructible quiet, indestructible peace. "If one is weary a little at midday, that is all part of the natural and happy course of the day. These gentlemen have continual midday", K. said to himself.'[34] And this is an important reflection, if one thinks of how often Kafka spoke in his diaries of 'the Indestructible': it is one of the most striking concepts that he uses.[35] Yet as Kafka goes on, in the next sentence, there appears a lighthearted element in the mood, which disturbs any normal notion of peace and quiet. It is not simply that the pleasure is childlike:

'The babble of voices in these rooms had something extremely joyful about it. At one moment it sounded like the rejoicing of children getting ready for an excursion, at another like the first stirrings in a hen-coop, like the joy of being in complete accord with the awakening day; somewhere one of the gentlemen even imitated the crowing of a cock.'[36]

– it is rather that this crowing like a cock (a sound which carries overtones of Peter's denial of Christ as well as of daybreak – both the depths of disgrace and the announcement of a new era) heralds a whole series of actions that are childlike to the point of zaniness. The officials are petulant, refractory, impatient, they stamp their feet, clap their hands, keep shouting the number of the file they want; one pours a basin of water over one of the distributing clerks, another throws a whole file over the partition-wall so that its contents spill all over the floor, others refuse to open their doors at all, despite repeated shoulder-charges. It is all like a mad cartoon, or some Chaplinesque comedy, and quite amusing in its way, though it turns K.'s benevolent reflections on the officials' serenity into nonsense. They are behaving like Bürgel, more than like the people K. supposes them to be. Yet that point about indestructibility seemed to have a special significance, coming just after the climactic interview.

Then again, K. witnesses the moment when the chief distributing clerk, having got rid of all his files, is left with one small scrap of paper, which has somehow come adrift, and which the clerk destroys apparently because he does not know what else to do with it. 'That might very well be mine', is K.'s comment, and whether it is or is not, the comment has the effect of drawing attention to the possibility that K.'s case is now over and done with. It is only a possibility. K. does not know, and Kafka does not tell us, whether the document is his. If it is, there is still no telling whether it has been destroyed simply because the clerk is impatient, or because K.'s case has been dismissed, and if it has been dismissed, whether this is because he is beneath contempt or above reproach. All the same, the possibility is there, that his case, the Bürgel interview being finished, is now over and done with.

This possibility is then reinforced, though still ambiguously, by the behaviour of the officials as soon as the clerk has left. One begins to press his electric bell, others join in, and soon there are so many bells going that they seem to be expressing not some need for help, but 'an excess of joy'[37] and even to be celebrating a victory, though it is not said what victory, and the idea of *electric* bells doing this, as distinct from church bells, is not too easy to grasp. K. soon learns what the ringing means from the landlord and landlady, who come running in comic haste to answer the summons of the bells, and who explain to K. very forcefully that it is only his presence in the corridor that has caused all the trouble. The officials have had too much delicacy to require K. to leave, but so long as he was present the distribution of files could not take place in due order, and only now, when the distribution is over, have the officials decided to have him sent away. This explanation is unsatisfying. The officials have shown no sign of delicacy; they have behaved more like spoiled children than men of tact, and K. ought to have no difficulty in pointing this out. That he does not do so may be due to Kafka's determination – conscious or otherwise – not to allow any positive suggestion that is not immediately negatived. But the fact is, the landlord simply does not negative what the reader has seen: the officials remain foolish from start to finish, and nothing they have done suggests any sensitivity or decent shame at having their private behaviour scrutinised – on the contrary, they have made an exhibition of themselves before K.'s eyes. So the bare thread of sense that could perhaps be observed running through the various events is turned into nonsense. If one takes the view that K. has done well (though not virtuously well) in not falling for Bürgel's offer of power, that he then comes to see the officials in a more positively good light, that as a result of all this his file disappears, or is abolished, and that the officials celebrate this by ringing their bells, one has at any rate a logical sequence of events to point to. On the other hand, the notion that K. is deceived about the indestructible peace, that the officials are glad to see the back of him, and that, though not sensitive as the landlord makes out, they are more likely to rejoice at the death – or at least frustration – of a sinner, than at anything else, is really more potent. So far as the Castle is concerned, it seems, K.'s case is finished, and that is the victory that is being celebrated.

Yet, given the nature of the Castle as it has appeared especially in the latter half of the novel, that would not be at all a bad thing. All this ceaseless attempt at penetrating to the innermost depths and conquering them, has characterised European thinking, or a good deal of it, for a very long time. So long, that failure to enter the Castle, failure to dominate, is easily taken as a sign of a defeat worse than any other that could be imagined. Yet, given the nature of K.'s Castle, the shifting image as he has seen it, there is no need to see defeat as a loss. Ceasing to have dealings with an organisation like this is rather a gain, and if K.'s document has in fact been destroyed, so much the better, one may say, whatever the officials and the landlord may think about it. This moment in the novel is rather like the moment in 'In the Penal Colony', when the machine of torture breaks into pieces. The machine seemed to be a means of enlightenment, as the Castle seemed to K., yet when placed to the final test it could only break down. Is it the same here, or roughly the same – has not K.'s potential challenge to the Castle reached its maximum, so that now only a complete severance is possible?

If Kafka had been fully conscious of that implication, he might have been able to finish the novel. In fact, it is doubtful whether he had more than an unconscious grasp of it; in other words, his mind, groping in darkness, deliberately remaining 'unknowing', not planning out the novel in advance, but following where his torments took him, went as far as to outline a kind of parody of deliverance, a parody that still belongs to the world of the Castle and is still at best an inversion of real deliverance. Real deliverance, Kafka himself knew, was to know the indestructible in oneself and not to strain after it, to let it be, as he wrote in his aphorisms. This he could not do within the novel without straining to breaking-point his integrity: this work, to remain whole as a work of art, had to continue as it had begun and developed, for once the Bürgel interview had taken place the die was cast, the dominant evil in the Castle had irrevocably made its mark. Had K. accepted Bürgel's offer it would have been like a pact with evil, on which there was no going back. But his failure to accept was not a refusal, it was merely a weariness of spirit, and his lack of interest in 'things that concerned himself' was not a choice, not a real self-denial, but a drifting, quietistic absence of self-regard. A sane man, however self-denying he may be, must have that essential self-regard, or the quick of life in him dies. In K. it has very nearly died, as the novel draws to an end.

That Kafka is still not, as an artist, a free man, is shown by the tedium of the final chapter, at least for the first twenty pages, a stream of hesitations and modifications, denials and concessions, which run on without so much as a paragraph division. We are back again, after the comparatively lively sequence of events since K. first entered Bürgel's room, in a world of 'indeed', 'probably', 'it is true . . .' and 'for that matter'. They are not K.'s words, and this makes an important difference. They are the words of Pepi, the barmaid who has succeeded Frieda temporarily in the tap-room at the Bridge Inn, and who now prattles on with a self-indulgence which must be ascribed in some part to Kafka too, since he seems to have abandoned all control as a novelist in order to give Pepi her head. And yet, despite this tedium, one can just see, even within Kafka's abandonment to the darkness, a glimmer of acceptable sense. Pepi's sole preoccupation is with herself, her prospects of promotion within the hierarchy, her jealousy of Frieda's relation with Klamm, her conviction that she could do better. She is self-regard personified, one might say. And the curious fact is that her name is like one used so often by Kafka for his fictional *alter egos* that it must surely have been significant to him. One could have done with more of an indication than this rather obscure one, it is true. Yet there it is: Pepi is the usual abbreviation or nickname for girls called Josephine, and Joseph is not only the name of K.'s counterpart in *The Trial*, it is also the name given by K. in *The Castle* on one occasion, though he is not otherwise referred to except by his initial; Josephine is also of course the name of the singing mouse in the short story which seems meant to comment ironically on Kafka's (and other writers') artistic pretensions. So it is not at all improbable that Kafka had in mind, in introducing Pepi, a confrontation of himself by Joseph K. Here all K.'s determination to get on, to reach the highest point, and enter the Castle, is parodied – or perhaps 'reflected' is the better word, when the manifest intention is so slight – in the figure of this childish young woman whose absurdities become more and more unbearably apparent as her monologue (much of it, like Hans Brunswick's, in the form of reported speech) continues.

Kafka does not control this. Yet K., confronted, as it were, with this caricature of himself, does remain remarkably calm and sane. Whatever the truth may be about the document and the behaviour of the officials – a truth so smudged over with unrefuted absurdities that all discussion of it must remain in confusion – it does seem at least very likely that the unconscious process which brought Kafka to write of the destruction of the document had been a move towards liberation of some sort, even though it was still much less than a full liberation. It is moving to find K. using words like these, when Pepi has been complaining that both he and she have been deceived, since it reflects back on K.'s earlier gratification at having his hopes frustrated:

'So long as you go on complaining about being deceived', said K., 'I can't come to any agreement with you. You always want to make out you have been deceived, because it flatters you, and because it moves you. But the truth is, you are not suited to this job. How clearly unfitted you must be, if a man like me, who in your opinion is more ignorant than anyone, can see it.'[38]

Again, K.'s friendly criticism of Pepi's absurd costume, telling her that she dresses up like an angel, or as she thinks angels are, because of her overweening pretensions, strikes an unusually humble note, besides reintroducing the religious note that has been absent for some time.

Similarly, K.'s lack of jealousy towards Klamm shows a new generosity in him that can surely only be the fruit of some deep-seated change. But though there is humility and generosity not only in this, but in several other of K.'s observations to Pepi, the change is still only partial, and his ideals still remain as much concerned with gaining power as ever. In contrasting Pepi with Frieda, K. shows that he is concerned with some kind of moral values, but they are still the values associated with his old determination to pursue and destroy Klamm:

'Have you ever noticed her eyes?' K. asks Pepi. 'Those weren't the eyes of a barmaid, they were very nearly the eyes of a landlady. She saw everything, and yet each individual at the same time, and the look she kept for a single individual was still strong enough to dominate him.'[39]

The odd idea of a hierarchy in the tap-room comes as near explicitness here as it ever does: one wonders just what land-ladies' eyes do look like. But the essential point is still this admiration for power, for the ability to subject a lover to one-self, which seems to have been in K. from the start, and which runs alongside his praise of Frieda's matter-of-factness and equanimity.

There is, then, a remarkable change in K., something that has no parallel in *The Trial* or in any other of Kafka's works, and this change has come about not through any conscious willing, though the strange unconscious process by which it is reached is detectable. He is now more generous, not vindictive or jealous at all, more willing to believe in other people's superiority to himself, and in the ineptitude of his approach to the Castle, than he was at the beginning, and all this comes at a point when he may (or may not – the issue is not one that can ever find an answer) have had all relationship with the Castle severed, when he has ceased to seek either to penetrate or to destroy it. The game of attack and counter-attack is over, and in these circumstances K. emerges a different man.

But the sense of frustration which still continues is due to K.'s continuing preoccupation with Pepi, if Pepi represents, as I have suggested, a kind of *alter ego*. K. can confront this caricature of himself that comes looming up out of the depths at him, but he has no alternative but to go down into them with her. Pepi's underground quarters are constricting, if cosy, and the suggestive overtones they carry must be obvious enough. K. will not move out into a freer world by joining Pepi, as he now half proposes to do: at most he will confront his own self without continual self-laceration, an achievement he may be glad to settle for. It may even be that he will not stay there for good. Pepi, it seems, is bound to the underground room, which is scarcely a statement to take absolutely literally. K., on the other hand, may leave when spring comes, he is bound only for the winter, and again a parallel from Rilke comes to mind:

> Doch unter Wintern ist einer so endlos Winter,
> Daß überwinternd dein Herz überhaupt übersteht.

But among all winters there is one that's so endlessly winter, that outwintering it your heart will outlast.

There is a part of K., at least, which may rise again, but that is the briefest of hints, scarcely even a speculation. Essentially, K. has emerged from the quest for the Castle with only death in sight, and a bare hope of something beyond. Equally important,

the writing continues as it has been through the greater part of
the novel, fluid, incessantly conceding and retreating from all
definiteness of statement, never differentiating between characters (or only minimally: the Superintendent is rather more
inclined to use jargon than others are), spreading a mist of doubt
which is there not because doubt is justified but because it has
become a regular principle to deny whatever is affirmed.
Momentarily, towards the end, Kafka seems on the point of
abandoning this principle, which is the principle of the Castle
itself. But because the movement of the novel is dreamlike, the
conscious recognition can never be made. To have recognised
where the undertow of the dream was taking him, Kafka would
have had to wake up, and to have woken up would have destroyed the unity of the novel, or rather the uniformity, the
oppressive nightmarish repetitiveness which is the kind of unity
it has. The character he has created can only go on to meet the
now sinister landlady, with her half-promise to 'come and fetch
him' next day, and then to the old crouching figure of Gerstäcker's mother (in the final fragment released by Max Brod
for the later editions), in whom the breath of corruption almost
touches him. The novel breaks off in mid-sentence, probably
because Kafka could not take it relentlessly on to the deathliness
which was all he had left for K. Yet there has been sufficient
indication of a reversal even within the uncontrollable dream,
even in the quietistically acquiescent K. who perseveres only in
acquiescence. One glimpses the truth in Hölderlin's lines:

> Herrscht im schiefesten Orkus
> Nicht ein Grades, ein Recht noch auch?

Even in most crooked Hades, does not a straightness, a rightness prevail?

Kafka's novel takes the reader a long way down into the
hopelessness of Orcus, but though it never, so far as its own content is concerned, lets him emerge again, it does suggest a dull,
yet insistent pull towards the reversal of all the values the Castle
stands for. More than that one can't claim on its behalf. It did
not take Kafka to the reversal of fortunes he sometimes looked
for, and it will not, of itself, help any reader there either.

10

LATER STORIES

The volume *Marriage Preparations in the Country* contains among other things over three hundred pages of brief fragments of stories, sentences, scraps, many of them reprinted from exercise-books which Kafka used for drafting his ideas. These exercise-books contain many of the later published stories, but there is a great deal that never was published in his lifetime, most of it dating from 1917 or after. The published items were very few, once the selection for *A Country Doctor* had been made: five more before his death, if one includes such a mystifying piece as 'The Bucket-Rider' (or 'Coal-Scuttle Rider'), which was written in 1917 as a fantasy about the wartime coal-shortage, published in the Christmas number of the *Prager Presse* in 1921, and not re-issued by Kafka. The remaining four came from the period immediately before, during and after the writing of *The Castle*: 'First Sorrow' in late 1921, 'A Little Woman' probably in 1923, 'A Hunger-Artist' (or 'A Fasting Showman') in 1922, and 'Josephine the Singer' in 1924, the year of his death.

Of these, Kafka singled out only 'A Hunger-Artist' as being fit to stand with his other works, but though there are clearly reasons for this, 'A Little Woman' is also interesting for the insight it gives into Kafka's normal state of mind. The little woman herself is said to be based on a Berlin landlady, though the insistent pressure she exerts suggests also a metaphorical figure.

This is a portrayal, in the form of a monologue, of a woman of extremely critical habits, so critical as to make the life of the speaker, who has to submit to her criticisms, unendurable. The woman herself may be meant allegorically, though it would be difficult to find an equivalent for her. More probably, she is a projection by means of which Kafka objectifies his mental tor-ment, and this seems to be the most satisfactory account of her. To judge by Kafka's diaries, it was just such a continual criticism of himself, from within rather than from without, which he had to endure, and the personification of the criticism in the form of a woman only vivifies the situation. Reading Kafka's other works with this one in mind, one gains some awareness of how he came to create his situations, the fittingness of the Trial and of the forms of torture that occur.

By the time *The Castle* was written, however, Kafka's critical defences had been so reduced that his style was often repetitive in the way already described. 'Josephine the Singer' is written in just this style, and continues, exhaustingly, for over twenty pages in the same vein. Its subject-matter gives some grounds for thinking that Kafka's original sense of isolation and uselessness had undergone a partial reverse, so that, while still feeling isolated and useless, he was tempted to feel himself by virtue of this very fact a kind of leader of men. So far as he personally was concerned, this need never have been more than a temptation, but one sees traces of it in his diary. This, for instance, is probably in its context meant partly for himself, no doubt with some degree of humorous irony :

'You lead the masses, great, tall general, lead those who are in despair through the passes of the mountains, hidden under the snow, which no-one else can discover. And who gives you the strength? He who gives you your clear vision.'[1]

The knowledge that he was moving in depths of despair beyond any normally known gave him strength to think that perhaps his mission was to explore the bottomless pit of *Angst* till it did, of its own accord, allow him to rise up again into freedom:

'. . . only forwards, hungry animal, does the path lead to edible food, breathable air, free life, even if it is beyond life.'[2]

This never appears, in the diaries, as a proud boast, rather as a grain of comfort in a life of continual melancholy. But for Kafka the mere occurrence of such a thought was enough to start a series of self-recriminations. Ideally he wanted to maintain a serene confidence even when everything seemed to have been lost. Sarah, Abraham's wife, he reminded himself, thought that all prospect of ever bearing a child had gone, yet she bore one.

In his own case, by parallel implication, even the fact he knew he was banging his head against the wall of a cell without door or window need not mean that he was right to despair. Thus the phrase from 'Conversation with the Suppliant' still comes to mind: 'Ich jause im Grünen' – the possibility of such a carefree existence was still not to be dismissed. But it seemed increasingly like a remote island, above and beyond the dialectic of self-assertions and withdrawals of his usual life. Thus the thought of being a leader had to be crushed, and this is what happens in the Josephine story.

Josephine, as a name, recalls the use of similar names by Kafka for *alter egos* in his fiction.[3] A certain self-projection into characters of this name is quite likely to have happened. But whether this is so or not, the idea of a singing mouse seems to have suggested a means of ironising while at the same time not destroying the pretensions of writers to have something of importance to say.

The narrator who speaks the monologue about Josephine is never consistent from one moment to another. Josephine's squeaking is powerful in the extreme, filling everybody who hears it with enthusiasm; on the other hand it is doubtful whether it is different in any way from the squeaking of ordinary mice, and may not be art at all. Yet again, the mere fact that Josephine does what everybody does, but draws attention to it in a special way, could be a justification of her devoting so much time to it and making such extravagant claims. But before long, the narrator is reduced to saying that some mice prefer to pay no attention, and that, though Josephine is said to be a bulwark of national solidarity, there have been occasions when the enemy has been able to be victorious precisely because her audiences were too attentive to her singing to pay attention to their own defence.

As a story of the pros and cons of art and artists in relation to society, 'Josephine' merely rehearses the familiar situations. From Hölderlin onwards there have been poets who claimed to be prophets, and who had similar doubts to those expressed here. By making the protagonist a mouse, Kafka knocks the bottom out of any serious claims, and seems to assume that any human greatness must appear as trivial as this, viewed *sub specie aeternitatis*. It is too crushing. Josephine never rises to anything approaching human sympathy or pity; she is not much more than a pretentious prima donna, as the narrator presents her. So the pendulum swings from melodramatic assertion to ironical denial: the possibility of a genuine art with human dignity is never entertained. The humour of the piece is on the boyish side (there are references to being 'still as a mouse', and to Josephine's saying 'Ich pfeife auf euren Schutz' 'I don't give a damn for your protection': literally 'I whistle (or squeak) at your protection', punning on the double sense of 'pfeifen'). Any breakthrough that might be achieved – and there is talk of the squeaking being 'liberated from the trammels of daily life' – is thus belittled from the start, and the belittling is too easily achieved. Here more than anywhere in Kafka one has the impression that his self-doubtings have got the better of his serious purposes – the attempt at overcoming self-assertion which his condition really required has resulted in a whimsy, and the writing itself, circling and circling round the same theme, produces at its worst such passages as this:

If this were so, all Josephine's claims would be completely intelligible, and one could see in this freedom which the people would accord her, in this extraordinary gift, never granted to anyone else, which actually infringes the law, a confession that the people do not, as they claim, understand Josephine, but feebly gape at her art, do not feel worthy of it, attempt to counterbalance the sorrow it causes Josephine by a really desperate performance and just as her art is beyond their comprehension, place her person and its wishes outside their power to control.

There are too many sudden twists of direction – as in this passage – too many unaccountable leaps from one subject or topic to another, to allow anything but a cold determination to sort out the logic or the reasons for the hiatuses, and this is not an interest compatible with art.

Kafka is not, of course, the narrator in this story, and none of the narrator's faults need be attributed to him. On the contrary, it is much more likely to be with Josephine that he identified himself, to however small a degree, and the narrator is there to provide a certain distance from something like Kafka's own position. But since the narrator has the entire account to himself, suffers no correction either by dispute or by the presence of some other personage, counterbalancing him, the story is for once more like a document of neurosis than a fashioned work of art.

A similar kind of belittling takes place in 'First Sorrow', the very brief account of a trapeze-artist who lives in almost complete isolation, on his trapeze. The opening sentence has a note that one would want to call sarcastic, were it not that such a mood is very far removed from anything Kafka normally expresses. It is probably, then, because of the implications Kafka saw in the art of the trapezist that he included the parenthesis:

as is well known this art, carried on in the domes of the great variety-theatres, is one of the most difficult achievable by Man.

There is, in the last four words, a suggestion that human achievement has here just about reached its limits, as though other forms of art might well exist, but beyond any man's power to realise them. The same suggestion is worked out further in the phrase, shortly afterwards, 'out of a striving for perfection'. It is clear that a trapezist would not normally spend days and nights continually on the trapeze out of any desire for perfection – quite the contrary result would be likely, if only for want of sleep – and thus the words suggest that the story is a parable with much more general implications, that it is really about a man who is 'an extraordinary, irreplaceable artist', who tries to maintain 'his art in its perfection'.

Not that Kafka is only interested in the allegory: there are touches of his characteristic humour and pathos in passages such as the one in which the fireman shouts across the roof to the trapezist:

True, his human contacts were limited, and it was only now and then that an acrobatic colleague would climb up to him; then they would both sit on the trapeze, leaning to the right and left on the safety-ropes and chatting, or workmen would come and repair the roof and exchange a few words with him through an open window, or a fire-man would be testing the emergency lighting in the top gallery and shout a few respectful but not very intelligible words to him.

There is something expansive in passages like this, a mood of genial self-criticism (for that is what it amounts to) quite unlike the grim mood of earlier stories, and this humour continues in the passage about the trapezist's sleeping in the luggage-rack on journeys, and racing through towns at high speed, to get back to a circus tent and a trapeze again.

But though the humour continues to the end, it is in a slightly different vein, later, and the intention overcomes the execution. The trapezist's biting his lips and bursting into tears because he has only one trapeze instead of two is childish in a way that Stan Laurel could have acted. But Kafka seems not simply to be writing comedy, even when the impresario puts his face so close to the trapezist's that the tears flow onto his own cheek, or when he concurs so solemnly in the trapezist's wish. The whole business of wanting two trapezes, which the end of the story brings as a crowning realisation, seems to have some special significance – perhaps the trapezist is an artist in his ivory tower, who realises at long last that two is company, though this would be a trite moral to put into the story – or perhaps he is a man about to fall in love. All in all, one would rather not stress the possible symbolism too hard. When the trapezist sobs 'Only this one rod in my hands – how can I live!', the overtones are all too clear. But either way, the tone of the humour is rather too crude for any notable significance: Kafka rubs in the after all not very subtle point, with his caricature of the trapezist's grief and the impresario's alarm and concern. One has the impression that Kafka turned to castigating himself too much here: had he not been so intent on mocking his own solitude and seclusive-ness, as he felt them to be, he might have allowed the 'artist' more scope and more dignity.

In neither 'Josephine' nor 'First Sorrow' are any pretensions of the artist allowed to go uncriticised. Nor are they in 'A

Hunger-Artist', though the general import of the story is different. Here once again, the almost irrelevant designation '-artist' (the trapezist is often called 'the trapeze-artist', or just 'the artist') draws the reader's mind from the professional starver to art in general. Yet it is not precisely art that Kafka has in mind. The story (distantly related to Melville's 'Bartleby' in *Piazza Tales*) begins with the observation that hungering has gone out of fashion in recent times, which certainly would not be appropriate if art were the subject of the allegory, so that one begins to cast about for some further sense. The idea soon presents itself that something like 'hungering and thirsting after righteousness' is a phrase to bear in mind, especially when the starver is said to fast for a Biblical forty days. It would make sense if Kafka were saying there had been an increase in materialism, and some disregard of righteousness in modern times (whether or not this was actually true). And certainly there seems to be a parallel with 'In the Penal Colony', in the contrast between effete, lax modernity and the discipline, or self-discipline, of earlier days, reflected in the self-discipline of the 'hunger-artist'.

Once again the humour is noticeable – the refusal of some laymen, set to watch the starver, to adhere strictly to the rules, and his frustration at their generosity, or the affable complaisance of the foreman. But once again, the allegory doesn't quite work in all respects. Hungering after righteousness, it soon appears, is not what the starver is doing at all: righteousness never comes into the matter, and if it did, it would be an insincere man who paraded *that* hunger for people's admiration, as the starver does. Hungering, as the story goes on to relate, is 'the easiest thing in the world', and that could not be said of the Biblical beatitude.

Kafka quite often speaks of 'food' as the object for which his characters are looking, and it is the absence of food of the proper kind that drives the starver to his extreme lengths. As he explains towards the end, it is simply because he could not find the kind of food he fancied that he went on starving in the midst of plenty. Had he found any, he would have fed to the full like all the rest. Nowhere does the starver explain what is wrong with

ordinary food – it is entirely a matter of taste. There is no right
or wrong here, no righteousness or unrighteousness, no turning
away from men's evil ways, such as a Biblical prophet might
have made. The starver simply does not take to what the rest
take to, and his reasons must remain as much a mystery to us as
to them.

The mysteriousness of the starving is something of a disappointment. Granted that hungering has certain overtones in
itself, it is frustrating to discover that the starver's motives are
almost arbitrary, or compulsive – it takes away from the
generalised application that the story seemed about to be given.
Is it hungering from such motives, or lack of motives, as these,
that has gone out of fashion? When? and where? one wants to
ask. When was this taste so prevalent and so unaccountable?
In the religions of renunciation there have always been particular
perceptions of human viciousness, and it has been a turning
away from this that the ascetic has practised. Kafka's starver has
no comparable stature, or any such general relevance, as the
traditional deniers of the world.

It is true that the starver makes some spiritual progress, in
that, at his dying moment, he is no longer proud of his achievement. 'Those were his last words, but in his failing eyes there
was still the firm, if no longer proud conviction that he was
going on hungering.' But lack of pride in such an achievement
is not one of the greatest triumphs of virtue. Again, it seems that,
just as Gregor Samsa and Georg Bendemann die thinking
affectionately of their families, so the starver learns to love by
the end. At any rate, he makes a gesture of love when he speaks
'with lips shaped as though for a kiss straight into the foreman's
ear, so that nothing should be lost'. But even this is sceptically
reduced to a minimum: it is only the necessary physical shaping
of the lips that makes it appear that the starver is offering a kiss,
and there is no suggestion of any inward mood in him that
would have made it almost an intentional gesture. On the other
hand, by observing the moment, Kafka seems to invite a feeling
that love has now entered the starver's life, even if only at the
last instant.

Finally, the story takes a turn like that at the end of 'The Metamorphosis'. Both the starver and Gregor Samsa are swept away after they die; in Gregor's story there is a return to life as his sister stretches her body; in 'A Hunger-Artist' the starver's place in the circus-cage is taken by the panther, who plays, thematically, a similar though not identical part with the part played by the sister. The starver's ascetic denial of life is replaced almost too symmetrically with the 'affirmation' of the panther. Kafka has some difficulty with the beast, it is true, mainly on account of the fact that it has to stay in a cage. There is none of the leaden dullness of Rilke's panther here, though at one point it seems that there well might be:

> Nur manchmal schiebt der Vorhang der Pupille
> Sich lautlos auf – dann geht ein Bild hinein,
> Geht durch der Glieder angespannte Stille
> und hört im Herzen auf zu sein.

Only now and then the curtain of the pupil pushes itself silently up. Then an image enters, travels though the tense silence of the limbs, and, in the heart, ceases once for all to be.

Surely the panther would be dissatisfied with its captivity? Kafka tries to meet the point, but not really successfully:

He lacked nothing. The keepers brought him the kind of food he liked without much thinking about it; he did not even seem to miss his freedom. This noble body, equipped almost to bursting point with all it needed, seemed to carry its own freedom around with it; it seemed to be somewhere in its teeth.

The last words quoted seem to mean that the panther is free to eat cheerfully any creatures that may fall in its way, free to be dangerous and uncontrollable. This is a merely anarchic freedom, not a serious alternative to the starver. Indeed the contrast seems to be between a meaningless asceticism and a pure savagery. The extremes are too polarised. Kafka seems once again, as in 'First Sorrow', though with more sympathy for his *alter ego* than in that story, to have dismissed the *alter ego* too abruptly, to have scorned his own pretensions in favour of what he shortly after calls 'joy in life', without taking a full look at both. The panther is treated with some irony, certainly. But the transition from the denier to the affirmer has a categorising sharpness about it that suggests too much determination in Kafka to demonstrate his dissatisfaction with his own condition. The subtleties of the ending of 'The Metamorphosis' would be overwhelmed by the comparatively blatant note of 'A Hunger-Artist'. And the genuinely observed people who filled the earlier story have yielded to grotesques and caricatures. In his struggle to maintain himself in a mental state as bad as any that can be imagined this side of insanity, Kafka had had to yield on many fronts.

Apart from these published stories there are thirty-two short pieces in the posthumous works from the period after 1915, most of them only a page or two long, but including among the later items the longer stories 'The Village Schoolmaster' (or 'The Giant Mole'), 'Blumfeld, an Elderly Bachelor', 'Building the Great Wall of China', 'Investigations of a Dog', and 'The Burrow'. All of these except 'Investigations of a Dog' are unfinished. Twenty-five of the thirty-two were written between 1915 and 1920, so that Kafka had ample opportunity of completing and including most of the pieces in his published collection if he had wished to do so.

Most of the longer pieces suffer from Kafka's exhaustion, as the later published stories do, being marked by the same compulsive style as 'Josephine'. 'The Burrow' is perhaps an indeterminate effort to review the whole of his creative work, by way of allegory,[4] while some phrases indicate it is probably also meant to represent Kafka's own body, undermined with tuberculosis, and threatened by the hissing sound which is, though it does not know it, its approaching death. The sound is also linked with other ideas of sound in Kafka's work – the story 'A Great Noise' comes to mind here, as well as Kafka's privately expressed belief that the overwhelming noise which sometimes assailed him was a prelude to the liberation of a great harmony. Whether the story included such a liberation is not known:

there is good reason to believe that it was completed, but the ending is now lost, or destroyed, and the manuscript breaks off in mid-sentence at the foot of a page.

The idea has been put forward that 'The Burrow' derives from Dostoevsky's *Letters from the Underworld*, and there is no occasion to dispute that, in general terms. Much more immediately relevant, however, is *Robinson Crusoe*, which Kafka refers to more than once in his final years, and which affords very close parallels in the episode where Crusoe flees to a cave after seeing a naked footprint on the beach. Crusoe's fear of the unknown maker of this footprint put him in a state of fear very much like that of Kafka's animal: he thinks of destroying all the civilised arrangements he has made, makes another wall outside his first wall, and sets osiers in the ground outside that, till his habitation is completely concealed. All this corresponds to the frenetic attempts of the animal to secure its safety in the burrow against the constantly approaching threat. Again like the animal, Crusoe is possessed with vindictive savagery, when he finds remains of a cannibal feast and revels in the thought of slaughtering the cannibals from ambush. Kafka could well have felt an echo responding from his own experience when Crusoe reflects on his lot: 'I, whose only affliction was that I seemed banished from human society, that I was alone, circumscribed by the boundless ocean, cut off from mankind, and condemned to what I called silent life; that I was as one whom Heaven thought not worthy to be numbered among the living, or to appear among the rest of his creatures.' But where Kafka makes the meaning clearly refer to his own inward condition, mental and physical, Crusoe is possessed with equally fantastic fears of an outwardly real enemy. And where Kafka's animal is constantly driven from one expedient to another, Crusoe masters his fears by rational reflection, as well as by his more and more elaborate protective measures: he persuades himself not to ambush the cannibals, reflecting that the custom of theirs which revolts him is no crime to them, and that he cannot tell how God judges their case; moreover, they have not attacked him yet. In his resilience and self-mastery he differs widely from the animal.

Defoe's prose, too, is, though as unadorned as Kafka's, without his repetitiveness. New devices continually crowd into Crusoe's mind, and his practical skill provides him with many comforts. As Malcolm Pasley says of Kafka's story, on the other hand, it 'exhibits in extreme form the chief characteristic – and perhaps the weakness – of Kafka's last works: the endless play with possibilities, the "mühselige Rechnungen" ["toilsome calculations"], the tireless building and demolishing of hypotheses'.[5] Yet Crusoe's concern is not only practical: the whole of his isolation is seen by him as much in the light of a moral and spiritual test as Kafka's.

'Investigations of a Dog' is an allegory needing little comment. The dog speculates on the way it receives its food, in much the same way as human beings speculate about their religious nourishment. As in 'A Report for an Academy', the situation is much clearer from the human point of view, so long as the comparison is made merely with the animal. As soon as the human being reflects on his own situation, however, he must see that an angelic or divine figure might regard him in the same light.

The remainder of the stories written in or after 1917 are very short, being for a large part either sketches for the larger work *Building the Great Wall of China* (apart from the story so entitled, also 'The City Coat of Arms', 'The Rejection' (but not the piece with the same title included in *Meditation*), 'The Problem of our Laws', and 'The Conscription' belong to this) or simple, clear statements of a few lines like 'Prometheus', 'The Vulture', 'A little Fable', and 'Give it up!' The most telling are perhaps those in which Kafka is thinly disguising his own condition, and especially one entitled 'The Truth about Sancho Panza', for it is one pole of Kafka's attitude to his own work that is reflected here:

Sancho Panza, who never made any fuss about it, succeeded over the years, by accumulating a large number of novels about knights and robbers, in diverting during the evening and the night [Kafka's normal hours for writing] his devil, to whom he later gave the name of Don Quixote, so well, that the latter then uninhibitedly performed the craziest deeds, though these, in the absence of any particular object, which ought in fact to have been Sancho Panza, did no harm to anybody. Sancho Panza, a free man, followed Don Quixote on his expeditions good-temperedly, perhaps out of a certain sense of responsibility, and derived a great deal of useful entertainment from it to his life's end.

The Kafka who preserved an external composure, who fell in love several times over, and who was from time to time able to direct his work where he wanted it to go, is the subject of those few lines. Yet this was a Kafka who could only fitfully maintain himself. With the great weight of his spirit he was sunk with the huntsman Gracchus, the dead man who appears on his bier to the mayor of Riva, the lakeside resort in Northern Italy which Kafka knew from his holidays (the word 'gracchio', it has been pointed out by Wagenbach, is Italian for 'chough', or 'daw', and is thus related to the Czech 'Kavka', used for the same bird). It is a proper way to end this account with Gracchus' own words, affording as they do the constant and outbalancing counterweight to Sancho Panza's contentment. Memories of the officer in the penal colony, still as he was in life, but transfixed with the spike, must come to mind here.

'Are you dead?'
'Yes', said the huntsman. 'As you see. Many years ago, but it must have been a great many years ago, I fell off a rock in the Black Forest – that's in Germany – while I was chasing a chamois. Since then I have been dead.'
'But you are alive, too', said the mayor.
'To a certain extent', said the huntsman. 'To a certain extent I am alive too. My ship of death missed its turn, the rudder was turned the wrong way, the steersman had a moment's inattention, we made a détour through my beautiful homeland, I don't know what it was, I only know I stayed on earth, and that since then my ship has sailed earthly waters. So I, who only wished to live among my mountains, now after my death journey through all the countries on earth.'
'And you have no part in the other world?', asked the mayor, frowning.
'I am always', said the huntsman, 'on the great staircase, ascending. On this infinitely wide staircase I cast about, now up, now down, now

to the right, now to the left, always on the move. The huntsman has turned into a butterfly, Don't laugh.' 'I am not laughing', protested the mayor.

The final words of the story are the most telling of all. What call could a man like this feel, to publish his story? If he thought of publishing it at all, it could only be because the story did not after all represent the whole truth about him:

'Nobody will read what I am writing here, nobody will come to help me; even if the duty of helping me were to be imposed on people, every door of every house would stay shut, every window shut, everybody would lie in bed with the clothes over his head, the whole earth a night-time hostelry . . . The idea of wanting to help me is a sickness and must be cured in bed.

I know that, and so I don't cry out to get help, even though at times – uncontrolled as I am, for instance, at this very instant – I think very much of doing so. But it is sufficient to drive such thoughts away if I simply look round and make myself aware where I am, and – I may say, I think – have been for centuries.'

'Extraordinary', said the mayor, 'extraordinary. And now you are thinking of staying with us in Riva?'

'I am thinking of nothing in particular', said the huntsman, smiling, and laying his hand on the mayor's knee to atone for the mockery. 'I am here, more than that I do not know, more than that I cannot do. My ship is without a rudder, it is running before the wind that blows in the lowest regions of death.'*

But though the final words of that piece were not the whole truth about Kafka at that time, they were close to it. Nothing he wrote conveys the dominant mood near the end of his life as that does.

---

* Conrad knew this mood, and used a similar image throughout *The Nigger of the 'Narcissus'*, though that story records a triumph over despair.

11

RELIGIOUS IDEAS

Friedrich Beissner takes the view that what Kafka says by means of his stories is never actually said, but is suggested, as the obverse of the words used, or as the unexpressed silence hovering in the background.[1] Martin Buber holds that Kafka's attack on divine providence, if that is what it is rightly to be called, is made from within the certainty of the unity of Israel, by virtue of which nothing whatsoever can detract from God's splendour:

If the whole world should tear the garment of His honour into rags, nothing would be done to Him. Which law could presume to demand anything from Him? – surely the highest conceivable law is that which is given by Him to the world, not to Himself: He does not bind Himself and therefore nothing binds Him.[2]

Kafka, Buber believes, was writing within this tradition, ready to say anything that might seem blasphemous, so long as it was true, in the certainty that 'from the darkness of heaven the dark ray comes actively into the heart'. 'Paradise is still there', Buber continues, and 'that means it is also here where the dark ray meets the tormented heart.'

These are mystical views, not relying on anything actually to be found in Kafka's writings, but on an independent and irrefutable conviction – irrefutable, since nothing could ever by any means refute it, but not valuable or meaningful on that account, since nothing could demonstrate it either.

On the other hand Max Brod maintains that, while the novels and stories show men as having lost contact with 'the Indestructible', the religious thought of Kafka shows him as recognising that metaphysical kernel of the world. Kafka, writes Brod, is 'a religious hero of the rank of a prophet who wrestles for his faith against a thousand temptations, yet is essentially certain of heaven and of the transcendental'. While these two currents in Kafka occasionally flow together, at other times they are poles apart, Brod holds, and yet Kafka can never be understood unless both currents in him are recognised and taken account of.[3] It has been part of Brod's purpose all along to stress the 'positive' aspects of Kafka over against the 'negative' aspects which Kafka's detractors, in Brod's view, made too much of. The religious thought is thus a means towards opposing the kind of irrational view put forward by Buber: here is the positive Kafka, Brod claims, not in some mystical paradox, but in his own unmistakable words.

Kafka's own beliefs are not necessarily shown in his fictional works at all, though his trend of thought is. His habitual self-distancing is shown by the title of the collection, 'He'. In his many aphorisms, however, those scattered throughout his diaries and those assembled under the heading 'Meditations [or: Reflections] on Sin, Suffering, Hope and the True Path', there is an opportunity to compare one's interpretation with ideas or beliefs which Kafka was inclined to entertain. None of them can be taken as definite expressions of faith, since Kafka habitually tried ideas out; the assembly of Meditations was selected from passages apparently written in 1917 and 1918, written out in a fair copy, and numbered, but then not finally approved in every respect, since some of them (marked in the posthumously published edition with an asterisk), were scored through in pencil, as though meant to be excluded, revised, or rearranged. Since none were published anyway, it would be pedantic to insist on these small signs of hesitation, or to concentrate only on the selected aphorisms. All that can be gleaned is the tenor of Kafka's reflections.

There is no system underlying all the passages, though there is a certain coherence between a large number, a complex and sometimes a paradoxical coherence almost amounting to a system. One idea constantly reiterated is that good and evil, truth and deceit or falsehood are divided by a sharp line, as clean-cut as that between the physical and the metaphysical world. In itself, this is an idea which Kafka could have found in Goethe, whom he greatly admired. The 'Prologue in Heaven' of Goethe's *Faust* presents just such a world, where the earth is subjected to the dialectical change and the dichotomy of creation and destruction, while the Lord sits aloof in splendour. As Kafka develops this idea, however, it takes on colours Goethe never dreamed of. If the real, the essential, the 'noumenal' world is cut off from the world of our ordinary experience, the world of phenomena, – a position Kant would have denied, pointing to the categorical imperative of the conscience as conferring awareness of the noumenal, and which Goethe would have refuted with his conviction that the whole of the real world is a manifestation of the divine, an 'open secret' conveyed in a form accessible to human perception – then the human situation is completely undependable: 'Truth', as Kafka writes, 'is one and indivisible; anyone who pretends to recognize it must be a lie (Lüge).' Kafka's premise here is derived from an idea like the so-called *principium individuationis*, frequently met with in German thought. Since men are separate from one another, and less than the whole in which they live, they must always be partial, and become presumptuous when they attempt to speak truth in an absolute sense. This is, of course, assuming that absolute truth, in a metaphysical sense, is what men do believe they are expressing when they 'speak the truth', which some philosophers would regard as a mistaken notion. But Kafka is thinking on the same lines when he writes 'Everything is deceit' (no. 55) and 'Can you know anything but deceit?' (no. 106). The view of the world here is akin to that of the officer in 'In the Penal Colony', when he declares that guilt is beyond doubt. If truth is out of reach, so far as men are concerned, so too is innocence, and all are always guilty. That is not to say that the gulf between the two sides precludes any relationship at all. 'Evil', reads another aphorism, 'knows of good, but good does not know of evil.' Thus one might imagine that an evil creature might go on recognising the evil in itself simply by virtue of the fact that it knew of good as a contrast to its own state, and similarly Kafka could see his own recriminations against himself as part of this process. If ever he achieved direct knowledge of good, however, he would cease to know evil. The difficulty here lies in saying whether the hitherto existent evil at such a moment of achievement becomes good, or is merely recognised as a subjective and mistaken impression. The danger would be that after all the efforts made, the *status quo ante* would be accepted, on grounds like 'whatever is, is right'. In Kierkegaard the ultimate state of one who has passed through 'infinite resignation' is indistinguishable in every respect from the state of those who have never begun any spiritual pilgrimage.[4] That Kafka was tempted to think in these terms is shown by the quotation from Flaubert he is said by Max Brod to have murmured on seeing a bourgeois family contentedly enjoying itself: 'ils sont dans le vrai,' ('they are living in the truth'). If he meant by this that lack of self-awareness is innocent, he might have been merely sentimental, projecting onto the bourgeois what he could not find in himself. But this is leaping some steps in the argument, introducing a little early the paradox that, despite the gulf between man and God, the condition of the most godlike can be outwardly indistinguishable from all others, and perhaps totally indistinguishable (if the others are in fact 'dans le vrai').

Kafka returns to the idea of a deep cleavage in his speculations on the creation of the world. Here it becomes apparent that no amount of self-examination and recognition of guilt can ever lead to the moment when self vanishes, and the vision of good takes its place. 'The world can only be regarded as good from the place at which it was created, for there alone was it said, 'Behold, it was good' – and only from there can he world be judged and destroyed.'[5] This would seem to remove all possibility of discrimination out of human power. But to understand Kafka better, it has to be seen that for the Creator to pronounce the world good is not an act of discrimination, since it is made in a mind which knows nothing of evil, and so approves without distinction. In Kafka's cosmos, knowledge of good and evil is a possession acquired by human beings, as the Bible says, at the Fall from Paradise. By virtue of the Fall, men have become essentially equal to one another in this kind of knowledge: each knows what is good, each knows what is evil, but each is convinced that his own knowledge is greater than others, and 'we seek precisely in this [knowledge] our own advantage' (no. 86). In other words, each imagines he has the basis for becoming as God, in fulfilment of the serpent's promise 'ye shall be as gods', and this is what Kafka calls the 'comfortless horizon of the evil man', for the evil man 'believes he sees his godlikeness in the very recognition of good and evil',[6] whereas in reality they are enough to destroy him. Thus man goes on to falsify even his knowledge of good and evil, taking the knowledge itself for the goal, whereas the real differences begin beyond this knowledge, in the sphere of faith. Where faith exists, there is no longer any concern with evil, which has vanished from consciousness, but faith is not reached by any amount of increase in knowledge.

The episode of the Whipper in *The Trial* seems to be related to these ideas of good and evil. Wrong has been done to K., in his view, and he complains of it to the Court at his first interrogation. As a result, though not in accordance with any expressed wish of his, the warders are flogged – and everlastingly flogged, it appears, since they are still there whenever he opens the cupboard. Within the world, the desire for justice inspires injustice, and K. is showing his all-too-human concern by objecting to the injustice of the trial at all. Yet when he sees the flogging he is indifferent, at least as regards the suffering of the warders, and is anxious only that the whole affair should be kept quiet. This is a mean kind of acquiescence: were K. more advanced in the direction of Kafka's own thought he might display a total indifference not only to the flogging, but to the question of its being publicly known.

The most characteristic utterance of Kafka's and the one which links him most closely with the *poètes maudits*, is about the issue of 'succumbing' to evil. Here the centre of the debate on the value of his thought must lie, for in arguing that men go astray by considering questions of good and evil, Kafka lays bare the roots of his own passive acquiescence. 'One of the most effective means of temptation that Evil possesses', he writes, 'is the challenge to struggle against it. This is like struggling with women and ending up in bed with them.' There need be no such struggle, he implies, unless one chooses to fall for the temptation. Alternatively, one need make no struggle in the first place, simply allowing evil its own way. As Oscar Wilde said, the best way to overcome a temptation is to succumb to it – but Kafka does not take so blasé a view of human pleasures. 'There are surprises in Evil,' he writes. 'Suddenly it will turn round and say, "You have misunderstood me", and perhaps it really is so. Evil transforms itself into your own lips, lets your own teeth rub against it, and with these new lips – none that you had before ever sat so snugly against your gums – to your own astonishment you pronounce the good word.'[7] This sounds too automatic to be true. If Kafka had decided to publish it, he might have considered guarding against misinterpretation along the lines of such distantly related disciples of the marquis de Sade as Artaud and Genet. Certainly, so far as his own fiction is concerned, there is never any question of his central characters inflicting evil in the belief that it will enable good to happen, unless perhaps it is the officer in the penal colony (but he has no use for good). Kafka's heroes are, rather, passive in enduring the evil inflicted by others. Still, in so far as Kafka believed that such evil as that could be a prolonged prologue to a self-transformation, it is a clue to why he allowed the last chapter in *The Trial* to push forward to its gruesome ending. Only in the closing pages of *The Castle*, in fact, when K. achieves some degree of real self-awareness, does anything like a good word emerge in his fictional work, and on the whole one would say that that work, in its failure to produce what he expected of it, is a refutation of his paradox.

There is, however, no coherence between the aphorisms. If at times Kafka believes in the miraculous metamorphosis of evil into good, at others he insists that there can be no metamorphosis, that to look for any is to go against the notion of infinite suffering and infinite endurance. If one of his definitions of faith is the ultimate expectation of a change, another is the firm persuasion that no change can take place and that this is all part of the life to be accepted. 'How much more oppressive it is', reads another aphorism, 'than even the most thoroughgoing conviction of our present sinful state, to have even the faintest conviction that our life in time will eventually be justified in eternity' (no. 99). This sounds as though it might have been inspired by Ivan

Karamazov, in his refusal to believe that anything can ever happen in eternity to atone for all the crimes of humanity, to make it possible not only to forgive but to justify all that has happened in human history. Unlike Dostoevsky's character, however, Kafka goes on: 'Faith can only be measured by the strength with which this second conviction, which in its pure form completely includes the other one, is borne.' That is to say, faith is a matter of being persuaded that the sins committed on this earth will not be forgotten, or redeemed, or purged away, but simply justified as they are. For this thought seems to be allied to others in which Kafka speaks of the notion that the present human condition may be not different from the supposedly original state of primal bliss, but may be identical with it: 'If what is supposed to have been destroyed in Paradise was destructible, then we are living in a false belief' no. 74). This seems to mean that the state of Adam and Eve before the Fall, to have been really blissful, must have been eternal, so that if we believe it was destroyed, we are wrong, and their state is still with us. Indeed, as other aphorisms imply, it is the mark of our fallen condition that we are not aware of this paradise within us, as Ivan Karamazov was not aware, or as Kafka was not aware when he heard the woman speaking so serenely of taking tea in the garden. Kafka would not deny that the expulsion from the Garden was eternal, and therefore final, but regarded it as an act eternally repeated at every moment, so that it was still possible, as he put it, 'that we not only might be able to remain in Paradise, but actually are permanently there, whether we recognize it or not' (no. 64/5). This is the reverse of the thought that faith might be shown by constancy in believing that this present life is justified in eternity. By thinking of the Fall and the state preceding it as eternally present, Kafka eternises the here and now in a permanent ambiguity. On such terms as these, where paradise and hell are conceived as possibly indistinguishable (this is the implied sense also of Leverkühn's music in *Doktor Faustus*), no escape is ever possible: escape is acceptance.

'The Good is in a certain sense comfortless' (no. 30). With those words Kafka introduces the idea implicit in the whole story of the penal colony, that there is, for the modern man, no way out. The prisoners on the machine in former days were rewarded at least by their transfiguration, as they read the law they had unknowingly broken, before being cast into the pit. In the days the story tells of there is not even transfiguration, and the officer remains transfixed, his face as it was in life. There is no relief from suffering: 'You can hold back from the sufferings of the world, that is left open to you and agrees with your nature, but perhaps this very holding back is the one suffering you could avoid' (no. 103). On the other hand, the paradoxical nature of Kafka's ideas does not permit any straightforward interpretation. The essential point is, perhaps, that there never is any glorious rebirth. 'Only here', he says of this world, 'is suffering suffering. This is not to say that those who suffer here will be raised up elsewhere on account of this suffering, but that what in this world is called suffering, in another world, where it remains unchanged, and is merely freed from its opposite, is bliss' (no. 97). By 'freed from its opposite', Kafka may mean 'freed from any conception that a world of happiness or liberation from suffering could possibly exist'. In these circumstances, presumably, Joseph K.'s final words 'like a dog' ring on into the future life, in which Kafka seems to have believed very strongly. 'It was as though he meant the shame of it to outlive him', the final words of the novel itself, could then imply that in the next world K. enters the bliss of suffering pure and simple. It sounds like a hell in which no hope exists.

Seeing no possible way out from the condition he found himself in, Kafka seems to have opted for the paradox of identifying it with the best possible condition. The result is always – except when he finds some totally different, unparadoxical solution – to render him more and more passive. Where there is no distinguishing between opposites, there is no virtue in anything: 'Anyone who loves his neighbour within the world does no more and no less wrong than one who loves himself within the world. The only question is, whether the former is possible' (no. 61). This is one of the aphorisms crossed through in pencil, but its derivation from Kafka's usual cosmology is visible, in that 'loving within the world' is of no particular account (the possibility of it being good is not mentioned) in comparison with the other world. Love is a virtue only of the other world, and only within that sphere is the love of others a real possibility. 'Anyone who renounces the world must love all men, for he is renouncing their world too. He therefore begins to have a glimpse of the true essence of humanity, which cannot be other than loved, provided one is on a level footing with it'(no. 60). If this particularly difficult aphorism is to be elucidated, it perhaps means that by renouncing the world, entering the essence of things, one comes to see the essence of humanity also, and 'must love' all men in this sense. But such love is only possible if one is on equal terms (*ebenbürtig* – literally 'of equal birth') with that essence. In short, only when self and other selves are abstracted from the bric-à-brac of individual personalities is it possible for love to exist between the two.

Kafka's fiction says nothing of this, since a novel cannot deal with essences. That is why there is only frustration and ultimately condemnation of the individual, whether innocent or guilty, as he said of the two heroes of *America* and *The Trial*. The novel can only deal with individual events and destinies, it can only remain within the world. The beliefs here outlined cannot be expressed by it, though it is necessary, to gain the whole picture of what Kafka intended, and of the spirit in which he wrote them, to take account of these beliefs.

They amount in fact to the old 'German inwardness', which many Germans have lamented often enough: the belief of Luther that the externals did not matter, that political allegiances were indifferent, so long as the inward man had faith and was saved; the belief of Kant, that every conceivable intellectual experiment was open to men, so long as they did not allow it to influence their social and political conduct; the belief reiterated by philosophers and artists with a wide range of general views, that this world is divorced from the only world that matters, the metaphysical one, and that on that account the externals can be neglected.

That Martin Buber is right in his view of Kafka's beliefs

(though not necessarily on the score of their being representative of Judaism) is shown by an aphorism, from which I omit a final sentence not relevant to this point, in which Kafka is willing to speak not only of a sphere beyond human knowledge, but of the trust in this sphere being similarly beyond anything man can know: 'Man cannot live without a permanent trust in something indestructible within himself, though both that indestructible something and his own trust in it may remain permanently concealed from him' (no. 50). This is literally saying that a man may not put any trust in the Indestructible, yet this absence of trust is trust all the same. Here Kafka takes a step further towards the total paradox where, as in the figure in his 'A Wish to Be a Red Indian', the final strut is kicked away, the last vestige of a reality is removed, and the essence itself revealed. Even the man who lives his life in suffering, who lets evil sit snugly against his gums, guiding his speech, who has no trust, is in eternity blissful, good, and trustful, without any detectable change in the original condition. 'The Indestructible', Kafka writes, 'is one; it is every individual man, and at the same time it is common to all, and this is the reason for the unparalleled, inseparable union of mankind' (no.70/71). This paradisal state is beyond all cognizance, one can only 'be' it, but in this 'being' one shares in the whole human essence. Punning on the word 'sein' in German, Kafka remarks that it means both 'to be', and 'to belong to Him'; in short true being is here associated with a unity not so much with all men (though with them, too) as with a personal God, as though he and the Indestructible were one and the same.

Throughout these thoughts must remain the unhappy reminder that there is nothing for the individual but progressive acceptance of annihilation, even of evil. 'One must cheat no-one of anything, not even the world of its victory.' That can only be said from a position within a secure citadel, where such a victory is of no consequence. Nothing that happens within the world is ultimately of significance: the repercussions of all actions reverberate infinitely, without meaning. 'Christ suffered for mankind, but mankind must suffer for Christ,'[8] that is to say, Christ's life was not the redemption of mankind; it was a suffering which in the course of history produced further suffering, and must do so, being within the bounds of space and time. The Crucifixion generates an infinity of crucifixions, just as loving one's neighbour (if it is possible at all) is to be seen as generating as much wrong as loving one's own self.

Kafka sometimes seems not to adhere to these paradoxes and mystical assertions. There are times when he seems to speak in more accustomed language of enduring suffering until relief comes, of holding on in the face of defeat until victory is granted. On closer inspection, this is seen not to be the case, as in such an aphorism as this:

A first sign of enlightenment beginning is the wish to die. This life seems unbearable, another life unattainable. One is no longer ashamed to die; one begs to be taken out of the old cell, which one hates, into another which one will come to hate later on. During all this, a trace of the belief is still present, that during the transfer the Lord will come along the corridor, look at the prisoner and say 'This man is not to be imprisoned again. He is to come to me.' (no. 13)

If at first sight that appears to be cast in more or less conventional terms, the irony in it has not been observed, The man who still holds such a belief shows that he has not advanced far beyond the beginning he has just reached, that of wishing to die. The total acceptance of death, which Joseph K. is able to make, will at least save him from any such expectation of preferential treatment.

At yet other times, the whole basis of Kafka's endurance seems undermined, as when he writes in his diary in terms that reject all that normally gives him a paradoxical comfort:

The Negative alone, however strong it may be, cannot suffice as I believe it can in my unhappiest periods. For when I have mounted the smallest step and am in some sort of security, however dubious, I stretch myself out and wait – not for the Negative to step up and join me, but for it to pull me down again. So it is a defensive instinct, that does not tolerate the provision of the smallest lasting comfort for me, and, for instance, smashes the marriage-bed before it has even been set up.[9]

197

There Kafka seems to show the clearest insight into the self-defeating nature of his beliefs (once again with their sexual implications) – though what he would have done, how he would have escaped suicide, if he had not had such paradoxes to fall back on, is hard to say. But then a closer reading of the passage shows that it may have been meant not as a rejection of 'the Negative', but as one more act of acquiescence in it. Not wanting anything to 'suffice', not wanting comfort or marriage, Kafka could see in it even a kind of defence of the really negative element deeper down.

Nothing approaching such views as these is ever expressed in any of the fictional work, published or unpublished, until a late work like *The Castle*, or an even later one like 'A Hunger-Artist'. The reference to the children's voices as the only dependable source of contact with the Castle is clearly a hint at the remote and absurd nature of any contact with the Indestructible, since the voices are of no conceivable help to K. Similarly, the progressive abstraction of meaning from the hunger-artist's performance, the way in which it is shown to be unmeritorious, and the absence even of love in the lips of the artist 'shaped as though for a kiss', are conceived in the same spirit of stripping all value from the events of this world. On the other hand, although these two are late works, it is clear that Kafka's mind was running on these lines as early as the 'Wish to Be a Red Indian' – the evanescence of the individual is a theme almost from the start.

My argument has been directed, however, not to the truth or desirability of Kafka's religious beliefs in themselves. The issues involved in them would need a discussion of both Christianity and Judaism, and the purely self-destroying religions of the Far East, into which I am not competent to enter. What concerns me is Kafka's achievement as a writer of fiction, and the case has been that he was at his best, in that respect, in the story in which he most completely recognised his own condition and mastered it for art not by dwelling on it, but by taking it as one *donnée* of his whole tale, and exploring the situation that then arose. 'The Metamorphosis' has no overt metaphysical claims or overtones, and can have them only by importation, by accepting (for reasons outside the present debate) the principles of Kafka's thought as revealed separately from the stories. On the other hand, the other stories show increasing signs of artistic deterioration as the claim to metaphysical significance becomes greater. The writing in Kafka's early stories is vivid and subtle in a way that the later stories reveal only patchily, and the early ones have very little of the compulsive writing to which I have drawn attention. The art shows more signs of uncontrolled neurosis in the last six or seven years of Kafka's life than it does in the preceding years, which is not to say that the greater ambitiousness of the later works, especially *The Castle*, is of no consequence.

Surveying Kafka's writing as a whole, one is, I believe, forced to conclude that the one thing he was able to fashion so that it will always stand was the account of his own degradation, projected into fiction. Nothing more than that degradation is visible in the fictional work: we are not shown and cannot be shown how the degradation is bliss in another world, we are only shown that it happens. But having experienced the degradation intensely, both as a man and as a writer, Kafka did not do what other generations have done, and turn to new things, in a hope of re-emerging. He went on to intensify the realisation, and as he intensified it, he increased the chances that he would not be able to write, since he was left more and more in the grip of a debilitating self-laceration. At no point could he really claim, though he did in effect claim it, that he was beyond the infinite point of resignation: the infinite point could never be reached, only the increasingly loose hold on life could manifest itself, and did manifest itself in his fiction. The evidence of the fiction is that the beliefs did not spark off the kind of work which would confirm them.

NOTES TO THE TEXT*

1. Kafka the Writer, pp. 1–28

1 Max Brod, Afterword to the first German edition of *The Castle*.
2 W. H. Auden, as quoted in *Franz Kafka Today* (edd. Flores and Swander), p. 1.
3 Paul Claudel, *Le Figaro Littéraire*, 18 Oct. 1947.
4 Thomas Mann, quoted in *Franz Kafka* by Klaus Wagenbach, Rowohlt, Hamburg 1964, p. 144.
5 André Gide, quoted in *Franz Kafka et les lettres françaises 1928–1955* by Maja Goth, Paris 1956, p. 43.
6 Maja Goth, *op. cit.* p. 253.
7 F. Beissner, *Kafka der Dichter*, Stuttgart 1958, p. 8.
8 Beissner, *ibid.* p. 8.
9 H. Politzer, 'Problematik und Probleme der Kafka-Forschung', in *Monatshefte für deutschen Unterricht, deutsche Sprache und Literatur*, Madison, Wisconsin, 42 (1950), 273–80.
10 Max Brod, *Franz Kafka, eine Biographie*, 1954, p. 160.
11 See p. 32 below.
12 Brod, *Biographie*, 1954, p. 160.
13 *Saturday Review*, 12 April 1930.
14 *Times Literary Supplement*, 19 June 1930.
15 *New Statesman*, 12 April 1930.
16 *Saturday Review*, 12 April 1930.
17 *Life and Letters*, Dec. 1930.
18 Félix Bertaux, *A Panorama of German Literature*, New York 1935.
19 Kurt Tucholsky, *Gesammelte Werke*, Hamburg 1960, II, 372–6.
20 *Times Literary Supplement*, 11 May 1933.
21 *Ibid.* 3 July 1937.
22 *Ibid.* 8 Oct. 1938.
23 *Ibid.* 16 June 1945.
24 *Ibid.* 13 Nov. 1948 and 29 July 1949.
25 See further Dieter Jakob, 'Das Kafka-Bild in England. Zur Aufnahme des Werkes in der journalistischen Kritik 1928–1966', in *Oxford German Studies*, vol. 5, 1971.

* References to Kafka's works are to the pagination in the *Gesammelte Schriften*.

26 'Faut-il brûler Kafka?' in *Action*, no. 90, 24 May 1946; also replies in later issues up to no. 100.

27 Erich Heller, *The Disinherited Mind*, Bowes, Cambridge 1952, p. 160.

28 Günther Anders, *Franz Kafka*, translated and adapted by A. Steer and A. K. Thorlby, London 1960, p. 99. Originally *Kafka, pro und conta. Die Prozeß-Unterlagen*, Munich 1951.

29 Edmund Wilson, *Classics and Commercials*, 1950, reprinted in *Franz Kafka. A Collection of Critical Essays*, ed. R. Gray, Englewood Cliffs, N.J. 1962 (p. 96).

30 Hannah Arendt, 'Franz Kafka: A Revaluation', in *Partisan Review*, 1944, p. 416.

31 See p. 1 above.

32 Arendt, *op. cit.* p. 412.

33 *Times Literary Supplement*, 24 May 1947.

34 R. O. C. Winkler, in *Scrutiny*, VII, 357–8.

35 See W. Sansom, *Fireman Flower*, Hogarth Press, London 1944.

2. *Towards Understanding, pp. 29–47*

1 Diary, 19 Jan. 1911.

2 Thomas Mann, *Doktor Faustus*, Stockholm 1947, p. 382.

3 Diary, 21 July 1913.

4 *Briefe an Milena*, p. 208.

5 Diary, 6 Aug. 1914.

6 Diary, 27 Apr. 1915.

7 Diary, 24 Jan. 1922.

8 Diary, 4 May 1915.

9 *Erzählungen*, pp. 17–18.

10 *Beschreibung eines Kampfes*, p. 183.

11 Diary, 27 May 1914.

12 Diary, 18 Jan. 1922.

13 Diary.

14 Diary for 1911 (not precisely dated: *Tagebücher 1910–1923* in *Ges. Werke* 1948, p. 185).

15 Diary, 21 June 1913.

16 Diary, 27 Nov. 1913.

17 Diary, 25 Sept. 1917.

18 Gustav Janouch, *Gespräche mit Kafka*, Frankfurt a. M. 1951, p. 32.

19 *Hochzeitsvorbereitungen*, p. 202.

20 *Ibid.* p. 204.

21 *Ibid.* p. 193.

22 Diary, 20 July 1916.

23 Diary, 2 Aug. 1917.

24 Kierkegaard, *The Concept of Dread*, trans. W. Lowrie, Princeton 1957, p. 139.

25 *Ibid.* p. 144.

26 *Ibid.* p. 145.

27 Diary, 13 Dec. 1914.

3. Early Stories, pp. 48–66

1 Letter quoted in Brod's afterword to the first edition of *The Castle*.

2 *Briefe an Felice*, ed. Erich Heller and Jürgen Born (*Ges. Werke* 1967), p. 332.

3 *Briefe 1902–1924* (*Ges. Werke* 1966), p. 102.

4 Diary, 23 Sept. 1912.

5 Diary, 6 Aug. 1914.

6 C.-E. Magny in *The Kafka Problem*, ed. A. Flores, 1946, pp. 75–96.

7 Magny, *loc. cit.*

8 Kate Flores, in *Franz Kafka Today*, ed. A. Flores, p. 16.

9 Brod, *Biographie*, 1954, p. 140.

10 Kate Flores, *op. cit.* p. 17.

4. 'America', pp. 67–82

1 Diary, 19 Jan. 1911.

2 Diary, 30 Sept. 1915.

3 *Briefe an Felice*, p. 332.

4 *Loc. cit.*

5 Letter to Kurt Wolff, 4 April 1913.

6 Diary, 8 Oct. 1917.

7 Diary, 31 Dec. 1914.

8 Herbert Tauber, *Frank Kafka, eine Deutung seiner Werke*, Zürich and New York, 1941, p. 58.

9 Reprinted in R. Musil, *Tagebücher*, ed. A. Frisé, Hamburg 1955, p. 688.

5. 'The Metamorphosis', pp. 83–92

1 Letter to Kurt Wolff, 7 April 1915.
2 Kafka, *Die Verwandlung*, ed. M. L. Hoover, London 1962, p. vi.
3 F. D. Luke, 'The Metamorphosis', in *Franz Kafka Today*, p. 39.
4 Paul Goodman, preface to *The Metamorphosis by Franz Kafka*, Vanguard Press Inc. 1946, pp. 6, 7.
5 See below p. 180.
6 *Briefe an Felice*, 6/7 Dec. 1912.
7 Diary, 19 Jan. 1914.

6. 'In the Penal Colony', pp. 93–102

1 See p. 106 below.
2 Austin Warren, in *The Kafka Problem*, p. 70.
3 Hellmuth Kaiser, 'Franz Kafkas Inferno. Eine psychologische Deutung seine Strafphantasie', *Imago*, 1931, pp. 41–103.
4 Albert Schweitzer, *The Quest for the Historical Jesus*, London 1910 (2nd edn), p. 368.
5 Nietzsche, *Zur Genealogie der Moral*, 2 Abhandlung, 3 Absatz.
6 See p. 45 above.

7. 'The Trial', pp. 103–25

1 André Gide, Diary, 28 Aug. 1940.
2 Quoted by Martin Greenberg, *The Terror of Art*, London 1971, p. 113.
3 Greenberg, *ibid.* p. 117.
4 Johann Bauer, *Kafka and Prague*, London 1971, p. 106.
5 M. Pasley, 'Two Literary Sources of Kafka's *Der Prozess*', *Forum for Modern Language Studies*, III, 1967, 142–7.
6 Max Brod, Epilogue to *The Trial*.
7 See H. Uyttersprot, *Eine neue Ordnung der Werke Kafkas?*, Antwerp 1957.
8 M. Pasley, *loc. cit.*
9 Diary, 24 Jan. 1915.
10 de Sade, *Juliette*, II, 341–50, quoted in Mario Praz, *The Romantic Agony*, Oxford, 2nd edn 1951, pp. 102–3.
11 See p. 162 below.
12 See p. 58 above.

13 Diary, 2 Nov. 1911.
14 See p. 47 above.

8. 'A Country Doctor' and other tales, pp. 126–39

1 *Hochzeitsvorbereitungen*, pp. 440, 447; also *Briefe*, 20 Aug. 1917, 27 Jan. 1918 and 1 Oct. 1918.
2 *Briefe*, 7 July 1917.
3 *Briefe*, March 1918 (p. 237).
4 Same letter.
5 Malcolm Pasley (ed.), *Franz Kafka, Short Stories*, Oxford 1963, p. 26.
6 G. Janouch, *Gespräche mit Kafka*, p. 160.
7 W. Rubinstein, in *Franz Kafka Today*, p. 60.
8 Diary, 25 Jan. 1922.
9 *Briefe an Milena*, pp. 244–5.
10 Diary, 5 Oct. 1911.
11 Rubinstein, *loc. cit.*
12 See p. 155 below.
13 Letter, 5 Sept. 1917.

9. 'The Castle', pp. 140–72

1 K. Wagenbach, 'Wo liegt Kafkas Schloß?', in *Kafka-Symposion*, contrib. J. Born and others, Berlin 1965.
2 *Das Schloß*, 3rd edn, New York 1946, p. 92.
3 M. Pasley, 'Zür äußeren Gestalt des "Schloß-Romans"', in *Kafka-Symposion*.
4 *Das Schloß*, p. 72.
5 *Ibid.* pp. 292–3.
6 *Ibid.* p. 311.
7 *Ibid.* p. 139.
8 See p. 37 above.
9 *Das Schloß*, p. 120.
10 Kafka, *Briefe*, p. 401 (July 1922).
11 See Max Brod in *Franz Kafka Today*, pp. 161–4.
12 St Teresa of Avila, *Complete Works*, trans. Alison Peers, London 1946, vol. 2, p. 201.
13 *Das Schloß*, p. 49.
14 Erich Heller, *The Disinherited Mind*, Cambridge 1952, p. 169.

15 *Das Schloß*, p. 73.
16 *Ibid.* p. 110.
17 *Ibid.* p. 18.
18 *Ibid.* p. 27.
19 *Ibid.* p. 104.
20 *Ibid.* p. 201.
21 *Ibid.* p. 229.
22 *Ibid.* p. 258.
23 *Ibid.* p. 312.
24 *Ibid.* p. 105.
25 *Beschreibung eines Kampfes*, p. 183.
26 *Das Schloß*, p. 256.
27 *Ibid.* p. 172.
28 *Ibid.* p. 149.
29 *Ibid.* p. 160.
30 De Caussade, *Abandon à la divine providence*, ii.1. 1, quoted in C. Butler, *Prayer*, London 1961, p. 116.
31 *Das Schloß*, p. 309.
32 *Ibid.* p. 310.
33 *Ibid.* p. 311.
34 *Ibid.* p. 315.
35 See pp. 54, 64, 165, 168, 187, 196, 198.
36 *Das Schloß*, p. 315.
37 *Ibid.* p. 323.
38 *Ibid.* p. 352.
39 *Ibid.* p. 353.

10. Later stories, pp. 173–86

1 Diary, 10 Feb. 1922.
2 *Ibid.*
3 See p. 169 above.
4 Malcolm Pasley, *Franz Kafka. Der Heizer, In der Strafkolonie, Der Bau*, Cambridge 1966, pp. 24ff.
5 Pasley, *ibid.* p. 30.

11. Religious ideas, pp. 187–99

1 F. Beissner, *Kafka der Dichter*, passim.
2 Martin Buber, *Two Types of Faith*, 1951, reprinted in R. Gray (ed.), *Kafka. A Collection of Critical Essays*, pp. 157–62.

3   Max Brod, *Franz Kafkas Glauben und Lehre*, Winterthur 1948, p. 7.

4   Kierkegaard, *Fear and Trembling*, trans. W. Lowrie, Princeton 1945, pp. 52–7.

5   Kafka, *Hochzeitsvorbereitungen*, p. 114.

6   *Ibid.* p. 102.

7   *Ibid.* p. 76.

8   *Ibid.* p. 117.

9   Diary, 31 Jan. 1922.

CHRONOLOGICAL TABLE

Year	Life	Work (pieces of one page or less marked *)	Nature of work	Written	First published in Kafka's lifetime (marked † if first published in periodical)	Title of book-publication
1883	3 July, Franz Kafka born in Prague.	Stories in early youth, including plans for a novel (now lost)			—	
1889–93	Attended 'Volksschule'.					
1893–1901	Attended 'Gymnasium'.					
1901–6	German Univ. of Prague. Studied Law.	*Beschreibung eines Kampfes* (Description of a Struggle) (two versions; both unfinished)	novel	1904/5	—	
		Die Bäume* (The Trees)	extract from above	1904/5	1908†	*Betrachtung*
		Kleider* (Clothes)	extract from above	1904/5	1908†	*Betrachtung*
		Gespräch mit dem Beter (Conversation with the Suppliant)	extract from above	1904/5	1909†	*Betrachtung*
		Gespräch mit dem Betrunkenen (Conversation with the Drunken Man)	extract from above	1904/5	1909†	*Betrachtung*
		Kinder auf der Landstrasse (Children on the Highroad)	extract from above	1904/5	1912	*Betrachtung*
		Der Ausflug ins Gebirge* (Excursion into the Mountains)	extract from above	1904/5	1912	*Betrachtung*
1902	First met Max Brod. Introduced by him to literary circles in Prague	Die Abweisung* (Rejection)	prose-piece	1906	1908†	*Betrachtung*
		Das Gassenfenster* (The Street Window)	prose-piece	1906/9	1912	*Betrachtung*
1907	Took doctorate in Law. Began work at 'Assicurazioni Generali' (private insurance office), Prague.	Der Kaufmann (The Tradesman)	prose-piece	1907?	1908†	*Betrachtung*
		Hochzeitsvorbereitungen auf dem Lande (Wedding Preparations in the Country) (three versions; all unfinished)	novel?	1907/8	—	
		Zerstreutes Hinausschauen* (Absent-minded Window-gazing)	prose-piece	1907?	1908†	*Betrachtung*

Year		Work	Type			Publication
		Der Nachhauseweg* (The Way Home)	prose-piece	1907?	1908†	*Betrachtung*
		Die Vorüberlaufenden* (Passers-by)	prose-piece	1907?	1908†	*Betrachtung*
		Der Fahrgast* (On the Tram)	prose-piece	1907?	1908†	*Betrachtung*
1908	Began work at 'Workers' Accident Insurance Office for the Kingdom of Bohemia', Prague, and remained till retirement in 1922.					
1909		Die Aeroplane in Brescia (The Aeroplanes in Brescia)	reportage	1909	1909†	
		Zum Nachdenken für Herrenreiter* (Reflections for Gentleman Jockeys)	prose-piece	1909/10	1910†	*Betrachtung*
1910	Began diary. Interest in Yiddish theatre; Jizchak Löwy.	Unglücklichsein (Unhappiness)	prose-piece	1910	1912	*Betrachtung*
		Das Unglück des Junggesellen* (Bachelor's Ill-Luck)	prose-piece	1911	1912	*Betrachtung*
		Entlarvung eines Bauernfängers (Unmasking a Confidence Trickster)	short story	1911	1912	*Betrachtung*
		Richard und Samuel (with Max Brod; unfinished; one chapter published)	travel-diary	1911	1912†	
		Entschlüsse* (Resolutions)	prose-piece	1912	1912	*Betrachtung*
		Der plötzliche Spaziergang* (The Sudden Walk)	prose-piece	1912	1912	*Betrachtung*
		Wunsch, Indianer zu werden* (A Wish to be a Red Indian)	prose-piece	1910	1912	*Betrachtung*
		Grosser Lärm* (A Great Noise)	prose-piece	1911	1912	*Betrachtung*
		Der Verschollene (Lost without Trace)	first drafts	1911/12	—	*Betrachtung*
1912	Aug. First met Felice Bauer.	Das Urteil (The Judgement)	short story	Sept. 1912	1913†	*Das Urteil* (1916)
		Der Verschollene (=Amerika) (first 7 chapters of later version; last chapter written 1914)	novel	late 1912	—	
		Der Heizer (The Stoker)	extract from above	late 1912	1913	*Der Heizer*
		Die Verwandlung (=The Metamorphosis)	short story	late 1912	1915†	

Year	Life	Work (pieces of one page or less marked *)	Nature of work	Written	First published in Kafka's lifetime (marked † if first published in periodical)	Title of book-publication
1913	First read Kierkegaard. Visits to Felice in Berlin. Sept. In love with 'G.W.', a Christian girl, at Riva.					
1914	June. Engagement to Felice. (Broken off in July.) Aug. Unfit for military service in World War. Ceased to live in parents' home. Met Grete Bloch.	Der Prozeß (The Trial) (unfinished)	novel	July–Dec. 1914	—	
		Vor dem Gesetz* (Before the Law)	extract from above	Dec. 1914	1919	Ein Landarzt
		Ein Traum* (A Dream)	extract from above?	1914/15	1919	Ein Landarzt
		In der Strafkolonie (In the Penal Colony)	short story	Oct. 1914	1919	In der Strafkolonie
		Der Riesenmaulwurf (=Der Dorfschullehrer (The Giant Mole, or The Village Schoolmaster) (unfinished)	short story	Dec. 1914	—	
		Verlockung im Dorf (Temptation in the Village)	study for Das Schloß?	1914	—	
1915	Carl Sternheim gives prize-money from his Fontane Prize to Kafka. Son of Kafka's said later by Grete Bloch to have been born to her (unknown to Kafka).	Blumfeld, ein älterer Junggeselle (Blumfeld, an Elderly Bachelor)	short story	1915	—	
1916	Moved to the Alchimistengasse by the Hradschin, Prague.	Auf der Galerie* (In the Gallery)	prose-piece	late 1916 or 1917	1919	Ein Landarzt

1917	Ein Landarzt (A Country Doctor)	collection of stories, etc.	1917	1919	Ein Landarzt
	Der neue Advokat* (The New Advocate)	prose-piece	early 1917	1919	Ein Landarzt
	Schakale und Araber (Jackals and Arabs)	allegory?	early 1917	1917†	Ein Landarzt
	Ein Besuch im Bergwerk (A Visit to a Mine)	prose-piece	early 1917?	1919	Ein Landarzt
	Ein Brudermord (A Brother's Murder)	short story	early 1917?	1917†	Ein Landarzt
	Ein altes Blatt (An Old Manuscript)	short story	early 1917	1917†	Ein Landarzt
	Die Brücke* (The Bridge)	short story	early 1917	—	
	Der Jäger Gracchus (The Huntsman Gracchus) (unfinished)	short story	early 1917	—	
	Der Schlag ans Hoftor* (The Knock at the Manor-Gate)	short story	early 1917	—	
	Der Kübelreiter (The Bucket-Rider)	short story	early 1917	—	
	Beim Bau der chinesischen Mauer (Building the Great Wall of China)	novel?	early 1917	—	
	Eine kaiserliche Botschaft (A Message from the Emperor)	extract from above	early 1917	1919†	Ein Landarzt
	Das nächste Dorf* (The next Village)	prose-piece	1917	1919	Ein Landarzt
	Ein Bericht für eine Akademie (A Report for an Academy)	allegory?	spring 1917	—	
	Der Nachbar (The Neighbour)	short story	spring 1917	—	
	Eine Kreuzung (A Crossbreed)	prose-piece	spring 1917	—	
July. Second engagement to Felice Bauer. (broken off in Dec.)	Die Sorge des Hausvaters* (Troubles of a Householder, or, A Worry to the Caretaker)	prose-piece	1917	1919	Ein Landarzt
Sept. Tuberculosis diagnosed.	Elf Söhne (Eleven Sons)	prose-piece	1917	1919	Ein Landarzt
Lived at Zürau with sister Ottla.	Ein Landarzt (A Country Doctor)	short story	1917	1918†	Ein Landarzt
	Eine alltägliche Verwirrung (An Everyday Confusion)	prose-piece	Oct. 1917	—	
First plans for *Das Schloß*.	Die Wahrheit über Sancho Pansa* (The Truth about Sancho Panza)	prose-piece	Oct. 1917	—	

Year	Life	Work (pieces of one page or less marked *)	Nature of work	Written	First published in Kafka's lifetime (marked † if first published in periodical)	Title of book-publication
		Das Schweigen der Sirenen* (The Silence of the Sirens)	prose-piece	Oct. 1917	—	
		Aphorisms (see the collection 'Betrachtungen über Sünde, Leid, Hoffnung und den wahren Weg', so titled by Max Brod).		late 1917–early 1918	—	
		Der Gruftwächter (The Guardian of the Tomb)	play	1917?	—	
1918	At Zürau. Returned to Prague in summer. Winter at Schelesen, North of Prague. Met Julie Wohryzek.					
1919	Returned to Prague in spring. Engagement to Julie. (Broken off in 1920.)	Prometheus*	prose-piece	Jan. 1919	—	
		Brief an den Vater (Letter to his father)	personal letter	Nov. 1919	—	
1920	Fell in love with Milena Jesenská. Conversations with Gustav Janouch. Dec. To Matliary sanatorium in High Tatras till Sept. 1921.	Das Stadtwappen* (The City Coat of Arms)	for Beim Bau?	late 1920	—	
		Poseidon*	prose-piece	late 1920	—	
		Gemeinschaft* (Fellowship)	prose-piece	late 1920	—	
		Nachts* (At Night)	prose-piece	late 1920	—	
		Die Abweisung (The Rejection)	for Beim Bau?	late 1920	—	
		Zur Frage der Gesetze (The Problem of our Laws)	for Beim Bau?	late 1920	—	
		Die Truppenaushebung (The Conscription)	for Beim Bau?	late 1920	—	
		Die Prüfung* (The Test)	prose-piece	late 1920	—	

Year		Title	Type	Written	Published	
		Der Geier★ (The Vulture)	prose-piece	late 1920	—	
		Der Steuermann★ (The Helmsman)	prose-piece	late 1920	—	
		Der Kreisel★ (The Top)	prose-piece	late 1920	—	
		Kleine Fabel★ (A little Fable)	prose-piece	late 1920	—	
		Heimkehr★ (Home-Coming)	prose-piece	late 1920	—	
		Er (He)	aphorisms	Jan./Feb. 1920	—	
1921	Told Max Brod he would ask for all his work to be destroyed.	Erstes Leid (First Sorrow)	short story	1921/2	1922†	Ein Hungerkünstler
1922	July. Retired from work.	Das Schloß (The Castle) (unfinished)	novel	Jan.–Sept. 1922	—	
		Der Aufbruch★ (The Departure)	prose-piece	1922	—	
		Fürsprecher (Advocates)	prose-piece	1922	—	
		Forschungen eines Hundes (Investigations of a Dog)	allegory	1922	—	
		Das Ehepaar (The Married Couple)	short story	1922	—	
		Gibs auf!★ (Give it up!)	prose-piece	1922	—	
		Von den Gleichnissen★ (On Parables)	prose-piece	1922/3	—	
		Ein Hungerkünstler (A Hunger-Artist)	collection of stories	1921–4	1924	Ein Hungerkünstler
1923	Sept. To Berlin. Lived with Dora Diamant till spring 1924.	Ein Hungerkünstler	short story	1922	1924†	Ein Hungerkünstler
		Eine kleine Frau (A Little Woman)	short story	1923	1924	Ein Hungerkünstler
		Der Bau (ending lost) (The Burrow)	short story	1923/4	—	
		Josefine, die Sängerin, oder das Volk der Mäuse (Josephine the Singer, or the Nation of Mice)	short story	March 1924	1924	Ein Hungerkünstler
1924	3 June. Died at Kierling sanatorium near Klosterneuburg, Austria.					

NOTE: This list does not include the many fragmentary pieces scattered through Kafka's manuscripts but not printed as part of his collected stories or novels, or his few poems, or the unknown quantity of writings destroyed by him and Dora Diamant or confiscated by the Gestapo.

The dating of the works relies largely on *Kafka-Symposion*, contrib. J. Born and others, Berlin 1965 and on Kafka, *Sämtliche Erzählungen*, ed. Paul Raabe. These contain fuller details.

213

SELECT BIBLIOGRAPHY

Editions

The latest German edition is the *Gesammelte Werke*, edited by Max Brod and published by Fischer Verlag at Frankfurt, beginning in 1946. The English translations in the Definitive Edition are published by Secker and Warburg.

Textual criticism

Brod's editing of the text has been severely criticized. An account of the MS of *Das Schloß*, which is now in the Bodleian, Oxford, along with most of the other MSS of Kafka's works, is given by Malcolm Pasley in 'Zür Äußeren Gestalt des Schloß-Romans', in *Kafka-Symposion*, contrib. J. Born and others, Berlin 1965.

Anthologies of criticism

A. Flores and H. Swander (edd.). *The Kafka Problem*, New York 1946.
— *Franz Kafka Today*, Madison 1958.
R. Gray (ed.), *Kafka. A Collection of Critical Essays*, Englewood Cliffs, N.J. 1962.

Bibliographies

R. Hemmerle, *Franz Kafka, eine Bibliographie*, Munich 1958. (Works by Kafka and some secondary literature.)
H. Järv, *Die Kafka-Literatur. Eine Bibliographie*, Malmö and Lund 1961. (Secondary literature.)

Biographies

M. Brod, *Franz Kafka, eine Biographie*, 3rd edn, Berlin 1954 (Eng. trans. London 1947).
K. Wagenbach, *Franz Kafka. Eine Biographie seiner Jugend (1883–1912)* Berne 1958.
— *Franz Kafka in Selbstzeugnissen und Bilddokumenten*, Rowohlt, Hamburg 1964. (Paperback with many illustrations.)

INDEX

INDEX